New York
United States

EVERYMAN
CITY GUIDES

EVERYMAN CITY GUIDES

ISBN 1-85715-894-6

First published April 1998
Revised and updated Feb 1999

Originally published in France by Nouveaux Loisirs, a subsidiary of Gallimard, Paris 1997, and in Italy by Touring Editore, Srl., Milano 1997.

SERIES EDITORS
Seymourina Cruse/Marisa Bassi
NEW YORK EDITION: Sophie Lenormand, with Mélanie Le Bris, Lucie Milledrogues, Alexandra Rose
GRAPHICS
Élizabeth Cohat, Yann Le Duc
LAYOUT: Gérard Dumas, Olivier Lauga, Yann Le Duc
AIRPORT MAPS:
Kristoff Chemineau
NEW YORK MAPS:
Édigraphie
STREET MAPS:
Touring Club Italiano
PRODUCTION
Catherine Bourrabier

Translated by Susan Mackervoy

Edited and typeset by Book Creation Services, London

English edition revised by First Edition Translations Ltd, Cambridge, UK

Printed in Italy by Editoriale Lloyd

Authors
NEW YORK

Getting there: Christine Silva (1)
Silva has lived in Manhattan since 1991 and worked on the editorial team of several Havas and Gallimard guides to New York.

Where to stay: Benjamin Morse & Anna Jefferys (2)
A columnist and a journalist specializing in hotels for the magazine *Condé Nast Traveller*, Morse and Jefferys travel the globe and are familiar with all aspects of the hotel world, especially the hotels in New York.

Where to eat: Andy Birsh (3)
Birsh has been a restaurant critic for the American magazine *Gourmet* for more than ten years, a position that has required him to try out many of New York's 17,000 restaurants. His reputation has crossed the Atlantic, too: he is a regular contributor to *The Tatler*.

After dark:
Jeannette VanDeusen Troiano (4)
VanDeusen Troiano is public relations manager for the New York Convention & Visitors Bureau, and author of several guides including the *Big Apple Visitor Guide*. Since 1997 she has been in charge of the Bureau's Internet site, which means she is up to date with the latest cultural developments in New York.

What to see and Further afield:
Stuart Miller & Sharon Seitz (5)
Miller and Seitz are columnists for *Variety* and *The Home News* and have co-authored *The Other Islands of New York City: A Historical Companion* (The Countryman Press). They write on their city's cultural heritage for *The New York Times Sunday Magazine* and *Time Out*.

Where to shop: Francis Lewis (6)
Lewis is assistant chief editor of the magazine *Where New York* and has contributed to a number of New York publications. His passion for shopping and intimate knowledge of the fashion world were reinforced through his management experience at the department stores Bloomingdale's and Macy's.

> *Note from the publisher:*
> *To keep the price of this guide as low as possible we decided on a common edition for the UK and US, which has meant American spelling.*

Steve Max

Contents

Symbols

- ☎ telephone
- fax
- ● price or price range
- opening hours
- credit cards accepted
- credit cards not accepted
- toll-free number
- @ e-mail/website address
- ★ tips and recommendations

Access

- subway stations
- bus (or tram)
- private parking
- parking attendant
- no facilities for the disabled
- train
- car
- boat

Hotels

- telephone in room
- fax in room on request
- minibar
- television in room
- air-conditioned rooms
- 24-hour room service
- caretaker
- babysitting
- meeting room(s)
- no pets
- breakfast
- open for tea/coffee
- restaurant
- live music
- disco
- garden, patio or terrace
- gym, fitness club
- swimming pool, sauna

Restaurants

- vegetarian food
- view
- formal dress required
- smoking area
- bar

Museums and galleries

- on-site store(s)
- guided tours
- café

Stores

- branches, outlets

The Insider's Guide is made up of **8 sections** each indicated by a different color.

Things you need to know (mauve)
Where to stay (blue)
Where to eat (red)
After dark (pink)
What to see (green)
Further afield (orange)
Where to shop (yellow)
Finding your way (purple)

Practical information is given for each particular establishment: opening times, prices, ways of paying, different services available

How to use this guide

In the area
The grand buildings bordering Ce
York's past, also immortalized by t
uxury hotels. In their lo
gnates mingle with curi
3 ■ After dark ➥ 88 ■

The section **"In the area"** refers you (➥ 00) to other establishments that are covered in a different section of the guide but found in the same area of the city.

Central Park South **D** A2 - B3

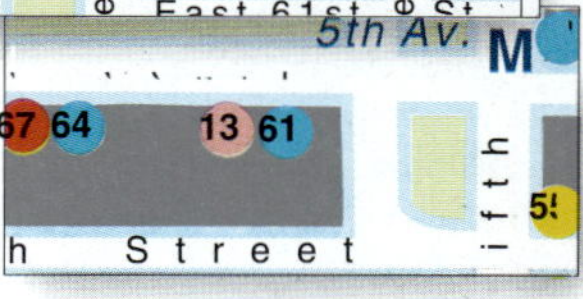

The small map shows all the establishments mentioned and others described elsewhere but found "in the area", by the color of the section.

The name of the district is given above the map. A grid reference (**A** B-C 2) enables you to find it in the section on Maps at the end of the book.

Not forgetting
■ **Sherry Netherland (63)** 7
☎ (212) 355-2800 ➠ (212) 319-430

The section "Not forgetting" lists other useful addresses in the same area.

"Bargain!"
This star marks good value hotels and restaurants.

The opening page to each section contains an index ordered alphabetically (Getting there), by subject or by district (After dark) as well as useful addresses and advice.

The section "Things you need to know" covers information on getting to New York and day-to-day life in the city.

Theme pages introduce a selection of establishments on a given topic.

The "Maps" section of this guide contains 9 street plans of New York followed by a detailed index.

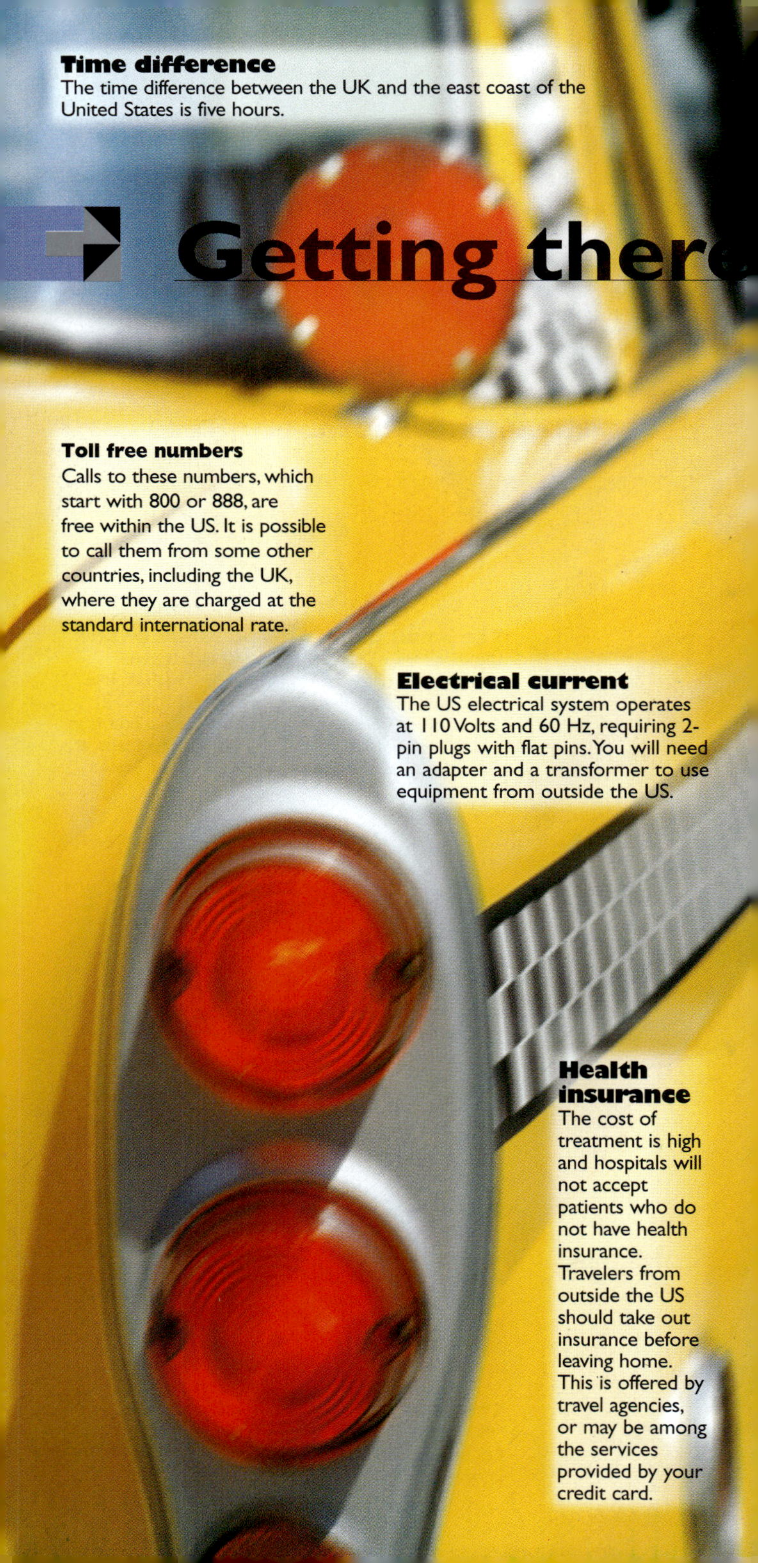

Time difference
The time difference between the UK and the east coast of the United States is five hours.

Getting there

Toll free numbers
Calls to these numbers, which start with 800 or 888, are free within the US. It is possible to call them from some other countries, including the UK, where they are charged at the standard international rate.

Electrical current
The US electrical system operates at 110 Volts and 60 Hz, requiring 2-pin plugs with flat pins. You will need an adapter and a transformer to use equipment from outside the US.

Health insurance
The cost of treatment is high and hospitals will not accept patients who do not have health insurance. Travelers from outside the US should take out insurance before leaving home. This is offered by travel agencies, or may be among the services provided by your credit card.

Formalities

UK citizens do not need a visa for stays of less than 90 days, but your passport must be valid six months after the date of return. It is illegal to bring in any plants or perishable produce.

42 Things you need to Know

Public holidays

On these days most institutions and public services are closed.
Christmas & New Year's Day December 25 and January 1
President's Day Third Monday in February
Memorial Day last Monday in May
Independence Day July 4
Labor Day First Monday in September
Veterans Day November 11
Thanksgiving Day Fourth Thursday in November

INDEX

Basic facts

New York has three airports. Two of them are international: John F. Kennedy Airport (JFK) on Long Island and Newark Airport (EWR) in New Jersey. La Guardia Airport (LGA), in Queens, is for domestic flights.

Getting there

Information

JFK
☎ *(718) 656-4444*
Newark
☎ *(201) 961-6000*
La Guardia
☎ *(718) 476-5000*

Concorde

The fastest UK-US flight takes only four hours. 🕒 *London Heathrow (terminal 4) departures 11.15am, 7pm* 🕒 *New York JFK (terminal 4W) departures 8.45am, 1.45pm* ☎ *0345 222100; (212) 247-0100*

Airlines

American Airlines
📠 *800 433-7300*
British Airways
☎ *(718) 397-4000*
Continental Airlines
📠 *800 231-0856*
Delta Airlines
📠 *800 241-4141*
Canada Airlines
📠 *800 426-7000*

Hotels

JFK
Hilton
☎ *(718) 322-8700*
Holiday Inn
☎ *(718) 659-0200*
Ramada Plaza Hotel
☎ *(718) 995-9000*

Newark
Marriott
☎ *(973) 623-0006*
Holiday Inn
☎ *(973) 589-1000*
Hilton
☎ *(908) 351-3900*

La Guardia
Marriott Hotel
☎ *(718) 565-8900*
Holiday Inn Crown Plaza
☎ *(718) 457-6300*
Courtyard
☎ *(718) 446-4800*

Car rental

Toll-free numbers
Avis
📠 *800 831-2847*
Hertz
📠 *800 654-3131*
Budget
📠 *800 527-0700*
National
📠 *800 227-7368*
Dollar
📠 *800 800-4000*

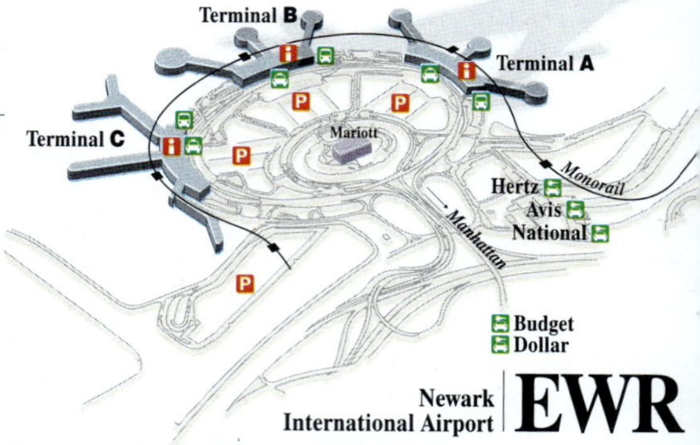

Airport connections – Manhattan

Ground Transportation Center
Information on all types of connection
📠 *800 247-7433*
Taxis
"Dispatchers", identifiable by their uniform, are in charge of allocating cabs. Only yellow cabs are authorized
● *Flat fee for the journey, plus $3.50 toll and 15% tip*

Limousines
These are not always more expensive than a cab. Price varies according to size
● *$20 / hr approx., plus tolls and 15–20% tip*
Carmel Limo
📠 *800 922-7635*
☎ *(212) 666-6666*
Town Car
📠 *800 411-4477*
☎ *(212) 873-4477*
Bus
Departures every 30 mins.
From **JFK and La Guardia**
Stops: Grand Central Station (Park Ave and 42nd St.), Port Authority Terminal (Eighth Ave and 42nd Sts)
Carey Bus
● *$13 (JFK); $10 (La Guardia)*
🕒 5am–11pm
📠 *800 632-0500*
From Newark
Stops: Grand Central, Pennsylvania Station, Port Authority Terminal, World Trade Center
Olympia Trails
● *$10*
☎ *(212) 964-6233*
Minibus
Stops to suit you between 23rd and 125th Sts
Gray Line Air Shuttle
● *$16.50 (JFK); $13.50 (La Guardia); $18.50 (Newark)*
📠 *800 451-0455*
☎ *(212) 315 3006*

- Ground Transportation Center
- Taxi rank
- Car rental
- Buses
- Water Shuttle
- Parking

Arriving in New York by plane

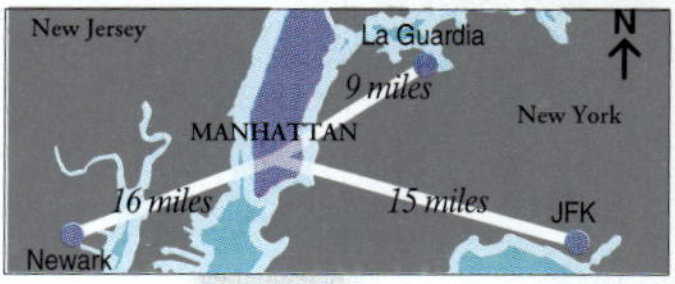

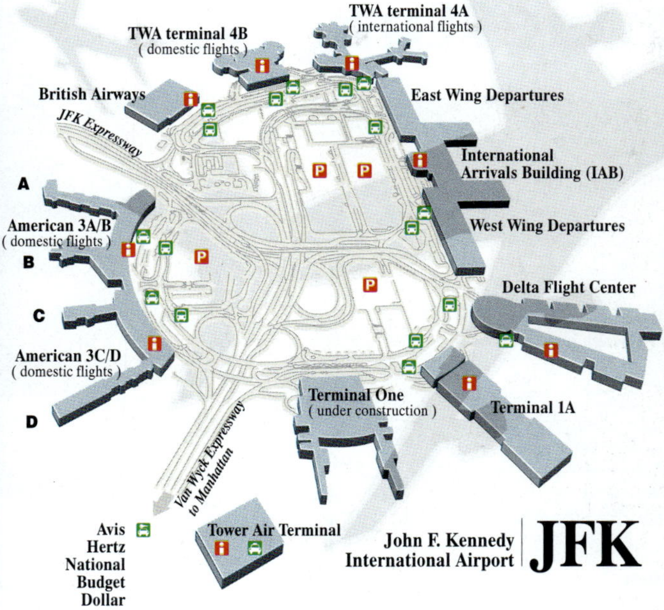

John F. Kennedy International Airport | **JFK**

JFK connections

Helicopter (10 mins) A rapid and dramatic way to arrive in Manhattan. Not too expensive if shared between six people. Book 24 hrs ahead. Arrives E. 34th St. or W. 30th St.
● $299 *per flight*
Liberty Helicopter
888 692-4354
(908) 474-9700

Taxis (60 mins approx.) Flat rate from airport to Manhattan
● *$30;* round trip *$30–$40.*

Subway (60 mins approx.) Line A The cheapest form of transport. Free shuttle to Howard Beach station
● *$1.50*

La Guardia Airport | **LGA**

La Guardia connections

Cabs (30 mins approx.)
● *$18 approx.*

Boat (20 mins approx.) Stops on East River on 62nd, 34th or Wall Sts., pier 11
● *Single $15; Round trip $25*
Delta Water Shuttle
800 543-3779
6.30am–5.30pm

Basic facts

Thousands of commuters pass through the main hall of Grand Central Station (1) every day. Trains from other states and Canada arrive at Penn Station (2); city buses (6) arrive at Port Authority Terminal. And you can still travel from Europe by boat (4)!

Getting there

1

Train

The train may not be the quickest form of transport to New York, but it is reliable and relatively cheap. Manhattan has only two main stations, Grand Central Terminal and Penn Station.

Grand Central Terminal (1) *42nd St. and Park Ave* ☎ *(212) 532-4900* This splendid station ➡ 106 serves the suburbs and New York state and Connecticut. **Metro-North** is a rapid commuter service for Westchester County, the Hudson Valley, and Connecticut and carries thousands of people into New York City every day.

🍴 Oyster Bar & Restaurant ➡ 70

Penn Station (2) *34th St. and Seventh Ave* ☎ *800 872-7245* Serves Long Island as well as Boston, Chicago, and Washington.

LIRR (Long Island Rail Road) ☎ *(718) 217-5477* Trains for Long Island

Amtrak ☎ *800 872-7245* Amtrak is the national rail operator that connects New York with other cities in the US and Canada. Some trains have reclining seats, a buffet service, and saloon cars. Sleepers are available on long-distance trains.

- *Boston–New York in 4 hrs 25 mins, $50-65 one way*
- *Washington–New York in 3 hrs by Metroliner $112 one way Mon.–Fri.; $90 Sat.–Sun. Northeast Direct is slower and cheaper: 3 hrs 30 mins, $61–84.*
- *New York–Montreal in 9 hrs 30 mins, $49–62 one way*

Car

Getting there

The New Jersey Turnpike (I-95) gives access to Manhattan from the west and south. From the east, use the Lincoln Tunnel (or the Holland Tunnel for Midtown). From the north, access is via the George Washington Bridge • tolls *$3.50* each bridge. The New England Thruway (I-95) links the Triborough Bridge and the Cross Bronx Expressway. From the north, I-87 connects with the Triborough Bridge as well as the other bridges over the East River and the Harlem River.

In the city

Most streets and avenues are one-way, and the system is easy to understand. Odd-numbered streets flow from east to west; evens from west to east. 14th, 23rd, 34th, 42nd, and 57th Streets are two-way. In odd-numbered avenues traffic flows from north

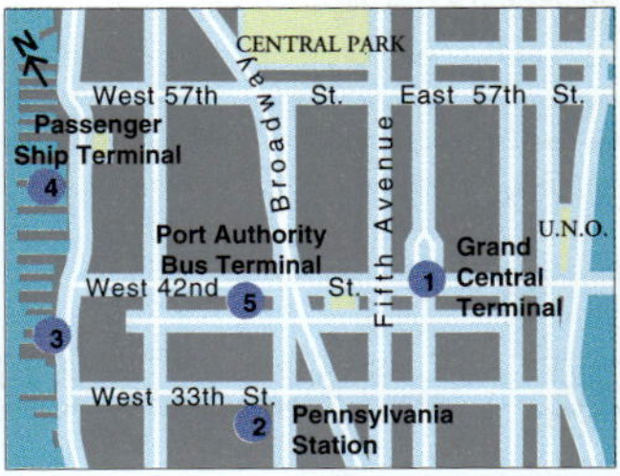

4

6

to south; even-numbered avenues flow from south to north (exceptions are Second, Third, and Park Avenues). The speed limit is 35mph (56kph). It is illegal to turn right when the lights are red.

Parking
Difficult and expensive. Private parking lots show their hourly rates at the entrance. Street parking is metered and limited to one hour. Don't be tempted to park at a meter that is out of order: you will get a ticket. In streets where parking is free, alternate side of the street parking rules usually apply: parking is prohibited between certain hours on one side one day and on the other the next.

Parking Violations Bureau
☎ *(212) 477-4430*
🕒 *Mon.–Fri. 8am–5pm*

Towing (3)
Cars are often towed away on the island, and one third of them are damaged in the process.
Traffic Dept. Tow Pound *Pier 76, W. 38th Street (Twelfth Ave)*
☎ *(212) 971-0772*
• *$150 tow fee plus $10 per day and the cost of unpaid tickets exceeding $229*
🕒 *General information Mon.–Fri. 9am–11pm; Parking Violation Window Mon.–Fri. 9am–5pm*

Boat

An expensive and slow way to travel, but a memorable one. The Queen Elizabeth II (QE2) crosses the Atlantic 17 times a year, from Southampton. After a six-day journey you arrive at the ***Passenger Ship Terminal* (4)**
Piers 88–92 (55th Street)
☎ *(212) 246-5450*

Long-distance bus

A cheap way to travel, but slow and tiring. Allow eight to nine hours from Montreal, four to five hours from Washington D.C. or Boston, slightly less than three days from Los Angeles and around 26 hours from Miami. All buses arrive at:
***Port Authority Terminal* (5)**
West 40th Street (Eighth Ave)
☎ *(212) 564-8484 (10am–10pm)*
Lost property
☎ *(718) 625-6200*

Greyhound
800 231-2222 (24 hrs)
• *Washington D.C.–New York and Boston–New York one way $28; round trip $53*
• *Los Angeles–New York one way $132; round trip $216*
• *Miami–New York one way $105; round trip $159*
• *Montreal–New York one way $69; round trip $89*

Accidents

In an emergency call *911* (police, fire service).

Basic facts

Red and green globes mark subway entrances (1); a token (2) and an old transfer ticket (3) now replaced by a MetroCard – valid for the bus and the subway; signs representing the Americas on Avenue of the Americas (or Sixth Avenue) (4); in Chinatown the signs are also written in Chinese

Getting around

1

2

8

New York

New York City has five boroughs: Manhattan, Queens, Brooklyn, Staten Island and the Bronx. Only the last of these is joined to the mainland: the others are islands.

Manhattan

Every district in this borough has a name (Harlem, Chelsea, Murray Hill...). The island is divided into three major areas.

Downtown
The area to the south of 34th St., which includes: *Financial District, TriBeCa, SoHo, Little Italy, Chinatown, Greenwich Village* and *East Village, Chelsea and Gramercy Park.*

Midtown
The area between 34th and 59th Sts includes *Murray Hill, Theater* and *Garment Districts.*

Uptown
To the north of 59th St., *Upper East Side* and *Upper West Side* are separated by Central Park.

East and West Sides
Manhattan is divided into East and West sides, split down the middle by Fifth Avenue and Central Park.

Addresses

The streets
The streets run from east to west. Except in Financial District and Greenwich Village, streets are numbered rather than named, with numbers from 1st to 215th, running from south to north.

The avenues
The avenues run from north to south, and mostly have a number rather than a name: exceptions are Lexington, Park, and Madison Avenues. Sixth Avenue was renamed Avenue of the Americas in 1948: however the name is rarely used. Addresses on the avenues are numbered from south to north. Because the avenues are so long (about 14 miles) it is usual to give the closest cross-street when giving an address: for example, Fifth Avenue and 55th Street.

Blocks
A block is the area or distance between two streets or avenues. Beware: the blocks vary greatly in length.

Transport

Public and private transport generally operates 24 hours a day. The subway and the buses are efficient and inexpensive. Maps ➡ 176
A flat fare is charged regardless of distance. Buy tokens or the renewable MetroCard at ticket counters.
● *$1.50 per token; from $3 for a MetroCard; free for children less than 45 in. tall.*
☎ *(718) 330-1234*

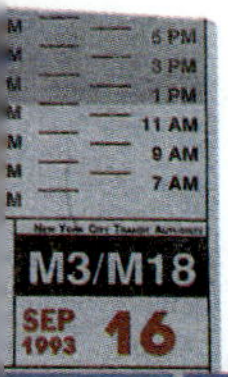

"Hey! taxi" (6), the statue in front of the Chemical Building (277 Park Ave); a New York cab (7) and the Staten Island ferry (8).

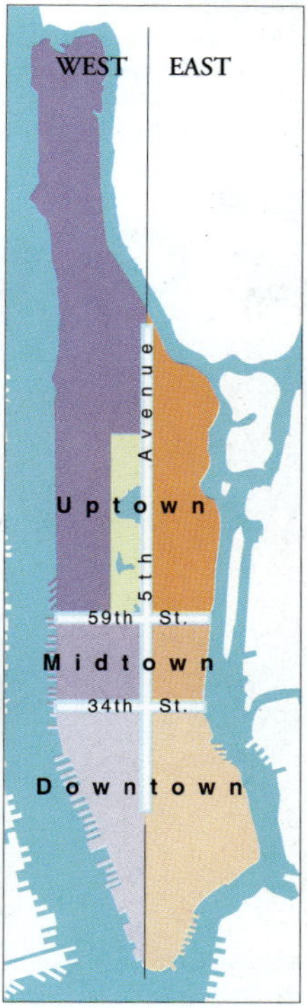

Buses

Buses are frequent, quite comfortable (air conditioning in summer) and relatively quick. They follow the north-south avenues, stopping every two or three blocks, with crosstown routes (east-west) on the main streets. When you get on a bus, ask for a transfer if your journey will continue on another bus. Bus stops have signs showing a bus against a blue and red background. The line number is marked on the buses and the bus stops. You can pay with a MetroCard or subway token; have the right change to pay cash.

Subway

Be careful: in many cases station entrances are for trains going in one direction only (uptown, to the north, or downtown, to the south). A green globe at the subway entrance indicates that the ticket counter is open 24 hours a day; a red globe indicates restricted opening hours. The subway is the fastest form of transport in Manhattan for north-south connections. The local trains stop at all stations; express trains only at main stations. For connections follow the transfer signs.

Taxis

New York's yellow cabs are instantly recognizable emblems of the city. When the sign on top of the cab is lit up you just have to hail it. Cabs can take up to four people. Don't forget to add the tip (15%) onto the price. Drivers are not obliged to accept banknotes larger than $20. Ask for a receipt.
● *basic charge $2 then 30¢ every 0.2 miles. Surcharge of 50¢ from 8pm–6am*
Lost property
☎ *(212) 221-8294*

Ferry

Manhattan is an island, and commuters use the ferries to travel to and from Staten Island or Hoboken (New Jersey). Take the ferry and admire some of the best views of the Manhattan skyline at an unbeatable price! ● *free* ➥ 104

New York Water Taxis

Water taxis circle around Manhattan. A pleasant way to avoid the gridlocks.
● *$8 each journey*

Bicycle

Many people ride bicycles or roller-blade in New York; Central Park ➥ 122 is the perfect place to do this.
Loeb Boat House
(East 72nd Street and Fifth Avenue)
☎ *(212) 517-2233*
● *$10 per hour*
Blades, Board, and Skates
➥ 166

Basic facts

The New York Convention and Visitors Bureau (1) at Columbus Circle has information on all events in the Big Apple; national papers are available from machines on street corners or at Hotalings (2), which also sells international papers; some facilities are open 24 hours a day in case of

Getting by

Tourist Information

New York Convention and Visitors Bureau
224 W. 42nd St. (between 7th and 8th Aves)
☎ *(212) 484-1222*
🕘 *daily 9am–6pm*

Big Apple Greeter
An original way of getting to know the city, devised by the mayor's office. A New Yorker will spend two or three hours with you to help you find your way round the city or to visit a particular district.
☎ *(212) 669-2896*
➠ *(212) 669-3685*

Money

Checks are rarely used.

Dollar bills and coins
The currency unit is the dollar ($), divided into 100 cents (¢). Banknotes are available in 100, 50, 20, 10, 5, and 1 dollar denominations. Avoid banknotes larger than $50 as these may not be accepted. Coins are called penny (1¢), nickel (5¢), dime (10¢), and quarter (25¢).

Banks
In addition to regular opening hours, most have automatic cashpoints that are open 24 hrs.
🕘 *Mon.–Fri. 9am–3pm, Sat. 9am–1pm*

Exchange rate
$1 = £1.6 (at time of going to press)
Thomas Cook Currency Service
1590 Broadway (Times Square)
🕘 *Mon.–Sat. 9am–7pm, Sun. 9am–5pm*
☎ *(212) 883-0400*

Credit cards
In addition to their regular use for purchases, they are essential for making bookings by telephone and for the deposit when renting a car.

Taxes
Not included in prices. Add 8.25% for most goods and services. Taxes in hotels vary between 14.25% and 19.25%.

Tips
Tips are never included in the bill and should be added separately. Bars and restaurants: between 15 and 20% (or double the tax: 8.25%), cabs 15%. Give $1 to hotel staff and $1 per item of luggage to the porter. No tips in theaters, cinemas, and gas stations.

The media

Papers
Sold in most hotels, in kiosks, and machines on street corners, and at Hotalings.
142 W. 42nd St. (between Sixth Ave and Broadway)
☎ *(212) 840-1868*
🕘 *Mon.–Fri. 7.30am– 9pm; Sat.–Sun. 7.30am–8pm*
Dailies: *The N.Y. Times; N.Y. Post; Daily News; N.Y. Newsday; Wall Street Journal* (finance)
Weeklies: *N.Y. Magazine; The New Yorker; N.Y. Observer; Time Out N.Y.; The Village Voice* (free).
Monthlies: *Forbes; Vogue; Harper's; Rolling Stone*

Travel bookstore
The Complete Traveler Bookstore

emergencies: Thomas Cook (3) for changing currency, the Genovese pharmacy (4) and the central post office (5).

199 Madison Ave (35th St.)
☎ *(212) 685-9007*
H *Mon.–Fri. 9am–6.30pm, Sat. 10am–6pm; Sun. 11am–5pm*

Television
In your hotel you will receive at least the three national channels, ABC, CBS and NBC. There is also a profusion of cable channels, with a huge variety of programming.

Radio
There are around 100 radio stations in the New York City area. Scan the AM dial for 24-hour news and eccentric call-in shows, and FM for music.

Telephone

Local telephone network operated by Bell Atlantic.

Information
☎ *411*
☎ *0* (operator)

Public telephones
● local calls are approx. 25¢ for 3 min. The cost of non-local calls is posted.

Dialing codes
212 Manhattan; *718* other boroughs.

International
To make international calls dial 011 followed by the country code and phone number without the first zero. Unless you have an international calling card, be prepared with a lot of quarters if you are calling from a public telephone.

Mail

Blue letter boxes marked U.S. Mail
● *domestic: 32¢; international letters: 60¢; international postcards: 50¢;*

Central post office
Eighth Ave (33rd Street)
☎ *(212) 967-8585*
H *24 hrs*

Express delivery
Federal Express
New York-London in 2 days max.
● *min. $25.50*
V *800 463-3339*

Telegrams and money orders
Service operated by private companies.
Western Union
V *800 325-6000*

Health

You will have to pay for any treatment you receive in hospital emergency rooms unless you have an acceptable health insurance policy, so it is important to arrange this in advance. There are a number or walk-in clinics in the city: contact your insurance company or check the phone book for information.

Pharmacy
Genovese
Second Ave (68th Street)
☎ *(212) 772-0104*
H *24hrs*

Consulates

Britain
845 Third Avenue
☎ *(212) 745-0200*

Canada
1251 Sixth Avenue
☎ *(212) 596-1600*

Ireland
515 Madison Avenue
☎ *(212) 319-2555*

Emergencies

Police, fire
☎ *911 (free)*

Traveler's Aid Services
☎ *(212) 944 0013*
H *24 hrs*

Credit cards
V *(410) 581-3836*

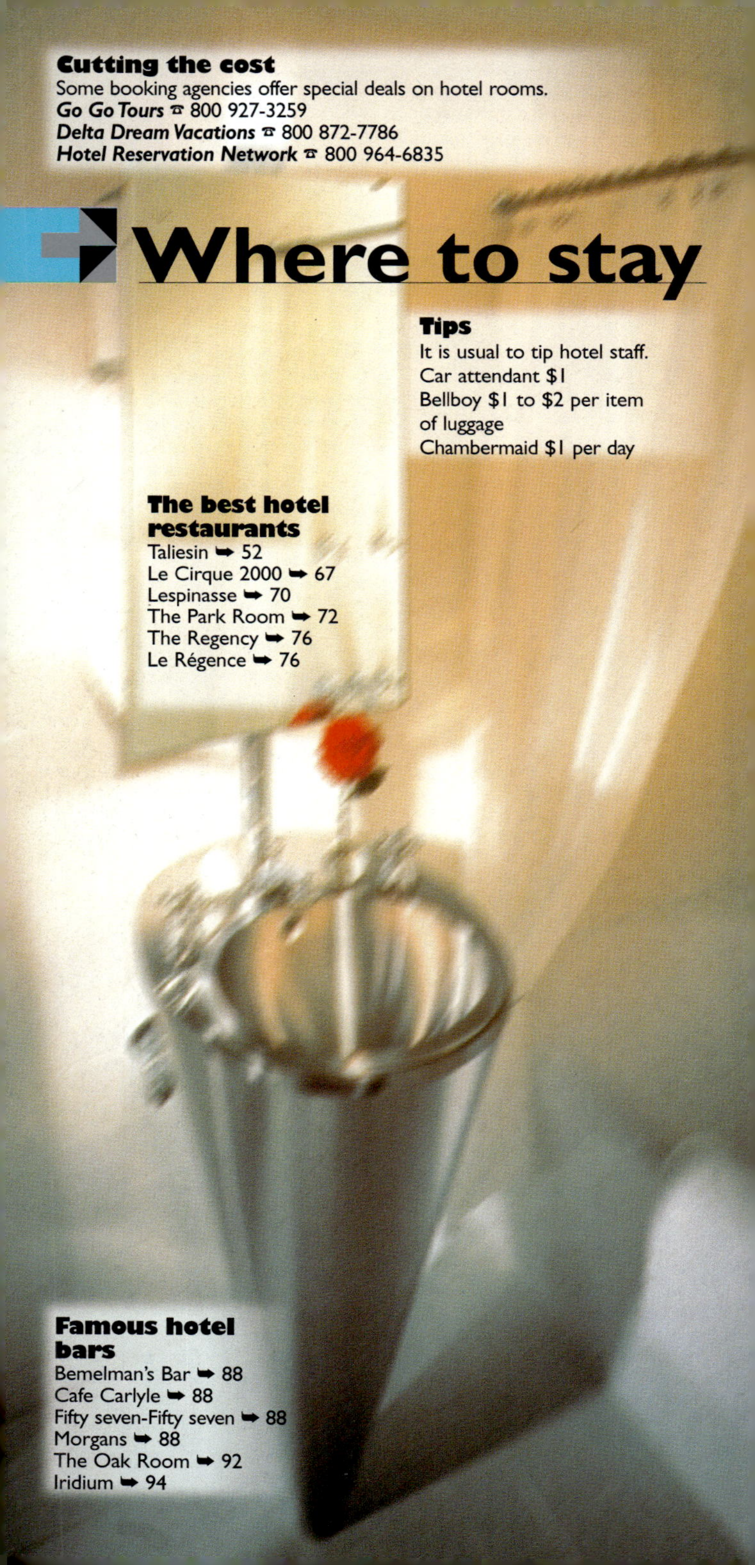

Cutting the cost

Some booking agencies offer special deals on hotel rooms.
Go Go Tours ☎ 800 927-3259
Delta Dream Vacations ☎ 800 872-7786
Hotel Reservation Network ☎ 800 964-6835

Where to stay

Tips

It is usual to tip hotel staff.
Car attendant $1
Bellboy $1 to $2 per item of luggage
Chambermaid $1 per day

The best hotel restaurants

Taliesin ➡ 52
Le Cirque 2000 ➡ 67
Lespinasse ➡ 70
The Park Room ➡ 72
The Regency ➡ 76
Le Régence ➡ 76

Famous hotel bars

Bemelman's Bar ➡ 88
Cafe Carlyle ➡ 88
Fifty seven-Fifty seven ➡ 88
Morgans ➡ 88
The Oak Room ➡ 92
Iridium ➡ 94

Prices

The following information is given for each hotel: number of rooms and price range; number of suites and top price; cost of the least expensive breakfast. Prices do not include hotel tax (14.25% plus $2 per night). Ask about special rates when you make your reservation.

76 Hotels

THE INSIDER'S FAVORITES

The man with the golden keys

How do you get a seat for a performance that's booked out? Or reserve the best table in a restaurant, find a babysitter or locate your lost luggage? The concierge knows the city and can help with all your problems: make use of him!

INDEX BY PRICE

5 PRICE CATEGORIES FOR HOTELS

● less than $150 for a double room
●● $151–$200
●●● $201–$250
●●●● $251–$300
●●●●● $301 or more

In the area

These two districts present a striking contrast. Downtown is the city's financial center, its narrow streets lined with skyscrapers. TriBeCa is the artistic center, home of New York's avant-garde, crammed with cast-iron industrial buildings from the 19th century. ■ Where to eat ➡ 50

Where to stay

SoHo Grand Hotel (1)

310 West Broadway N.Y. 10013 ☎ (212) 965-3000 ➡ (212) 965-3200

(Grand St.) M *Canal St.* ***369 rooms ●●●●●*** *5 suites $1049* *$8* *Canal House* *Grand Bar* *800 965-3000* @ *www.sohogrand.com*

A new and prestigious addition to TriBeCa's array of hotels. Bill Sofield's simple, elegant decor highlights the building's original cast-iron structure. The lobby is unconventionally located on the first floor. In the luxurious rooms, linens and decorative details have been chosen with care and include original photographs on loan from the neighboring Howard Greenberg Gallery. The penthouse balconies offer magnificent panoramic views over Manhattan.

The Millennium Hilton (2)

55 Church Street N.Y. 10007 ☎ (212) 693-2001 ➡ (212) 571-2316

(between Fulton and Dey Sts) M *Cortlandt St.* ***473 rooms ●●●●*** *94 suites $350* *free for guests* *The Grille, Taliesin ➡ 52* *Connoisseur* *800 752-0014*

The elegant black glass façade of this hotel, located opposite the World Trade Center, provides a foretaste of its modern entrance hall, a pleasant space decorated with precious woods. The spacious rooms combine teak and maple with opulent fabrics in shades of beige. There are splendid views over St Paul's Chapel ➡ 112 from the Taliesin restaurant ➡ 52 and the swimming pool on the 4th floor. For more personal service ask for one of the three penthouse suites on the 54th floor.

Marriott World Trade Center (3)

3 World Trade Center N.Y. 10048 ☎ (212) 938-9100 ➡ (212) 444-3444

(on West St.) M *Cortlandt St.* ***794 rooms ●●*** *14 suites $450* *$12* *Greenhouse Café* *Tall Ships Bar and Grill*

The design of the entrance is impressive; the rooms, by contrast, are somewhat lacking in character. However, direct access to the WTC Plaza ➡ 112 through the second floor gives you the feeling of being at the center of the world.

Marriott Financial Center (4)

85 West Street N.Y. 10006 ☎ (212) 385-4900 ➡ (212) 227-8136

(Albany St.) M *Cortlandt St.* ***491 rooms ●●*** *13 suites $400* *$12* *JW's* *Liberty Lounge, Pugsley's Pub*

The view over the Statue of Liberty ➡ 109 makes up for the unimaginative decor of the rooms, a disappointment after the opulence of the lobby, which features enormous Ming vases.

Not forgetting

■ **Seaport Suites (5)** 129 Front Street (between Wall and Pine Sts) N.Y. 10005 ☎ (212) 742-0003 ➡ (212) 724-0124 ●●●

➥52 ➥56 ➥76 ■ After dark ➥88 ■ What to see ➥110 ➥112 ■ Where to shop➥ 168

4

2

3

Luxury, quality, and service are the trademark of the hotels in Downtown and SoHo.

1

4

In the area

With their low brownstones, Chelsea and Greenwich Village still have a traditional, village-like character; at the same time their young, dynamic population ensures a vibrant, lively atmosphere. Here the hotels are among the most reasonable in the city ■ Where to eat ➡ 62 ➡ 64 ➡

Where to stay

Hotel 17 (6)

225 East 17th Street N.Y. 10003 ☎ (212) 475-2845 ➡ (212) 677-8178

(between Second and Third Aves) M *14th St.* P ***125 rooms*** ● *($180 per week) 5 suites $129* *on the roof*

The best deal in New York, as long as you don't mind having a room without a private bathroom or telephone. A former social center, it prides itself on being the only hotel to re-create the "genuine" New York atmosphere – in fact Woody Allen used it as a set for his *Manhattan Murder Mystery*. The rooms are decorated in an eclectic, bohemian style with satin quilted headboards and psychedelic wallpapers. It's a good idea to see the room first to make sure that it suits you. Children under 17 are not admitted.

Chelsea Inn (7)

46 West 17th Street N.Y. 10011 ☎ (212) 645-8989 ➡ (212) 645-1903

(between Fifth and Sixth Aves) M *Sixth Ave* P ***25 rooms*** ● *7 suites $149* *800 640-6469* @ *chelseainn@earthlink.net*

This delightful, intimate hotel occupies a 19th-century townhouse. The rooms are tastefully furnished with wooden furniture, and all of them have a kitchenette; the bathrooms are decorated with hand-painted flowers and animals, like something out of a child's storybook. The modest prices justify choosing a suite (large living room, bathroom, small kitchen, and small bedroom). Alternatively, choose a room facing the courtyard for peace and quiet.

The Larchmont Hotel (8)

27 West 11th Street N.Y. 10011 ☎ (212) 989-9333 ➡ (212) 989-9496

(between Fifth and Sixth Aves) M *14th St.* P ***55 rooms*** ● *free for guests*

A quiet, comfortable hotel with a thoroughly European atmosphere, perfectly situated in a shady street in the Village. Reasonable prices compensate for small drawbacks such as the eclectic decor and shared bathrooms.

Washington Square Park Hotel (9)

103 Waverly Place N.Y. 10011 ☎ (212) 777-9515 ➡ (212) 979-8373

(between Fifth and Sixth Aves) M *W. 4th St.* ***170 rooms*** ● *free for guests* *C III* 800 222-0418

Book in advance to guarantee a view over Washington Square and enjoy this lively spot. The lobby is elegantly decorated: marble flooring in contrasting colors, wrought ironwork, photos of New York in bygone days. The rooms facing the street are small but sunny, and decorated in a cheerful mint green.

Not forgetting

■ **Gramercy Park Hotel (10)** 2 Lexington Avenue (21st St.) N.Y. 10010 ☎ (212) 475-4320 ➡ (212) 505-0535 ●●

76 ■ After dark ➥ 86 ➥ 90 ➥ 98 ➥ 100 ■ Where to shop ➥ 168

8

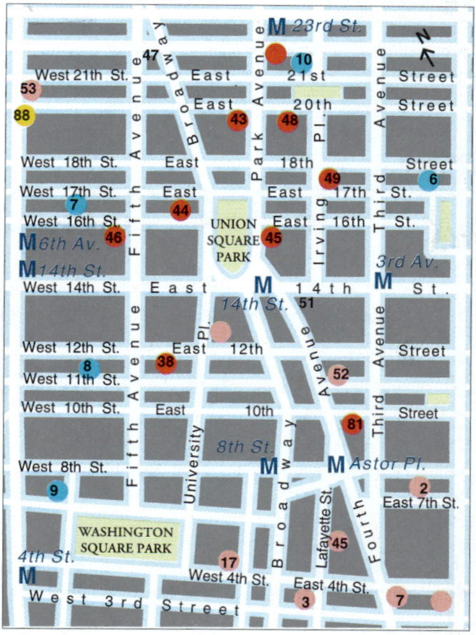

10

7

10

6

WASHINGTON SQUARE HOTEL

In the area

This district is neither glamorous nor residential. Since Macy's ➡ 147 opened in 1901 it has been the home of New York's ready-to-wear fashion industry, which is why it is known as the Garment District. The hotels here are good value, and the district is a favorite with bargain

Where to stay

Hotel Metro (11)

45 West 35th Street N.Y. 10001 ☎ (212) 947-2500 ➡ (212) 279-1310

(between Fifth and Sixth Aves) M *34th St.* P ***152 rooms*** ●● *22 suites $225* *free for guests* *on the roof* *800 356-3870*

The Metro has a great look. The art deco furniture, along with photos of 1930s starlets, gives the lobby a very Hollywood feel. The rooms could be larger, but crafted oak furniture and metallic Venetian blinds give them much more character than you would normally expect from a hotel in this price range. In winter you can relax in the library by the fire; in summer, lounge on the roof terrace, which offers a stunning view over the northwest corner of the Empire State Building ➡ 114.

Best Western Manhattan Hotel (12)

17 West 32nd Street N.Y. 10001 ☎ (212) 736-1600 ➡ (212) 790-2760

(between Fifth Ave and Broadway) M *34th St.* ***126 rooms*** ●● *26 suites $189* *$7.50* *Tullyos Dae Dong,* *800 551-2303* @ *applecorehotels.com*

The hotel's elaborate façade seems almost to flutter in the breeze along with the Japanese and Korean flags that hang from the front of the building. The entrance is designed in art deco style, with lighting effects and decorative details intended to transport your imagination into the world of the cinema. On the courtyard side the rooms in the upper floors have a view over the Empire State Building ➡ 114. Their elegant SoHo-style decor features framed posters of Marilyn Monroe by Andy Warhol, which make an interesting contrast with the flamboyant orange of the walls. An attractive feature for families is that children under 12 can stay free of charge.

Wolcott Hotel (13)

4 West 31st Street N.Y. 10001 ☎ (212) 268-2900 ➡ (212) 563-0096

(between Fifth Ave and Broadway) M *28th St* P ***109 rooms*** ● *50 suites $110* @ *sales@wolcott.com*

The Wolcott offers a curious mixture of faded grandeur and informality. The rococo lobby is positively exotic in effect, with a profusion of gilt, a magnificent chandelier, and rather rickety furnishings. Despite the ornamental hotchpotch and the long, dark corridors, the hotel has a friendly atmosphere, which carries on into the bedrooms, decorated in traditional American style with floral prints, and striking emerald-green carpets.

Not forgetting

■ **Hotel Stanford (14)** 43 West 32nd Street (Broadway) N.Y. 10001 ☎ (212) 563-1500 ➡ (212) 643-0157 ● ■ **Carlton (15)** 22 East 29th Street (between 5th and Madison Aves) N.Y. 10016 ☎ (212) 532-4100 ➡ (212) 889-8683 ●

hunters ➡ 168.
■ What to see ➡ 114 ■ Where to shop ➡ 146 ➡ 168

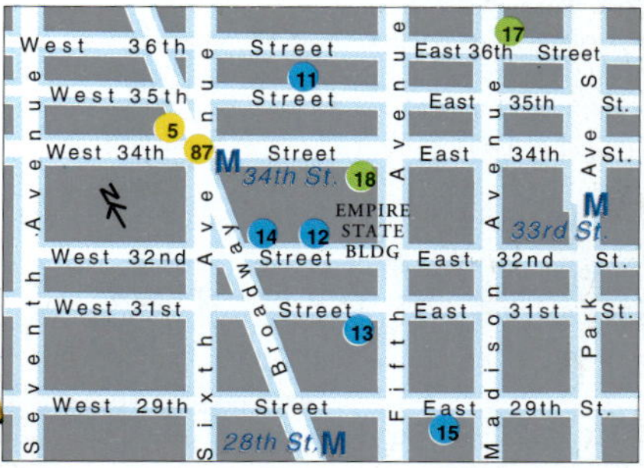

11

13

12

12

11

In the area

Murray Hill is named after an old country residence that once stood on this site; the great families of New York moved into the district in the early years of this century. The house of financier J.P. Morgan, whose library is now a museum ➡ 114, illustrates the grand style of this period.

Where to stay

Doral Tuscany (16)

120 East 39th Street N.Y. 10016 ☎ (212) 686-1600 ➡ (212) 779-7822

(Park Ave) M *Grand Central* P ***109 rooms*** ●●● *12 suites $450* *$9.50* *Adirondack Grille* *800 22 DORAL*

The public spaces feature exposed beams and walls in traditional Tuscan style – a striking but pleasant contrast to the New England-style decor of the spacious rooms, which are accented with fresh flowers.

Jolly Madison Towers (17)

22 East 38th Street N.Y. 10016 ☎ (212) 802-0600 ➡ (212) 447-0747

(Madison Ave) M *Grand Central* P ***245 rooms*** ●●● *6 suites* *$8* *Cinque Terre* *Whaler Bar* *800 225-4340*

The rooms are an elegant synthesis of European style with the warmth of traditional American rosewood furniture: they are pleasant and affordably priced although they are unlikely to make a lasting impression. More memorable is the delicious Northern Italian cooking that you can sample in the Cinque Terre.

Morgans (18)

237 Madison Avenue N.Y. 10016 ☎ (212) 686-0300 ➡ (212) 779-8352

(between 37th and 38th Sts) M *Grand Central* ***113 rooms*** ●●●● *27 suites $425* *free for guests* *Asia de Cuba* *Morgans Bar* *from Balcony Suite and PH Suite* *800 334-3408*

The rooms in this sophisticated hotel, a favorite with the fashion world, bear the hallmark of Andrée Putman's distinctively elegant designs. They appear more spacious than they really are, thanks to low-level furnishings and the cleverly camouflaged closets. Everything has been carefully thought out, down to the smallest detail. Special features and personal touches include signed works by Mapplethorpe, sofas below the windows, and luxury Kiehl's ➡ 144 toiletries for guests to pamper themselves with.

Shelburne Murray Hill (19)

303 Lexington Avenue N.Y. 10016 ☎ (212) 320-8025 ➡ (212) 779-7068

(37th St.) M *Grand Central* P ***272 suites*** ●●●● *$259* *Secret Harbor, Rooftop Garden* *800 637-8483*

The Shelburne's regulars come back time after time because this hotel makes them feel at home. All the rooms are suites with well-equipped kitchens, but dinner on the Rooftop Garden (where Fred Astaire used to practice his putting) is a delightful experience: the view over the Midtown skyline is the perfect appetizer.

Not forgetting

■ **Doral Park Avenue (20)** 70 Park Avenue (38th St.) N.Y. 10016 ☎ (212) 973-2500 ➡ (212) 973-2497 ●●

■ **Sheraton Russell (21)** 45 Park Avenue (between 36th and 37th Sts) N.Y. 10016 ☎ (212) 685-7676 *(212) 889-3193* ●●●●●

Today Murray Hill is one of the most select quarters of the city. ■ After dark ➥ 88 ■ What to see ➥ 114

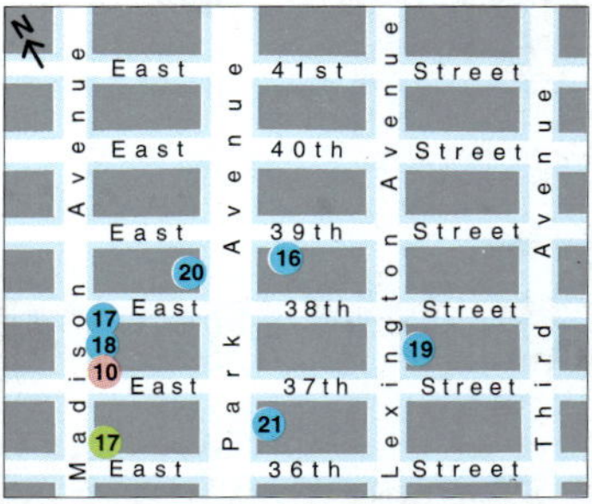

19

19

18

18

In the area
This district, flanked by Grand Central Station ➡ 106 and the UN headquarters ➡ 114, has a businesslike character (as its stores show ➡ 152). It comes to life during rush hour. ■ Where to eat ➡ 70 ➡ 82 ■ After dark ➡ 92 ■ What to see ➡ 114 ■ Where to shop

Where to stay

Hotel Lexington (22)
511 Lexington Ave N.Y. 10017 ☎ (212) 755-4400 ➡ (212) 751-4091

(48th St.) Grand Central **665 rooms ●●** *35 suites $275 $17 Dynasty, Vuli Raffles Suites 800 448-4471*

The hotel attracts an international business clientele, as can be seen from the clocks in the lobby, which show the different time zones around the world. This is not a luxury establishment, but the rooms are spacious and the huge marble bathrooms add an extra touch of class.

Roger Smith (23)
501 Lexington Ave N.Y. 10017 ☎ (212) 755-1400 ➡ (212) 319-9130

(47th St.) Grand Central **130 rooms ●●●** *21 suites $275 free for guests Lily's 800 445-0277*

This little Art Deco hotel prides itself on a taste for the beautiful things in life – it even organizes exhibitions of contemporary art. The hotel's curious mix of styles lends itself splendidly to this use: striking features include the oval-shaped lobby, the pink and purple frescos of Lily's restaurant, and the country-style charm of the comfortable rooms.

Grand Hyatt (24)
42nd between Park and Lexington N.Y. 10017 (Grand Central Terminal) ☎ (212) 883-1234 ➡ (212) 697-3772

(42nd St.) Grand Central **1347 rooms ●●●●●** *63 suites $335 $33 Crystal Fountain, Sun Garden Lounge, The Cigar Room at Trumpets*

A mecca both for families and for conference delegates, and a vast establishment. Despite the size this is a very attractive place, thanks to minimalist furniture, atmospheric lighting, and spacious rooms. The Chrysler Building ➡ 106 towers majestically over the glass roof of the Sun Garden Lounge. The Grand Hyatt is a listed building that still houses the Empire State Ballroom, which dates from the 1920s.

Crowne Plaza U.N. (25)
304 E. 42nd Street N.Y. 10017 ☎ (212) 986-8800 ➡ (212) 986-1758

(Between First and Second Ave) Grand Central **300 rooms ●●●●** *14 suites $349 $14.95 Cecil's*

This red-brick hotel does not reveal its character until you are beyond the elegant, austere entrance hall. The rooms on the top floors, decorated in subtle shades of beige, are larger than the others and have terraces and views over the East River.

Not forgetting

■ **Helmsley Middletown (26)** 148 East 48th Street (between Third and Lexington Aves) N.Y. 10017 ☎ (212) 755-3000 ➡ (212) 832-0261 ●●●
■ **Helmsley New York (27)** 212 East 42nd Street (between Second and Third Aves) N.Y. 10017 ☎ (212) 490-8900 ➡ (212) 490-8909 ●●●

➥ 152 ➥ 154

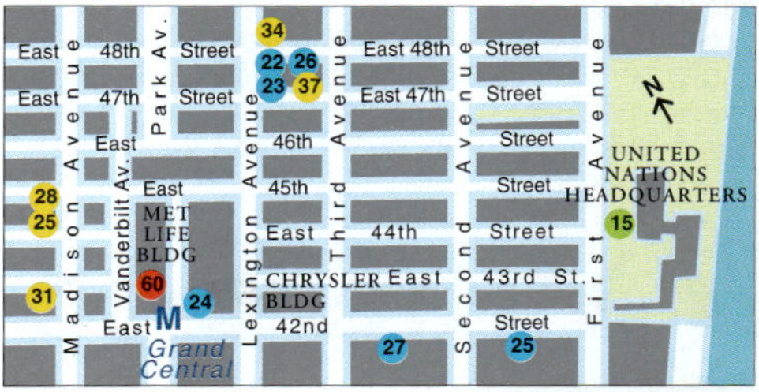

22

26

27

25

24

25

At the Crowne Plaza U.N., suites with jacuzzi and terraces overlook the Chrysler Building.

In the area

A few blocks away from Diamond District, this area has a distinctly elitist air: it is home to many prestigious private clubs. But Bryant Park hosts a variety of outdoor festivals and performances all summer.
■ Where to eat ➡ 68 ■ After dark ➡ 92

Where to stay

The Algonquin (28)

59 West 44th Street N.Y. 10036 ☎ (212) 840-6800 ➡ (212) 944-1419

(between Fifth and Sixth Aves) M *42nd St.* P ***142 rooms*** ●●●● *23 suites $429* *free for guests* *Oak Room* *Blue Bar, Lobby Bar* *Oak Room ➡ 92* *800 555-8345*

Dorothy Parker established the Algonquin as the heart of the literary scene in the 1920s, when her famous Round Table met daily in the Rose Room. Since then this has been a favorite haunt of the publishing and literary worlds. The recent renovation has preserved the atmosphere: comfortable and spacious lobby, wallpaper with drawings from the *New Yorker* and even a cat, Hamlet. Enjoy breakfast in the Oak Room ➡ 92 and order the soufflé of this legendary place.

Mansfield (29)

12 West 44th Street N.Y. 10036 ☎ (212) 944-6050 ➡ (212) 764-4477

(between Fifth and Sixth Aves) M *42nd St.* ***96 rooms*** ●●● *27 suites $279* *free for residents* *800 255-5167*

The Mansfield exudes an unforced elegance from every corner, especially the library where impressive dark wood shelves, iron tables, and leather armchairs create a very 1920s feel. Extremely friendly service makes up for the small size of the rooms. Altogether the hotel gives the impression of a small but chic private club.

Royalton (30)

44 West 44th Street N.Y. 10036 ☎ (212) 869-4400 ➡ (212) 869-8965

(between Fifth and Sixth Aves) M *42nd St.* P ***138 rooms*** ●●●●● *30 suites $425* *$25* *44* *Round Bar, Lobby Bar* *800 635-9013*

Staying at one of the trendiest New York hotels, designed by Philippe Starck, is for some the very last word in style. A fashionable crowd hangs out in the spacious lobby, with its theatrical decor of white drapery and goldfish bowls. The rooms are rather cramped, however.

Casablanca (31)

147 West 43rd Street N.Y. 10036 ☎ (212) 869-1212 ➡ (212) 391-7585

(between Sixth Ave and Broadway) M *Times Square* P ***48 rooms*** ●●● *4 suites $325* *free for guests*

A haven of exotic delights at the heart of Times Square. The lobby and walls of the bar-restaurant are covered with Moroccan tiles, and a fresco in the grand marble staircase depicts a romantic image of Casablanca viewed from a roof terrace.

Casablanca

Not forgetting

■ **Quality Hotel and Suites (32)** 59 West 46th Street (between Fifth and Sixth Aves) N.Y. 10036 ☎ (212) 719-2300 ➡ (212) 768-3477 ●●

■ Where to shop ➥ 152 ➥ 154 ➥ 168

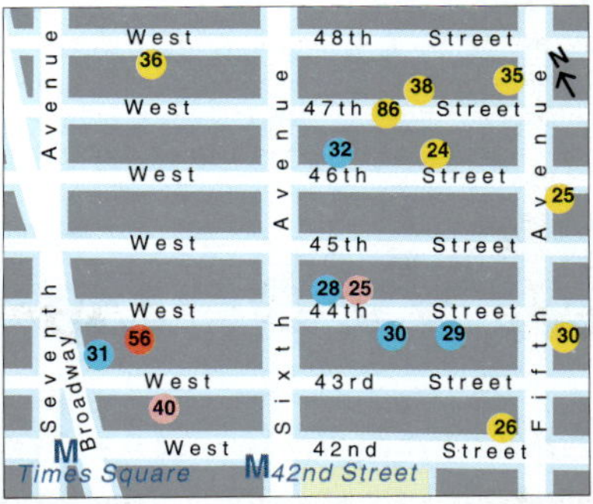

0

29

30

In the area

Times Square, at the heart of the Theater District, was named after the building belonging to the *N.Y.Times* in 1904. The area revolves around theaters and theatergoers. Enjoy walking through Times Square, and watch the neon lights come on all around. ■ Where to eat ➡ 68 ➡ 72

Where to stay

Edison Hotel (33)

228 West 47th Street N.Y. 10036 ☎ (212) 840-5000 ➠ (212) 596-6850

(between Broadway and Eighth Ave) *49th St.* ***850 rooms*** ● *30 suites $200* *free for guests* *Sofia's B* *Sofia's B Rum House* *Cafe Edison* *800 637-7070* *Edisonnyc@aol.com*

The Edison welcomes its guests in a huge art deco entrance hall, which is constantly busy; a collection of clocks shows the time all over the world. The spacious rooms are tastefully and simply furnished, becoming progressively brighter in the higher stories. A traditional deli ➡ 60 serves excellent borscht and Reuben sandwiches (towering concoctions of corned beef, sauerkraut, and melted swiss cheese on rye bread).

The Paramount (34)

235 West 46th Street N.Y. 10036 ☎ (212) 764-5500 ➠ (212) 575-4892

(between Broadway and Eighth Ave) *42nd St.* ***600 rooms*** ●●● *12 suites $395* *$15* *Le Mezzanine* *Whisky Bar* ➡ *86**, Library Bar*

Philippe Starck's other New York creation (Royalton ➡ 28) looks like something straight out of a 1950s spy novel. In the lobby the lighting is subtle; armchairs and sofas of all shapes and sizes are carefully arranged, brightened by colored cushions, inviting you to take a break. Old-fashioned telephones add to this John le Carré atmosphere. A humorous touch: mirrors outside the elevators light up and give you weather reports. The rooms are rather dark and cramped, with little or no view, but striking details make up for the lack of space: beds and washbasins standing on conical bases and spindly metallic wall lamps. Futurist-style telephones and two-tone furniture add to the distinctive style.

Broadway Inn (35)

264 West 46th Street N.Y. 10036 ☎ (212) 921-1824 ➠ (212) 768-2807

(Broadway) *50th St.* ***41 rooms*** ● *12 suites $195* *free for guests* *800 826-6300*

This delightful hotel is the perfect antidote to the bustle of this part of town. The lobby on the first floor is cozy and welcoming, with its brick walls, plants, and mahogany tables; tea and breakfast are served here. The rooms, decorated in a rather showy style, are well presented, very comfortable (some even have a jacuzzi), and extremely good value. On the whole the flashy style is more enjoyable than irritating. If you are a light sleeper avoid the rooms facing the street, where the noise of 46th Street is most audible.

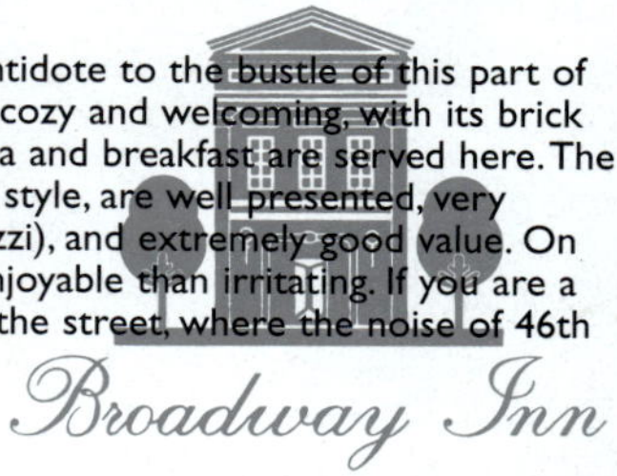

Not forgetting

■ **Michelangelo (36)** 152 West 51st Street (Seventh Ave) N.Y. 10019 ☎ (212) 765-1900 ➠ (212) 541-6604 ●●●●

■ **Renaissance New York (37)** 714 Seventh Avenue (between 47th and 48th Sts) N.Y. 10036 ☎ (212) 765-7676 ➠ (212) 765-1962 ●●●●

■ **Marriott Marquis (38)** 1535 Broadway (45th St.) N.Y. 10036 ☎ (212) 398-1900 ➠ (212) 704-8966 ●●●●

Theater District (42nd – 51st Streets) **D** C1-D2

■ After dark ➥ 86 ➥ 90 ➥ 92 ➥ 96 ➥ 98
■ Where to shop ➥ 154

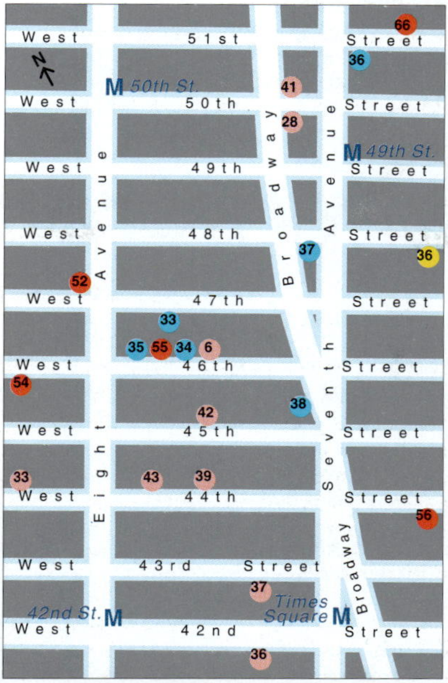

34

36

37

In the area

Between St Patrick's Cathedral and the UN building, magnificent residences and landmarks such as the General Electric building echo the splendors of a bygone age. ■ Where to eat ➡ 66 ➡ 70 ■ After dark ➡ 92 ■ What to see ➡ 116 ■ Where to shop ➡ 154

Where to stay

The Pickwick Arms (39)

230 East 51st Street N.Y. 10022 ☎ (212) 355-0300 ➡ (212) 755-5029

(between Second and Third Aves) *51st St.* ***350 rooms*** ● *$4.95* *on the roof* *800 742-5945*

A modest hotel, but sheltered from the din of the city. The rooms are small and a little stifling, decorated with old-fashioned prints and patterned carpets; the bathrooms are positively Lilliputian. However, it suits a smaller budget.

Waldorf Astoria & Waldorf Towers (40)

301 Park Avenue N.Y. 10022 ☎ (212) 355-3000 ➡ (212) 872-4784

(between 49th and 50th Sts) *51st St.* ***1380 rooms*** ●●●●● *200 suites $375* *$13.50* *Bull & Bear, Oscar's Peacock Alley, Inagiku* *Sir Harry's* *800 925-3673*

The Waldorf Astoria is the epitome of luxury and elegance. The impressive art deco lobby, which displays a clock made for the Chicago Exhibition of 1893, is a profusion of velvet, gilt, chandeliers, and mural paintings. However this decorative abundance does not carry through to the bedrooms, which are small and traditional. The suites of the Towers are larger, and also have magnificent views.

Beekman Tower Hotel (41)

3 Mitchell Place N.Y. 10017 ☎ (212) 355-7300 ➡ (212) 753-9366

(First Ave) *49th St.* ***174 suites*** ●●●● *$269* *$10* *Zephyr Grill, Top of the Tower*

The hotel offers spacious suites decorated in an English country-house style, furnished with burgundy-colored fabrics in the lounge and kitchenette. The unforgettable Top of the Tower restaurant has a panoramic view over the city.

The Box Tree (42)

250 East 49th Street N.Y. 10017 ☎ (212) 758-8320 ➡ (212) 308-3899

(between Second and Third Aves) *51st St.* ***13 rooms*** ●●● *free for guests* *The Box Tree*

This delightful hotel, which consists of two town houses, is more like an old-world inn. Huge armchairs, floors of brick and wood, a fireplace flanked by enamel caryatids, and a crackling fire contribute to the romantic atmosphere of the entrance hall. A splendid Art Nouveau staircase leads to opulent rooms with brocade drapery, fireplaces, and beautifully crafted four-poster beds.

Not forgetting

■ **Doral Inn (43)** 541 Lexington Avenue (49th St.) N.Y. 10022 ☎ (212) 755-1200 ➡ (212) 319-8344 ●●●

■ **Hotel Intercontinental (44)** 111 East 48th Street (Park Ave) N.Y. 10017 ☎ (212) 755-5900 ➡ (212) 644-0079 ●●●●

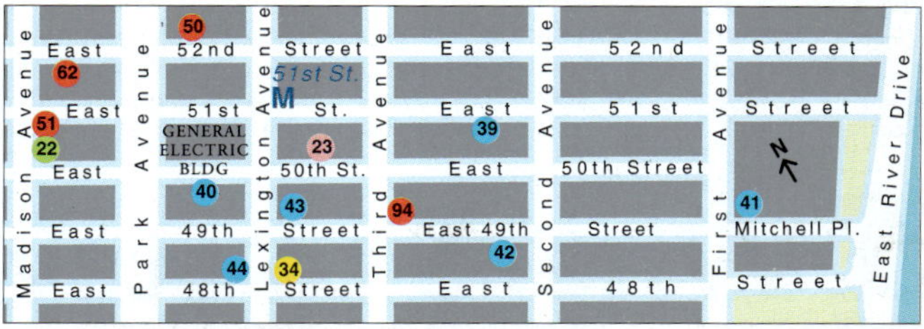
Madison Avenue
Park Avenue
Lexington Avenue
Third Avenue
Second Avenue
First Avenue
East 52nd Street
East 51st Street
East 50th Street
East 49th Street
East 48th Street
51st St.
M
GENERAL ELECTRIC BLDG
Mitchell Pl.
East River Drive
N
50
62
51
22
23
39
40
43
94
41
42
44
34

40

41

41

44 40

In the area

Midtown was once the district where New York's great families and magnates lived; gradually stores and large companies moved here in the early part of the century. Today this forest of skyscrapers is the city's second-largest business center after Downtown. ■ Where to eat ➡ 66

Where to stay

Elysée (45)

60 East 54th Street N.Y. 10022 ☎ (212) 753-1066 ➟ (212) 980-9278

(between Park and Madison Aves) M *Lexington Ave* ***88 rooms ●●●●*** *11 suites $325* *free for guests* *Monkey Bar* *800 535-9733* @ *elysee99@aol.com*

The main charm of the Elysée, apart from the haphazardly arranged hand-painted furniture, resides in the quality of the service. The hotel's seasoned staff have looked after the likes of Maria Callas, Marlon Brando, and Tennessee Williams and know how to be both attentive and discreet. The rooms are cleverly furnished in rococo and Empire styles; their marble bathrooms have monogrammed towels and subtle lighting. Chinese vases and 19th-century portraits line the corridors, while the elegant Clubroom and the famous Monkey Bar offer fashionable settings for a drink or dinner.

Omni Berkshire Palace (46)

21 East 52nd Street N.Y. 10022 ☎ (212) 753-5800 ➟ (212) 754-5020

(Madison Ave) M *Fifth Ave* ***325 rooms ●●●●●*** *47 suites $400* *$13* *Kokachin* *800 843-6664*

An elegant establishment, with Empire furniture adding a touch of European class. The Omni offers large, comfortable rooms and personal service. A quirky detail: this is one of the few hotels where the telephones are used to control the lights, television, and room temperature.

New York Palace (47)

455 Madison Avenue N.Y. 10022 ☎ (212) 888-7000 ➟ (212) 303-6000

(between 50th and 51st Sts) M *51st St.* P ***810 rooms ●●●●●*** *100 suites $425* *$22* *Le Cirque* ➡ *66*, *Istana* *triplex suite*

The hotel is a striking combination of a modern 54-story tower (1980) and Villard Houses (1882) ➡ 166, a landmark building in the style of an Italian palazzo. In the marble lobbies, classical features are combined with floors displaying Escheresque motifs. The hotel's different categories of rooms and suites are arranged by floor. The standard rooms occupy the 8th through the 28th floor; in the 29th through the 38th floor are the executive rooms and suites, with private living rooms and stunning views over the back of St Patrick's Cathedral ➡ 116 and the Hudson; from the 40th through the 54th floor are the towers and the four triplex suites, with their own entrances and butler service, and individual decor. The excellent restaurant, Le Cirque 2000 ➡ 67, in the landmark part of the hotel, has recently revised its menu. It has its own separate entrance from the beautiful courtyard.

Not forgetting

■ **Lombardy (48)** 111 East 56th Street (between Park and Lexington Aves) N.Y. 10022 ☎ (212) 753-8600 ➟ (212) 754-5683 ●●● ■ **The Drake Swissotel (49)** 440 Park Avenue (56th St.) N.Y. 10022 ☎ (212) 421-0900 ➟ (212) 371-4190 ●●●●

➥ 70 ■ After dark ➥ 88
➥ 92 ■ What to see ➥ 116
■ Where to shop ➥ 156
➥ 158 ➥ 160 ➥ 162

47

49

45

45

47

Old furniture and warm tones create peaceful retreats.

In the area

Midtown's most beautiful buildings are without doubt between Fifth and Sixth Avenues. This area has a distinctive refined and elegant atmosphere.
■ Where to eat ➥ 70 ➥ 74 ■ After dark ➥ 90 ■ Where to shop ➥ 147 ➥ 156 ➥ 158 ➥ 161 ➥ 162 ■ What to See ➥ 116

Where to stay

Shoreham (50)

33 West 55th Street N.Y. 10019 ☎ (212) 247-6700 ➟ (212) 765-9741

(between Fifth and Sixth Aves) M *55th St* **24 rooms ●●●●** *26 suites $305* *free for guests* *La Caravelle*

This hotel could be mistaken for an annex of the Museum of Modern Art ➥ 116, which is located two blocks away. Its unconventional decor is a happy combination of contemporary design (reception desk in resin and steel, gray marble floor, curved concrete-faced ceilings, paintings by Robert Fabricant) and a profusion of original works and furniture from the 1930s (aluminum tubular armchairs by Warren McArthur, futurist murals by Winold Reiss, including *Skyscrapers* and *Airplane*, and photoengravings by Karl Blossfeldt). The rooms, with their minimalist decor, offer a peaceful haven from city life and attract a clientele from the artistic and theatrical worlds.

St Regis (51)

2 East 55th Street N.Y. 10022 ☎ (212) 753-4500 ➟ (212) 787-3447

(Fifth Ave) M *Fifth Ave* ***241 rooms* ●●●●●** *19 suites $795* *$40* *Lespinasse* ➥ *70* *King Cole* *800 759-7550*

This is more than a temple of luxury, it is an institution. John Jacob Astor had the hotel built in 1904, in the Beaux-Arts style, for the then outlandish sum of six million dollars. After a costly restoration the sumptuous lobby has regained all its former splendor, with mahogany paneling, red velvet armchairs and Waterford crystal chandeliers. The high-ceilinged rooms are furnished in Louis XV-style, with a sitting area, a good deal of brocade, sofas, and a tea table with a fruit basket that is replenished daily. The two-tone marble bathrooms of the double rooms are stocked with Bijan ➥ 158 in the guest rooms and Tiffany ➥ 162 toiletries in the suites. A cocktail in the luxurious King Cole Bar makes a delightful prelude to dinner in the Lespinasse restaurant ➥ 70.

The Peninsula New York (52)

700 Fifth Avenue N.Y. 10019 ☎ (212) 247-2200 ➟ (212) 903-3949

(55th St.) M *Fifth Ave* ***186 rooms* ●●●●●** *56 suites $700* *$22.50* *Adrienne, Le Bistro* *Pen-Top Bar, Gotham* *800 262-9467* @ *pny@peninsula.com*

Cordless phones and marble bathrooms are just two of the luxuries enjoyed by guests in this superb Beaux-Arts style hotel, renovated in 1998 (reopening in November). After experiencing the opulence of its bedrooms, the Art Nouveau decor, the restaurants and roof-top bar, one is left with the discouraging impression that life has little left to offer.

Not forgetting

■ **Gorham (53)** 136 West 55th Street (between Sixth and Seventh Aves) N.Y. 10019 ☎ (212) 245-1800 ➟ (212) 582-8332 ●●●

■ **RIHGA Royal (54)** 151 West 54th Street (between Sixth and Seventh Aves) N.Y. 10019 ☎ (212) 307-5000 ➟ (212) 765-6530 ●●●●●

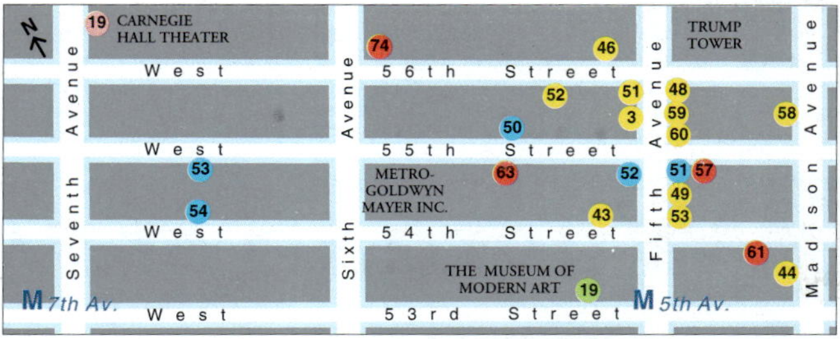
CARNEGIE HALL THEATER
TRUMP TOWER
West 56th Street
West 55th Street
West 54th Street
West 53rd Street
Seventh Avenue
Sixth Avenue
Fifth Avenue
Madison Avenue
METRO-GOLDWYN MAYER INC.
THE MUSEUM OF MODERN ART
M 7th Av.
M 5th Av.
19
74
46
52
51
48
59
58
3
60
50
53
63
52
51
57
49
54
43
53
61
44
19

50

51

51

52

52

In the area

For breakfast at Tiffany's, a manicure at Elizabeth Arden or a concert at Carnegie Hall ➥ 90, this is the district to visit. ■ Where to eat ➥ 74 ➥ 75 ■ After dark ➥ 88 ➥ 90 ■ Where to shop ➥ 146 ➥ 147 ➥ 158 ➥ 160 ➥ 161 ➥ 162

Where to stay

Helmsley Windsor (55)

100 West 58th Street N.Y. 10019 ☎ (212) 265-2100 ➠ (212) 581-1382

(Sixth Ave) M *57th St.* P ***192 rooms*** ●● *52 suites $260* *free for guests* *800 221-4982*

The Windsor is not in the same class as the other hotels in the Helmsley chain. However, it is unpretentious and well located, with reasonable prices for small rooms.

Four Seasons Hotel (56)

57 East 57th Street N.Y. 10022 ☎ (212) 758-5700 ➠ (212) 758-5711

(Madison Ave) M *59th St.* ***310 rooms*** ●●●●● *60 suites $825* *$25* *Fifty Seven-Fifty Seven* ➥ 88 *800 332-3442*

This masterpiece by I.M. Pei is the apex of the luxury hotel scene in New York. Once past the grand staircase you will discover a minimalist paradise made of precious materials. The walls of the rooms are covered with English sycamore, making them seem larger. The health and beauty center and the first-class cuisine of Fifty Seven-Fifty Seven ➥ 88 are among the luxury facilities on offer; the world's finest boutiques have taken up residence in the Four Seasons, too, so you can add to your wardrobe without even venturing outside. The Governor suite offers a splendid view over Central Park ➥ 122.

Salisbury (57)

123 West 57th Street N.Y. 10019 ☎ (212) 246-1300 ➠ (212) 977-7752

(between Sixth and Seventh Aves) M *57th St.* P ***128 rooms*** ●●● *82 suites $219* *free for guests* *888 692-5757*

In this conventiently located hotel, the rooms are pleasantly simple, even if some of the bathrooms are in need of renovation. Although there is no restaurant, guests are fully provided for: the suites include kitchenettes or you can have meals delivered to your room.

Le Parker Meridien (58)

118 West 57th Street N.Y. 10019 ☎ (212) 245-5000 ➠ (212) 708-7477

(between Sixth and Seventh Aves) M *57th St.* ***444 rooms*** ●●●●● *246 suites $375* *$16* *Seppi's, Norma's* *800 543-4300* @ *parkermer@aol.com*

As you go through the door you enter an impressive atrium, two floors high, with the reception on one side and Bar Montparnasse on the other. The rooms to the north, decorated in Greek/classical style, have a dizzying view over Central Park ➥ 122.

Not forgetting

■ **Wyndham Hotel (59)** 42 West 58th Street (between Fifth and Sixth Aves) N.Y. 10019 ☎ (212) 753-3500 ➠ (212) 754-5638 ●

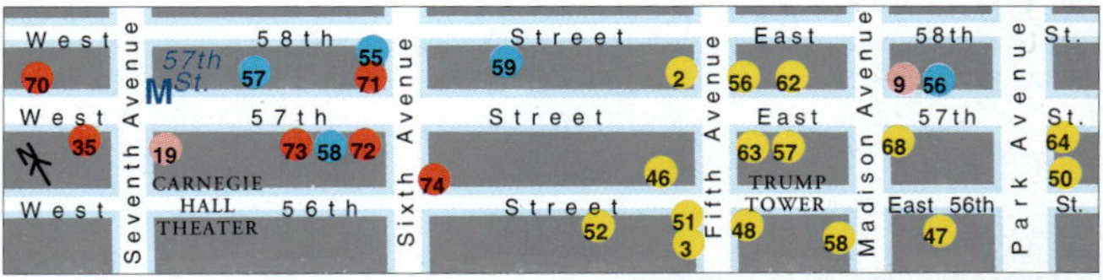

58

56

56

56

55

56

Harry and Leona Helmsley's hotel empire includes four of the grandest hotels in Manhattan.

In the area

The grand buildings bordering Central Park ➡ 122 are a slice of New York's past, also immortalized by these luxury hotels. In their lobbies, famous faces, film stars, and business magnates mingle with curious onlookers. ■ Where to eat ➡ 72 ➡ 78 ■ After dark ➡ 88 ■ Where

Where to stay

The Pierre (60)

2 East 61st Street N.Y. 10021 ☎ (212) 838-8000 ➡ (212) 758-1615

(Fifth Ave) M *Fifth Ave* ***177 rooms ●●●●●*** *25suites $695* *$18.50* *Café Pierre* *The Rotunda*

The Pierre deserved its Designers Circle Award for its fabrics alone. One of its dazzling public rooms, The Rotunda, is famous for its teas and especially for the trompe-l'oeil frescoes that match the Fragonard Room in the Frick Collection ➡ 120, a few blocks away on 70th Street. Some of the rooms seem rather uninspired by comparison, but the breakfast in bed, free local messenger service, beauty salon, the barber and around-the-clock service, extend the luxury hotel concept to the ultimate degree.

The Plaza Hotel (61)

Fifth Avenue N.Y. 10019 ☎ (212) 759-3000 ➡ (212) 759-3167

(Central Park South) M *Fifth Ave* ***780 rooms ●●●●●*** *70 suites $650* *$25* *Oak Room, Edwardian Room, Palm Court Oyster Bar,* *Oak Bar* *Palm Court* *800 759-3000*

Because of its location and reputation, The Plaza is rightly regarded as a New York landmark. It attracts a constant stream of famous visitors and remains an enduring symbol of the high life. The stunning Renaissance decor of the lobby bears witness to this, with crystal chandeliers hanging from dizzying heights above a mosaic floor; and in the Edwardian Room the opulent wood paneling is worthy of royalty. The suites, which include marble bathrooms decorated with bronze accessories, are equally impressive. At the other end of the scale, however the cheapest rooms are nowhere near as stylish, and some are so tiny that you can barely stand sideways between the wall and the foot of the bed.

The Westin Central Park South (62)

112 Central Park South N.Y. 10019
☎ (212) 757-1900 ➡ (212) 757-9620

(between Sixth and Seventh Aves) M *57th St.* ***199 rooms ●●●●●*** *15 suites $750* *$25* *Fantinos*

Formerly known as the Ritz-Carlton, the atmosphere in this hotel is so sophisticated that other luxury hotels may almost seem like 'nouveau riche' upstarts by comparison. Its peaceful drawing room and marble-topped furniture bring the stately and elegant New York of Henry James novels back to life. The rooms are spacious, decorated with antique lamps and bedspreads printed with pineapple motifs (which were formerly a symbol of wealth).

Not forgetting

■ **Sherry Netherland (63)** 781 Fifth Avenue (59th St.) N.Y. 10022 ☎ (212) 355-2800 ➡ (212) 319-4306 ●●●●

■ **Helmsley Park Lane (64)** 36 Central Park South (between Fifth and Sixth Aves) N.Y. 10019 ☎ (212) 371-4000 ➡ (212) 521-6656 ●●●●●

to shop
➡ 160
➡ 162
➡ 164

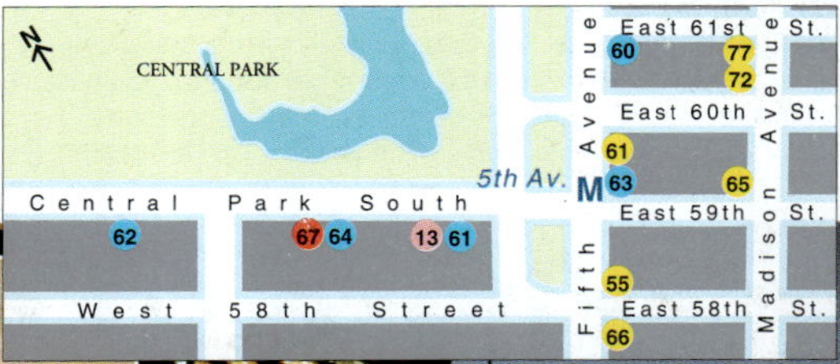

In the area

The Upper East Side has held its own with the passing of the years, retaining its majestic beauty, while Madison Avenue has plunged into the consumer age. The recent boom in "mega boutiques" has brought all the major designer names within the reach of fashionable New Yorkers.

Where to stay

The Mark (65)

25 East 77th Street N.Y. 10021 ☎ (212) 744-4300 ➠ (212) 744-2749

(between Fifth and Madison Aves) M *77th St.* ***120 rooms*** ●●●●● *60 suites $575* *$18* *Mark's*

The elegant marble entrance is just off Madison Avenue. Reproductions of Piranesi etchings hang in the rooms decorated in the Italian neoclassical style in hues of yellows and grays. Most of them have a view over Central Park ➥ 122 and many have kitchenettes for those who do not wish to visit the peaceful restaurant.

The Carlyle (66)

35 East 76th Street N.Y. 10021 ☎ (212) 744-1600 ➠ (212) 717-4682

(Madison Ave) M *77th St.* ***128 rooms*** ●●●●● *46 suites $600* *$17* *Gallery, The Carlyle* *Bemelmans Bar* *➥ 88* *Café Carlyle* *➥ 92*

In this timeless establishment, the rooms are elegant, with luxurious touches here and there: Fauchon biscuits in the bar, bottles of Givenchy eau-de-cologne in the bathrooms. The lobby is more like a museum than a hotel entrance, with Chippendale mirrors and 18th-century French tapestries. The frescoes in Bemelmans Bar ➥ 88 were painted by the eponymous illustrator.

The Barbizon (67)

140 East 63rd Street N.Y. 10021 ☎ (212) 838-5700 ➠ (212) 223-3287

(Lexington Ave) M *Lexington Ave* ***325 rooms*** ●●● *20 suites $425* *$17.50*

The Barbizon was once a women-only hotel, whose famous former residents include Grace Kelly. The rooms, completely renovated, are neat and stylish, with modern iron bedsteads, pine furniture, and pink floral carpets; the bathrooms are small and dazzlingly white.

The Regency (68)

540 Park Avenue N.Y. 10021 ☎ (212) 759-4100 ➠ (212) 826-5674

(61st St.) M *Lexington Ave* ***292 rooms*** ●●●●● *72 suites $625* *$25* *540 Restaurant* *The Library* *➥ 76*

The luxurious lobby, decorated in Louis XIV-style, has been updated with contemporary details: marble walls and floor, rare woods and alabaster chandeliers. The spacious rooms are targeted at business travelers, and the Library is perfect for business breakfasts or cocktails.

Not forgetting

■ **The Surrey (69)** 20 East 76th Street (Madison Ave) N.Y. 10021 ☎ (212) 288-3700 ➠ (212) 628-1459 ●●● *Room service available from neighboring restaurant: the Café Boulud.* ■ **Plaza-Athénée (70)** 37 East 64th Street (Madison and Park Aves) N.Y. 10021 ☎ (212) 734-9100 ➠ (212) 772-0958 ●●●●● ■ **Lowell Hotel** 28 East 63rd Street N.Y. 10021 ☎ (212) 838-1400 ➠ (212) 838-9194 60 ●●●●●

■ Where to eat ➡ 76 ➡ 78
■ After dark ➡ 88
➡ 92 ■ What to see ➡ 120
■ Where to shop ➡ 164

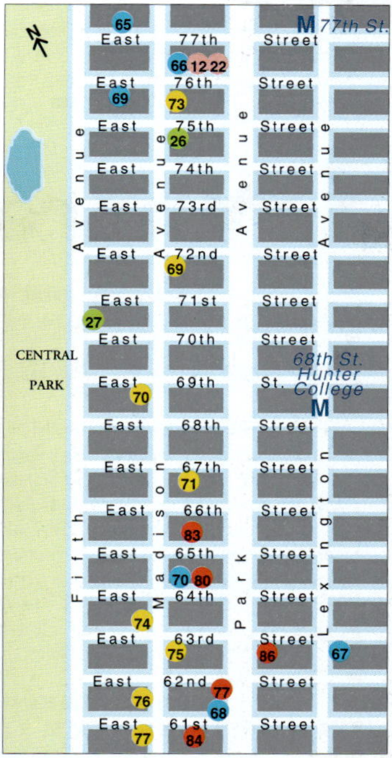

67

70

65

66

70

In the area

The Upper West Side is a quiet, residential area, flanked by Central Park West to the east and Riverside Drive to the west. Its cultural landmarks are Lincoln Center ➡ 102 and the Museum of Natural History ➡ 122. ■ Where to eat ➡ 76 ➡ 80 ■ After dark ➡ 94 ➡ 100 ➡ 102

Where to stay

Country Inn the City (71)

270 West 77th Street N.Y. 10024 ☎ (212) 580-4183 ➡ (212) 874-3981

(between Broadway and West End Ave) M *79th St.* P ***4 apartments*** ●

This brownstone has been carefully restored, comfortable yet elegant down to the smallest detail. It has four apartments, decorated in varying styles, including the Honeymoon Suite with its white floor, marble tables, and wisteria-covered terrace, ideal for breakfast. The Empire-style bedroom features a luxurious colonial bed made in Indonesia, sofas covered in red silk, and antique mirrors. Country Inn provides only minimal dining facilities: it is up to you to cook in your kitchenette, which is supplied with the basics. There are only two restrictions on this low-price luxury: children under 12 are not permitted, and you have to book for a minimum of three nights.

The Milburn Hotel (72)

242 West 76th Street N.Y. 10023 ☎ (212) 362-1006 ➡ (212) 721-5476

(between Broadway and West End Ave) M *72nd St.* P ***60 rooms*** ● *60 suites $170* *800 833-9622*

This small, discreet hotel is located in a tree-lined street one block from Central Park ➡ 122, and welcomes its guests in a Victorian-style lobby, with elegant mahogany paneling and oriental carpets. The rooms are generously sized and the decor is simple, in shades of olive green, creating a contemporary, if slightly antiseptic atmosphere. If possible book a room on the street side because there is little traffic and the views are pleasant.

Empire Radisson (73)

44 West 63rd Street N.Y. 10023 ☎ (212) 265-7400 ➡ (212) 245-3382

(between Broadway and Columbus Ave) M *Columbus Circle* P ***351 rooms*** ●●● *25 suites $275* *$14* *West 63rd St. Steakhouse* *Iridium* ➡ *92* *800 333-3333*

The Empire Radisson was the first hotel to open on this side of Central Park ➡ 122. Its high ceilings, wide staircase, grand paintings and wrought-iron candelabras give it the air of a Tudor manor. Models of opera stage-sets designed by Giuseppe Galli Bibiena and a rather unnerving portrait of Lady Macbeth will transport you into the theatrical world of the neighboring Lincoln Center ➡ 102. The rooms are airy and comfortable, with well-placed mirrors that make them look larger. The bar, with its deep armchairs, leather sofas, and billiard tables, has an English-style charm; here you can eat a delicious breakfast, or drink late into the night.

Not forgetting

■ **Excelsior (74)** 45 West 81st Street (Columbus Ave) N.Y. 10024
☎ (212) 362-9200 ➡ (212) 721-2994 ●●

■ **Beacon (75)** 2130 Broadway (75th St.) N.Y. 10023
☎ (212) 787-1100 ➡ (212) 724-0839 ●●

■ **Mayflower (76)** Central Park West (61st St) N.Y. 10023
☎ (212) 265-0060 ➡ (212) 265-5098 ●●

■ What to see
➥ 122
■ Where to shop
➥ 166

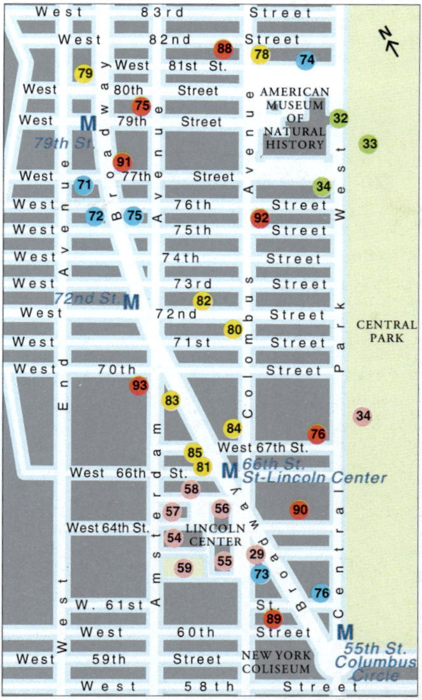

71

74

The hotels in the Upper West Side offer a more personal service.

75

75

73

More than just restaurants ...
All over Midtown and Downtown there are food carts where you can try hot dogs, soups, tacos, pretzels, baked potatoes, bagels ➥ 142 and all the other foods New Yorkers love for lunch.

Where to eat

Price categories
The prices given in this guide represent the average cost of a full meal for one person (appetizer, main course, dessert, and drinks), including tax.

Tips
Your tip should be between 15% and 20% of the bill, or twice the tax payable (8.25%).

Meal times
Americans take a light, quick lunch between noon and 2pm, and eat dinner after 5.30pm. Most restaurants in Midtown and the Financial District are closed on Sunday.

Modern American cuisine

American cuisine is currently undergoing a renaissance: the leading chefs are revitalizing traditional American dishes using local produce, new cooking methods, and French, Italian and Asian influences. This subtle mix of flavors is often combined with striking presentation, making a meal into a work of art.

99 Restaurants

THE INSIDER'S FAVORITES

INDEX BY TYPE

AND BY PRICE CATEGORY

- ● less than $15
- ●● $15–$30
- ●●● $31–$45
- ●●●● $46–$60
- ●●●●● $61 and over

Basic facts
The best way to appreciate the full effect of New York's high-rise world is by watching the sun set over the Manhattan skyline from the top of one of the city's skyscrapers. Witness the glowing colors of sunset and see the lights come on all over the city: a fairytale spectacle, with the

Where to eat

The Terrace (1)

400 West 119th Street N.Y. 10027 ☎ (212) 666-9490 ➟ (212) 666-3471

(between Amsterdam Ave and Morningside Dr.) M *116th St.* ***French*** ●●●●
Tue.–Sat. noon–2.30pm, 6–10pm

The Terrace, in Morningside Heights, offers a romantic setting with a relaxed, unpretentious atmosphere. It has a stunning view over Harlem and the northern tip of Manhattan, and the George Washington Bridge.

2

2

RAINBOW!

2

1

Empire State Building and the Chrysler Building as its two highlights. Having a drink or dinner in one of these restaurants is a luxury that is not to be missed.

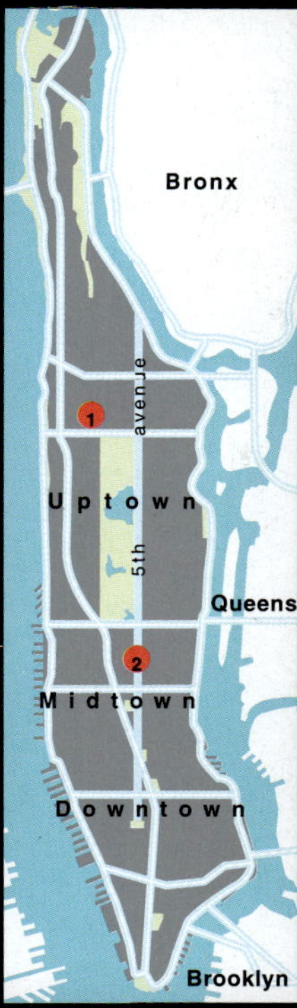

The Rainbow Room (2)

30 Rockefeller Plaza N.Y. 10112 ☎ (212) 632-5000 ➡ (212) 632-5072

(49th St., 64th floor) M *50th St.* ***Modern American*** ●●●●●
Tue.–Sat. 5–11pm; Sun. 11.30am–2.30pm (brunch), 6–9pm

As the dance floor rotates and the orchestra plays, you have Manhattan at your feet. The menu is traditional, but a new chef has improved the quality of the classics and added some innovations. Dress for the occasion and lose yourself in a world of dreams.

Basic facts

New Yorkers have long neglected one of the chief attractions of their city: the water all around them. Now a number of restaurants have opened to take advantage of this unique setting. Savor some of the best of American cooking while you enjoy views of the Hudson and East

Where to eat

3

4

Bryant Park Grill (3)

25 West 40th Street N.Y. 10018 ☎ (212) 840-6500 ➠ (212) 840-8122

(behind the Public Library) M *42nd St.* ***Traditional American*** ●●● ▣ ⊙ *Lunch Mon.–Sun. 11.30am–3.30pm; dinner Mon.–Sun. from 5pm, hours vary with the seasons.* Y ✱

This pavilion is a gastronomic jewel in Midtown's popular park. In the summer it can cater for hundreds of guests on the terrace and lawns. The menu offers original dishes drawn from as many different cultures as there are ethnic groups in New York.

Windows on the World (4)

1 World Trade Center N.Y. 10048 ☎ (212) 524-7000 ➠ (212) 524-7016

(West St., 107th floor) M *Cortlandt St.* ***Traditional American*** ●●●●● ▣ ⊙ *Mon.–Thur. 5–10.30pm; Fri.–Sat. 5–11.30pm; Sun. 5–10pm* Y *The Greatest Bar on Earth* ➡ *88*

Dinner in this restaurant with its panoramic view will leave you with your head in the clouds. The food is as delectable as the magnificent views, and the selection of wines from the Cellar in the Sky, which has more than 20,000 bottles in its stores, is impressive. Alternatively you can have lunch in the Greatest Bar on Earth ➡ *88*.

rivers, even more impressive by night; or dine on one of the boats that tour Manhattan and Hudson Bay. Contact *World Yacht, Pier 81, W. 41st Street* ☎ *(212) 630-8100.*

5

5

5

The River Cafe (5)
1 Water Street, Brooklyn N.Y. 11201
☎ (718) 522-5200 ➡ (718) 875-0037

(at the foot of the Brooklyn Bridge) ***Modern American*** ●●●●●
Mon.–Sat. noon–2.30pm, 6–11pm; Sun. 11.30am–2.30pm, 6–11pm

One of the birthplaces of modern American cooking, this floating restaurant offers varied and adventurous fare with unforgettable views of the East River and Manhattan.

In the area

Wall Street lives and eats at a hectic pace. Fast-food outlets abound, but you can find some more civilized places to eat, particularly in the World Financial Center and in South Street Seaport. ■ Where to stay ➡ 18 ■ After dark ➡ 88 ■ What to see ➡ 110 ➡ 112 ■ Where to shop ➡ 168

Where to eat

Hudson River Club (6)

4 World Financial Center, 250 Vesey Street N.Y. 10281
☎ (212) 786-1500 ➡ (212) 786-0103

(Vessey St) M *Cortlandt St.* ***Traditional American*** ●●●● *Mon.–Thur. 11.30am–2.30pm, 5–9.30pm; Fri. 11.30am–2.30pm, 5–10pm; Sat. 5–10pm; Sun. 11.30am–2.30pm*

This luxurious modern restaurant offers a view over the river and the big yachts moored at North Cove Yacht Marina at the World Financial Center. The menu pays tribute to the history of the Hudson River Valley, a fertile territory for fishing and agriculture. Specialties range from fresh foie gras of duck to American shad eggs, all washed down with wines from New York State. Situated close to the two Centers, the clientele is drawn mainly from the business world.

Taliesin (7)

The Millennium Hilton, 55 Church Street N.Y. 10007
☎ (212) 312-2000 ➡ (212) 312-2060

(between Dey and Fulton Sts) M *Cortlandt St.* ***Modern American*** ●●●● *Mon.–Thur. 6.30am–2.30pm, 6–10pm; Fri. 6.30am–2.30pm, 6–10.30pm; Sat. 6–10.30pm.*

Finding a restaurant that is both luxurious and comfortable in the Financial District is no easy matter. This is why Wall Street's financiers opt for this formal establishment at the Millennium Hilton ➡ 18, an elegant glass and steel block. The ambitious cuisine doesn't quite live up to the prices, but then this area has never been all that selective in culinary matters. The service is friendly and efficient, a detail that, on the other hand, does matter.

Bridge Cafe (8)

279 Water Street N.Y. 10038 ☎ (212) 227-3344 ➡ (212) 619-2368

(Dover St.) M *Brooklyn Bridge* ***Traditional American*** ●●● *Sun.–Mon. 11.45am–10pm; Tue.–Fri. 11.45am–midnight; Sat. 5pm–midnight*

This 19th-century wooden building at the foot of Brooklyn Bridge ➡ 106 has always had a café-restaurant trading under one name or another. The nearby Fulton Fish Market, at South Street Seaport ➡ 112, ensures that the produce is as fresh as it could possibly be; the memorable house specialty, served from April through September, is the delicate soft-shelled crab. The restaurant also offers excellent draught beers to go with its seafoods.

Not forgetting

■ **Morton's of Chicago (9)** 90 West Street (between Cedar and Albany Sts) N.Y. 10006 ☎ (212) 732-5665 ●●●● *Giant-sized steaks and excellent American Cabernet Sauvignon.*
■ **Harbour Lights (10)** Pier 17, South Street Seaport (3rd floor) N.Y. 10038 ☎ (212) 227-2800 ●●● *American cooking and seafood with a spectacular view of the Brooklyn Bridge.*

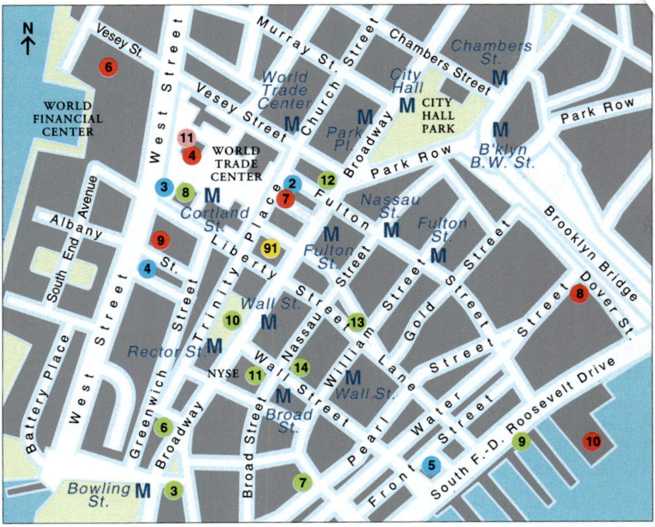

8

10

TALIESIN

Despite a large number of tourists, South Street Seaport has several high-quality and friendly restaurants.

7

6

In the area

One of the fastest-growing neighborhoods in New York City, Chinatown bustles day and night with an authentic Asian atmosphere. As it has grown, it has absorbed Little Italy, which is no longer an ethnic residential area: only a handful of Italian-Americans still live here. But the two districts have

Where to eat

Forlini's (11)

93 Baxter Street N.Y. 10013 ☎ (212) 349-6779 ➟ (212) 349-6779

(between Canal and Bayard Sts) M *Centre St.* ***Italian* ●●●** *daily noon–midnight*

This quiet, friendly, and traditional restaurant has long been a favorite with the occupants of the neighboring lawcourts: judges, attorneys, and journalists come here to stoke up on delicious house specials based on Italian home cooking: gnocchi, the unique "Fra Diavolo" spicy lobster, and freshly-baked Italian cheesecake.

Joe's Shanghai (12)

9 Pell Street N.Y. 10013 ☎ (212) 233-8888 ➟ (212) 233-8888

(between Bowery and Mott St.) M *Canal St.* ***Shanghai cuisine* ●●** *daily 11am–11.30pm*

This is the place that started the Manhattan craze for soup dumplings. The dumplings, called "steamed buns" on the menu, are patties containing a rich, delicious soup and a minced pork stuffing. Nowadays it also offers a more refined version of the dish, stuffed with flaked crab meat. The beautifully fresh Chinese-style seafood is another attraction. This is why the restaurant, in a narrow side street, is constantly packed.

Triple Eight Palace (13)

88 East Broadway N.Y. 10002 ☎ (212) 941-8886 ➟ (212) 925-6375

(between Division and Market Sts) M *Center St* ***Hongkong cuisine* ●●** *daily 8am–11pm*

The number 8 is considered a lucky number in China, and so the Triple Eight has made trebly sure of its good fortune. The house specialty is dim sum: plates of fritters, rolls, and other delicacies, many of which can be eaten with your fingers. Once dim sum was served with tea and the daily paper; now it is a way of relaxing with family or a group of friends. The restaurant prides itself on its service, backed up by a veritable fleet of tables and carts. It can be difficult to choose from the vast array of dishes on the menu, but waiters are on hand to help you.

Not forgetting

■ **Da Nico (14)** 164 Mulberry Street (between Broome and Grand Sts) N.Y. 10013 ☎ (212) 343-1212 ●● *Popular with lawyers who like Southern Italian cuisine served in a family atmosphere. A garden for summer dining.*
■ **Sweet 'n' Tart Cafe (15)** 76 Mott Street (Canal St.) N.Y. 10013 ☎ (212) 334-8088 ● *Cantonese-style soup and noodles in a tiny restaurant.*
■ **Mandarin Court (16)** 61 Mott Street (Bayard and Canal Sts) N.Y. 10013 ☎ (212) 608-3838 ●● *Dim sum during the day, seafood in the evening. Regular clientele.*
■ **Canton Formal (17)** 45 Division Street (Chatham Square) N.Y. 10013 ☎ (212) 226-4441 ●● *Excellent Cantonese cuisine. A place to see and be seen.*

one thing in common: excellent restaurants.

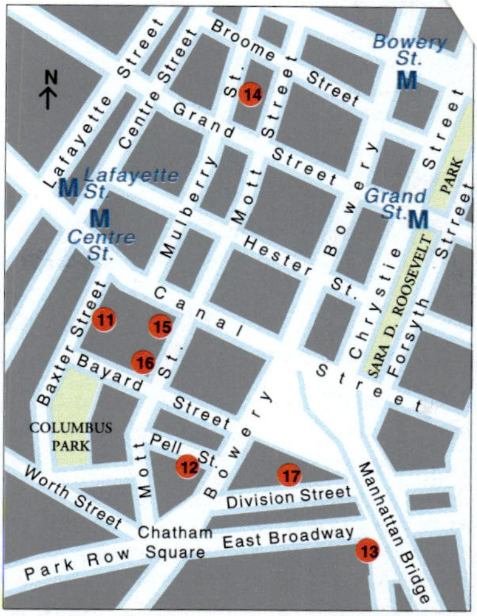

Try to visit Chinatown around the time of the Chinese New Year, in late January–early February.

13

11

13

13

In the area

TriBeCa is an acronym for TRIangle BElow CAnal Street, a chic district frequented by the film and fashion crowds, with a fairly small resident population. Gourmets enjoy its spacious and relatively cheap "canteens," buzzing with new and original ideas, and different from the more

Where to eat

TriBeCa Grill (18)

375 Greenwich Street N.Y. 10013 ☎ (212) 941-3900 ➟ (212) 941-3915

(Franklin St.) **M** *Franklin St.* ***Traditional American*** ●●●● *Mon.–Thur. 11.30am–2.45pm, 5.30–10pm; Fri. 11.30am–2.45pm, 5.30–11.30pm Sat. 5.30–11pm; Sun. 11.30am–3pm, 5.30–10pm*

This huge bar-restaurant is friendly and popular; it is jointly owned by actor Robert De Niro and restaurateur Drew Nieporent. Special attractions are the large paintings by Robert De Niro senior and the square bar rescued from the legendary (but now defunct) Maxwell's Plum. The menu is well conceived and contemporary. In all, this is a perfect place for dinner with friends.

Nobu (19)

105 Hudson Street N.Y. 10013 ☎ (212) 219-0500

(Franklin St.) **M** *Franklin St.* ***Japanese*** ●●●● *Mon.–Fri. 11.45am–2.15pm, 5.45–10.15pm; Sat.–Sun. 5.45–10.15pm; closed on Independence Day*

Nobuyuki Matsuhisa (known as Chef Nobu) is an innovative master chef operating within the sushi tradition. The decor is bizarrely eclectic, the clientele is noisy and fashionable, and the food is executed with an almost surgical precision. The list of dishes on the menu is endless and first-time diners are advised to go for house specialties such as the tuna tartare marinated in saké and decorated with Beluga caviar. Before eating, however, why not get into the mood by trying one of the 30 delicious house cocktails.

Chanterelle (20)

2 Harrison Street N.Y. 10013 ☎ (212) 966-6960 ➟ (212) 966-6143

(Hudson St.) **M** *Franklin St.* ***French and American*** ●●●●● *Mon. 5–10.30pm; Tue.–Thur. 11am–2.30pm, 5–10.30pm; Fri.–Sat. 11am–2.30pm, 5–11pm*

Dinner at Chanterelle is one of the most pleasurable culinary experiences New York has to offer. Chef David Waltuck is a true genius among the pots and pans, and the huge, bright dining room (designed by Bill Katz) along with the unobtrusive but immaculate service, carefully directed by Waltuck's wife Karen, combine to ensure that guests' enjoyment is complete. The fixed-price evening menus change every four weeks (with just one permanent fixture: the delicious seafood and white sauce sausage). In line with the other superlatives, the wine list and the cheeseboard are out of this world.

Not forgetting

■ **F.illi Ponte (21)** 39 Desbrosses Street (West St.) N.Y. 10013 ☎ (212) 226-4621 ●●●● *Excellent, generous Italian cuisine. View over Hudson River; smoking room for cigar lovers.* ■ **Montrachet (22)** 239 West Broadway (between Walker and White Sts) N.Y. 10013 ☎ (212) 219-2777 ●●●● *French cuisine, American chef, tremendous selection of burgundies.* ■ **Odeon (23)** 145 West Broadway (Thomas St.) N.Y. 10013 ☎ (212) 233-0507 ●●● *A traditional bistro and a place to be seen.*

conservative restaurants uptown. ■ Where to eat ➥ 76 ■ Where to shop ➥ 168

20

22

The fixed-price lunch at $35 is the perfect chance to experience the culinary delights offered at the Chanterelle.

20

20

19

In the area
SoHo is one of the liveliest parts of Manhattan. Its cafés, restaurants, stores, and art galleries exude an atmosphere of pure creativity, encouraging you to stroll through its streets. ■ After dark ➥ 86 ➥ 90 ➥ 98 ■ Where to shop ➥ 148 ➥ 150

Where to eat

Honmura An (24)
170 Mercer Street N.Y. 10012 ☎ (212) 334-5253 ➠ (212) 334-6162

(between Houston and Prince Sts) M *Broadway* ***Japanese*** ●●● *Tue.–Thur. noon–2.30pm, 6–10pm; Fri.–Sat. noon–2.30pm, 6–10.30pm; Sun. 6–9.30pm*

The owner, Koichi Jun Kobari, has revived the ancient craft of making soba (buckwheat) noodles – the noodles are rolled and cut by hand. The menu offers a range of variations on this buckwheat theme. Wash the noodles down with iced house saké or Japanese beer.

Savoy (25)
70 Prince Street N.Y. 10012 ☎ (212) 219-8570

(Crosby St.) M *Prince St.* ***Modern American*** ●●● *Mon.–Thur. noon–3pm, 6–10pm; Fri.–Sat. noon–3pm, 6–11pm; Sun. 6–10pm*

The inventive menus of chef-proprietor Peter Hoffman are enough to delight the most inquisitive gourmets. The Savoy is cozy and welcoming, with smooth and amiable service.

Zoë (26)
90 Prince Street N.Y. 10012 ☎ (212) 966-6722 ➠ (212) 966-6718

(between Broadway and Mercer St.) M *Prince St.* ***Modern American*** ●●● *Mon.–Thur. noon–3pm, 6–10.30pm; Fri. noon–3pm, 6–11pm; Sat. noon–3pm, 5.30–11.30pm; Sun. 11.30am–3pm, 5.30–10pm, closed the week of Independence Day*

Thalia and Stephen Loffredo have opened the restaurant of their dreams in an old industrial building hidden away among SoHo's fashionable stores and art galleries. They specialize in American cuisine, with a Californian bias, served in generous portions. Book well in advance.

Alison on Dominick Street (27)
38 Dominick Street N.Y. 10013 ☎ (212) 727-1188 ➠ (212) 727-1005

(Varick St) M *Spring St.* ***Country French and American*** ●●●● *Mon.–Thur. 5.15–10.30pm, Fri.–Sat. 5.15–11pm, Sun. 5.15–9.30pm*

Alison Hurt's peaceful, intimate restaurant is tucked away in a quiet corner of SoHo. Its chef, Dan Silverman, offers a menu based on the hearty cuisine of southwest France, reworked in the New York style. The result is lighter, but still substantial, and well accompanied by a selection of French wines.

Not forgetting
■ **Provence (28)** 38 Macdougal Street (between Houston and Prince Sts) N.Y. 10012 ☎ (212) 475-7500 ●●● *Provençal specialties.*
■ **Blue Ribbon (29)** 97 Sullivan Street (Spring St.) N.Y. 10012 ☎ (212) 274-0404 ●● *American cooking.* ■ **Aquagrill (30)** 210 Spring Street (Sixth Ave) N.Y. 10013 ☎ (212) 274-0505 ●●● *Seafood and raw bar.*
■ **Balthazar** 80 Spring Street (between Crosby and Broadway) N.Y. 10012 ☎ (212) 965-1414 ●●●● *Trendy French bistro.*

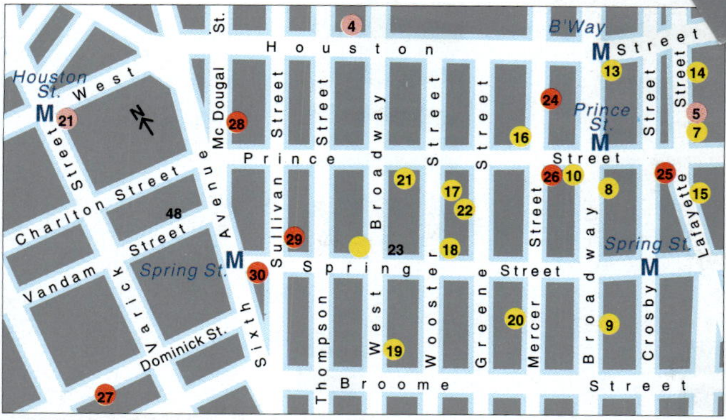

25

The Savoy occupies two floors of a small Federal-style house. Open fireplaces make it a pleasant refuge in winter.

24

30

24

26

Basic facts

Diner menus are encyclopedic. They offer the hungry eater a wide range of good-value options, from all-day breakfasts, to filling sandwiches and hot meals. They are ideal for a quick cup of coffee and a piece of pie, and meal portions are usually big enough to share. Delis, or delicatessens, are

Where to eat

EJ's Luncheonette (31)
1271 Third Avenue N.Y. 10000 ☎ (212) 472-0600

(E. 73rd St.) M *77th St.* ***American home cooking*** ● *Mon.–Thur. 8am–11pm; Fri.–Sat. 8am–11.30pm; Sun. 8am–10.30pm* *432 Sixth Avenue N.Y. 10000 ☎ (212) 473-5555 (W. 9th St.)*

A mini-chain in Manhattan that gives a 1950s touch to everyday dishes. The blue plate specials are generally good, as are the soups, the thick chilis and the ice-cream sundaes. Children are welcome. Unlike most luncheonettes (now a dying breed: once they were everywhere, in drugstores and in all Woolworth's branches), EJ's offers a range of beers and wines.

34

34

36

The Broadway Diner (32)
1726 Broadway N.Y. 10019 ☎ (212) 765-0909

(W. 55th St.) M *Seventh Ave* ***American home cooking*** ● *Mon.–Fri. 7am–midnight; Sat. 8–1am, Sun. 8am–midnight* *590 Lexington Ave (E. 52nd St.) N.Y. 10022 ☎ (212) 486-8838*

This is the classic New York diner: a simple coffee shop with a few art deco touches, fast service and good cooking, within the reach of any budget. Typical diner breakfasts include pancakes, omelettes, and French toast. For lunch and dinner choose burgers, sandwiches, salads, or fresh fish. Apart from regular mealtimes, part of the great tradition of diners is that they are places you can visit at any time for a slice of cake or apple pie with a cup of coffee.

of Jewish origin and are famous for their towering pastrami and corned beef sandwiches, best served on rye bread and with a sour pickle on the side.

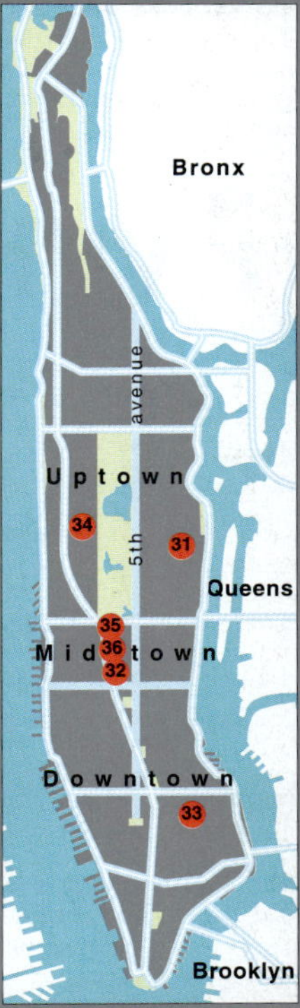

2nd Avenue Kosher Deli (33)

156 Second Avenue N.Y. 10003
☎ (212) 677-0606 ➠ (212) 477-5327

(E. 10th St.) Ⓜ *Astor Pl.* ***East European Jewish*** ●● *Sun.–Thur. 7am–midnight; Fri.–Sat. 7–2am (closed for Rosh Hashanah, Yom Kippur, Passover)*

This great delicatessen on the Lower East Side is the last of its type to survive on this stretch of Second Avenue, once the home of Jewish theater. The Matzo ball soup (chicken soup with dumplings) and the stuffed cabbage are the best in New York. Other delicacies of the house: the strongly-flavored chopped liver, spicy pastrami, and free sour and half-sour pickles. Everything is strictly kosher: the restaurant has no dairy products on the menu. Ask to sit in the Molly Picon room, which is a veritable museum of Yiddish theater.

3

34

34

35

Not forgetting

■ **Barney Greengrass (34)** 541 Amsterdam Avenue (between W. 86th and W. 87th Sts) N.Y. 10024 ☎ (212) 724-4707 ●● *Known as the sturgeon king. Smoked fish to take out or eat here. Lunchtime only.*

■ **Brooklyn Diner USA (35)** 212 West 57th Street (Seventh Ave) N.Y. 10019 ☎ (212) 581-8900 ●● *An American restaurant of quality disguised as a diner.*

■ **Carnegie Delicatessen & Restaurant (36)** 854 Seventh Avenue (W. 55th St.) N.Y. 10019 ☎ (212) 757-2245 ●● *One of the most famous of New York's delis, constantly packed, not kosher. Immortalized by Woody Allen in his film* Broadway Danny Rose.

In the area

The Village is Manhattan on a human scale: small, intimate restaurants nestling in old houses that are just a few stories high. Several generations of Italian immigrants once made this district their home, and this is reflected in the local culinary traditions. ■ Where to stay

Where to eat

Mi Cocina (37)

57 Jane Street N.Y. 10014 ☎ (212) 627-8273

(Hudson St.) M *Christophe St.* ***Mexican*** ●●● *Mon.–Thur. 5.30–10.30pm; Fri. 5.30–11.30pm; Sat. 5–11.30pm; Sun. 11.30am–3.30pm, 4.30–10pm*

Good Mexican restaurants are rare in New York, but Mi Cocina, owned by the excellent chef José Hurtado Prud'homme, is one of the few. Alongside popular tortilla-based dishes, Prud'homme offers a range from different regions of Mexico, on a menu that changes regularly.

Gotham Bar & Grill (38)

12 East 12th Street N.Y. 10003 ☎ (212) 620-4020 ➟ (212) 627-7810

(between Fifth Ave and University Pl.) M *14th St.* ***Modern American*** ●●●●● *Mon.–Thur. noon–2pm, 5.30–10.30pm; Fri. noon–2pm, 5.30–11.30pm Sat. 5.30–11.30pm; Sun. 5.30–10.30pm*

This big restaurant is famous for its French style of cuisine, presided over by Alfred Portale. Portale started the fashion for "culinary architecture": dishes presented with dazzling, sculptural virtuosity. His meals are a succession of delights, with outstanding fish and game dishes. Prices for lunch are moderate.

Home (39)

20 Cornelia Street N.Y. 10014 ☎ (212) 243-9579 ➟ (212) 627-1182

(between Bleecker and W. 4th Sts) M *W. 4th St.* ***American*** ●● *Mon.–Fri. 9am–3pm, 6–11pm; Sat. 11am–4pm, 6–11pm; Sun. 11am–4pm, 5.30–10pm*

A delightful, charming little bistro, just the kind you would hope to find in a quiet backstreet in the Village. The chef and his wife, David Page and Barbara Shinn, are passionate about American traditions: they prepare their own jam, ketchup, salami and side dishes.

Cent'Anni (40)

50 Carmine Street N.Y. 10014 ☎ (212) 989-9494

(Bleecker St.) M *W. 4th St.* ***Florentine*** ●●● *Mon.–Thur. noon–3pm, 5.30–11pm; Fri.–Sat. noon–3pm, 5.30–11.30pm; Sun. 5–10.30pm*

The name is a common greeting in Italy: "Live happily (and eat well!) for a hundred years." The simple decor of this Florentine restaurant shows that all its profits are reinvested in its food and wine. The highlights: the *zuppa ortolana*, one of the best soups in New York, as well as the home-made pasta and the succulent veal tripe.

Not forgetting

■ **Cafe Loup (41)** 105 West 13th Street (between Sixth and Seventh Aves) N.Y. 10011 ☎ (212) 255-4746 ●● *Bistro; French and American.*
■ **Da Silvano (42)** 260 Sixth Avenue (between Bleecker and Houston Sts) N.Y. 10014 ☎ (212) 982-2343 ●●● *Florentine cuisine served to a sophisticated clientele.*

➥ 20
■ After dark
➥ 90 ➥ 94
➥ 98

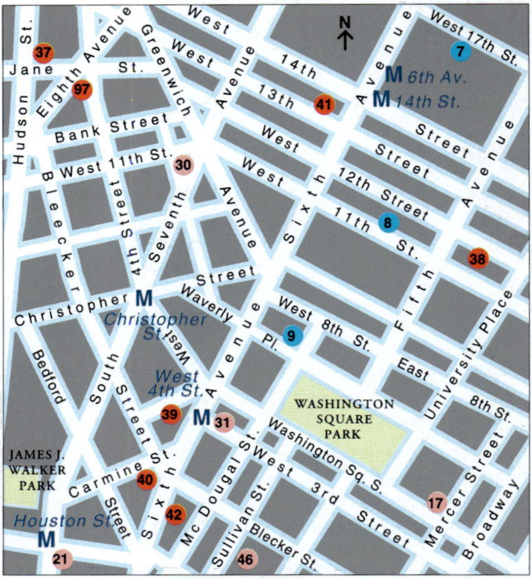

41

Cafe Loup is a favorite haunt of Villagers, both for its quiet atmosphere and for its unpretentious cuisine.

37

MI COCINA
RESTAURANT

37

39

In the area

This area, steeped in the history of New York, found a new lease of life when a number of young restaurateurs set up shop in its magnificent historical buildings. Union Square's splendid open-air market, known throughout the the city for its organic produce, also attracts food lovers

Where to eat

Patría (43)

250 Park Avenue South N.Y. 10003
☎ (212) 777-6211 ➠ (212) 777-0786

(E. 20th St.) M *23rd St.* ***Modern Latin American*** ●●● *Mon.–Thur. noon–2.45pm, 6–10.45pm; Fri. noon–2.45pm, 5.30–11.45pm; Sat. 5.30–11.45pm; Sun. 5.30–10.30pm*

Douglas Rodriguez, an eccentric Cuban-American chef, left Miami to manage this very festive New York restaurant. He has worked wonders, offering modern versions of great Latin American classics, such as yucca, *posole*, and *seviche*, served with popcorn or ribbons of fresh coconut.

Union Square Cafe (44)

21 East 16th Street N.Y. 10003 ☎ (212) 243-4020 ➠ (212) 627-2673

(Union Square West) M *14th St* ***Modern American and Italian*** ●●●● *Mon.–Thur. noon–2.15pm, 6–10.15pm; Fri.–Sat. noon–2.15pm, 6–11.15pm; Sun. 5.30–9.45pm*

Danny Meyer helped to change the character of the area when he opened this delightful restaurant. Today the cafe has a number of competitors, but it remains a favorite thanks to its distinctive Italian-American cuisine, its accessible wine list, and welcoming atmosphere.

Zen Palate (45)

34 Union Square East N.Y. 10003
☎ (212) 614-9291 ➠ (212) 614-9401

(E. 16th St.) M *14th St* ***Asian vegetarian*** ●● *Mon.–Sat. 11am–11pm; Sun. 5–9pm*

A strictly vegetarian restaurant, and one of the best in New York. The restaurant has a serene decor of Asian inspiration. The beautifully presented dishes would persuade even the most hardened carnivore to convert to tofu. The noodles with mushrooms are especially good.

Mesa Grill (46)

102 Fifth Avenue N.Y. 10011 ☎ (212) 807-7400 ➠ (212) 989-0034

(W. 16th St.) M *14th St* ***Modern Southwest American*** ●●●● *Mon.–Thur. noon–2.30pm, 5.30–10.30pm; Fri. noon-2.30pm, 5.30–11pm; Sat. 11.30am–3pm, 5.30–11pm; Sun. 11.30am–3pm, 5.30–10pm*

This huge, lively restaurant was the first to be opened by the young and original chef Bobby Flay. He uses the flavors and ingredients of the American southwest to produce delicious food, presented with flair. Tequila or iced beer make great accompaniments.

Not forgetting

■ **Union Pacific (47)** 111 East 22nd Street (Park Ave) N.Y. 10010 ☎ (212) 995-8570 ●●● *Modern American cooking.* ■ **Gramercy Tavern (48)** 42 East 20th Street (Between Broadway and Park Ave South) N.Y. 10003 ☎ (212) 477-0777 ●●●●● *Modern American.* ■ **Verbena (49)** 54 Irving Place (E. 17th St.) N.Y. 10003 ☎ (212) 260-5454 ●●●● *Modern American.*

(Mon., Wed., Fri., Sat. 8am–4pm).

■ Where to stay ➡ 20

45

Every detail of the design of Zen Palate, from the colors to the shapes of the rooms, reflects Japanese philosophy.

44

48

49

Two of New York's most prestigious restaurants are located just a few blocks from each other. They are different in terms of style (one has a modern setting and American cooking, the other a theatrical setting and European cuisine), but they both aspire to the highest standards.

Where to eat

The Four Seasons (50)
99 East 52nd Street N.Y. 10022
☎ (212) 754-9494 ➟ (212) 754-1077

(Park Ave.) M *Lexington Ave* ***American*** ●●●●● *Mon.–Fri. noon–2pm, 5–9pm; Sat. 5–11pm*

Picasso's beautiful painted backdrop for the ballet *Le Tricorne* hangs in the impressive entrance hall. The two dining rooms were designed by Philip Johnson in the 1950s, at the request of his mentor, Mies van der Rohe, architect of the famous Seagram Building, which houses the restaurant. But even if such features suggest a temple of twentieth-century architecture and art, the Four Seasons is not at all like a museum. This is most famous as the restaurant that perfected theart of American cuisine, using 100% American ingredients, a principle that still holds sway in the kitchens. The roast duckling is first class, as is the American lamb with accompaniments that vary with the seasons, sometimes including a fern garnish shaped like a violin scroll. A tall cart presents a sumptuous array of desserts, skillfully served. For business lunches, choose the Grill Room (where New York's leading publishers meet and exchange notes); for dinners book a table by the fountain in the more romantic Pool Room. It is the ideal spot for dinner before or after the theater as the special menus are the best value. Reserve a table ahead.

50

50

■ Where to stay ➥ 34 ■ After dark ➥ 92 ■ What to see ➥ 116 ■ Where to shop ➥ 156 ➥ 158

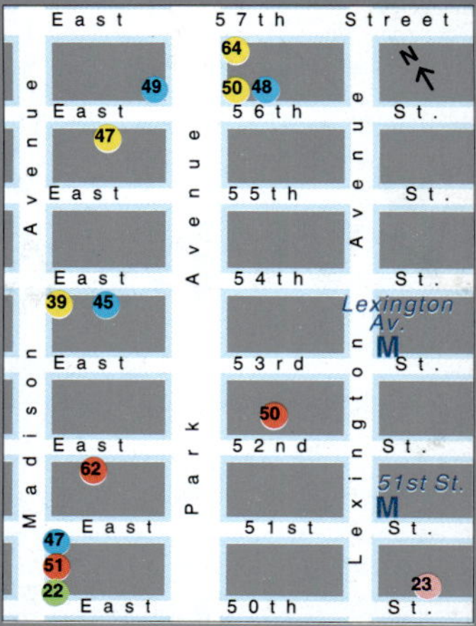

Le Cirque 2000 (51)

455 Madison Avenue
N.Y. 10022 ☎ (212) 303-7788

(East 50th St.) M *E. 51st* P
Eclectic French ●●●●●
Mon.–Sat. 11.45am–2.45pm, 5.45–11pm; Sun. 11.30am–2.30pm, 5.30–10.30pm (Sept.–June 5.30–10.30pm)

This restaurant opened its doors to the public on May 1, 1997: it is an outstanding achievement in terms of both design and execution. It occupies (some would say it has invaded) one of the wings of the Villard Houses ➥ 116, a magnificent Renaissance-style palazzo that symbolizes the city's golden age (and is part of the luxurious Palace Hotel). The bar is in the Gold Room, a sumptuous vaulted room with gilt-covered walls. The bold, theatrical decor, which plays on the circus theme, was designed by Iranian-American designer Adam Tihani. In the kitchen, Franco-Cambodian chef Sottha Khunn conjures up unique dishes, such as his Bollito Misto and the grilled lobster with artichoke and wild mushrooms that established the restaurant's reputation. Meanwhile, pastry chef Jacques Torres creates delicate desserts that are true works of art, sometimes using the clown theme, and a young American supervises the impressive list of wines belonging to the Maccioni family from Tuscany, the restaurant's proprietors. Advance booking is essential for this sought-after restaurant, which attracts many celebrities and the elite of New York.

51

51

51

In the area

For many years, Times Square had a less than salubrious reputation; now 46th Street is known as Restaurant Row, lined with eateries catering for the pre-, and post-theater crowd. ■ Where to stay ➡ 28 ➡ 30 ■ After dark ➡ 86 ➡ 92 ➡ 94 ➡ 96 ■ Where to shop ➡ 154 ➡ 168

Where to eat

B. Smith's (52)

771 Eighth Avenue N.Y. 10036 ☎ (212) 247-2222 ➡ (212) 582-3108

(W. 47th St.) M *50th St.* ***American*** ●●● *Sun.–Thur. noon–10pm, Fri.–Sat. noon–midnight*

A landmark for genuine American cooking, inspired by the soul food of the south. Despite being so close to the theaters of Broadway, the corner of Eighth Avenue where B. Smith's stands has so far escaped the general upgrading of Times Square. Its owner is Barbara Smith, a former model and actress.

Becco (53)

355 West 46th Street N.Y. 10036 ☎ (212) 397-7597 ➡ (212) 977-6738

(between Eighth and Ninth Aves) M *50th St.* ***Italian*** ●●● *Mon.–Sat. noon–3pm, 5pm–midnight; Sun. noon–3pm, 5–10pm*

The word Becco comes from the Italian *beccare,* which means "to nibble or taste delicately". This delightful and relaxed Italian restaurant is expertly managed by the Bastianich family. There is an excellent special offer to draw in the customers: for $21.95 the chef offers a substantial antipasto, a selection of baby vegetables accompanied by fish and seafood appetizers, or a classic Caesar salad. This first-class appetizer is followed by your choice of several pasta dishes, served by waiters wielding steaming pans.

Joe Allen (54)

265 West 46th Street N.Y. 10036
☎ (212) 581-6464 ➡ (212) 265-3383

(between Eighth and Ninth Aves) M *50th St.* ***American*** ●● *Mon.–Tue. noon–11.45pm; Wed. 11.30am–11.45pm; Thur. noon–11.45pm; Fri. noon–midnight; Sat. 11.30am–midnight; Sun. 11.30am–11.45pm*

Joe Allen's success has never faltered. The restaurant remains enduringly popular for its classic red-check tablecloths, its menu written on a blackboard, and the consistently high quality of typical American food such as the thick, delicious hamburgers, Caesar salad, fruit tarts, and cookies encrusted with chocolate chips or covered with icing. A meeting place for everyone who's anyone on Broadway, including producers, stars, and theatergoers alike.

Not forgetting

■ **Coco Pazzo Teatro (55)** Paramount Hotel ➡ 30, 235 West 46th Street (between Broadway and Eighth Ave) N.Y. 10036 ☎ (212) 827-4222 ●●●● *This new restaurant quickly won over fans of Italian cuisine; a light supper menu caters for theatergoers.*

■ **Virgil's Real BBQ (56)** 152 West 44th Street (between Broadway and Sixth Ave) N.Y. 10036 ☎ (212) 921-9494 ●● *Delicious wood-smoked meats (a subtle blend of walnut, oak, and fruit trees) and other "trapper" style dishes. A word of advice: the portions are huge, especially Virgil's Pig Out (full barbecue selection). Before you leave, buy a bottle of the house barbecue sauce ($5) to take home.*

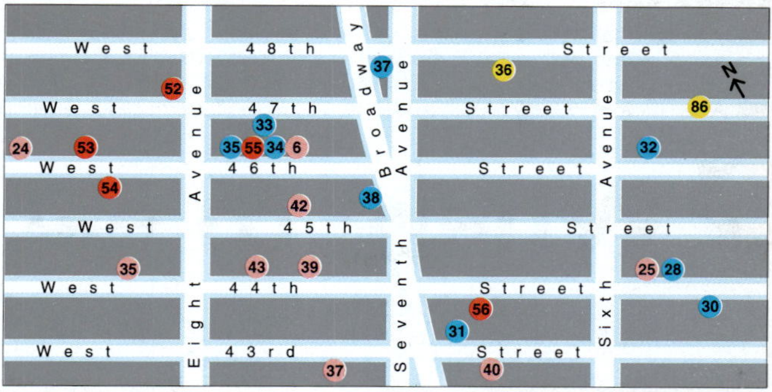

55

Virgil's Real BBQ serves the best smoked meats in Manhattan. A pleasant setting and a lively, varied crowd.

56

52

53

56

56

In the area

Many foreign companies have their offices in this part of Midtown, giving it a touch of international color as well as a host of excellent Japanese restaurants and sushi bars. ■ Where to stay ➡ 26 ➡ 32 ➡ 34 ➡ 36 ■ After dark ➡ 92 ■ What to see ➡ 116 ■ Where to shop ➡ 146

Where to eat

Lespinasse (57)

St. Regis Hotel, 2 East 55th Street N.Y. 10022
☎ (212) 339-6719 ➡ (212) 350-8722

(Madison and Fifth Aves) M *Fifth Ave* ***French*** ●●●●● *Mon.–Sat. noon–2pm, 5.30–10pm*

This is the jewel in the crown of the excellent St Regis Hotel ➡ 36, the setting for spectacular culinary skills and a unique gastronomic experience. The real centerpiece of the restaurant is not the spacious and comfortable dining room but the high-tech kitchen of Christian Delouvrier. The new chef – a former pupil of Alain Senderens, renowned for his unpretentious and distinctive cuisine – also has a special talent for preparing game.

Vong (58)

200 East 54th Street N.Y. 10022 ☎ (212) 486-9592 ➡ (212) 980-3745

(Third Ave) M *Lexington Ave* ***Thai and French*** ●●●● *Mon.–Thur. noon–2.30pm, 6–11pm; Fri. noon–2.30pm, 5.30–11pm; Sat. 5.30–11.30pm; Sun. 5.30–10pm*

Jean-Georges Vongerichten from Alsace is one of the most popular chefs in New York. He combines immaculate French cuisine with Thai exotica: ginger, galangal, lemongrass, mango, and chili meet foie gras, salmon and other western classics. The result is pure delight.

Hatsuhana (59)

17 East 48th Street N.Y. 10017 ☎ (212) 355-3345 ➡ (212) 308-0001

(Madison Ave) M *51st St.* ***Japanese*** ●●● *Mon.–Fri. 11.45am–2.45pm, 5.30–10pm; Sat. 5–10.30pm*

This is often considered the best sushi bar in New York. The chefs are first rate: they work with surgical precision, skillfully creating delicious sushi to order.

Grand Central Oyster Bar & Restaurant (60)

Grand Central Terminal N.Y. 10017
☎ (212) 490-6650 ➡ (212) 949-5210

(Level 1) M *Grand Central* ***Seafood*** ●●● *Mon.–Fri. 11.30am–9.30pm*

This *Beaux-Arts* masterpiece, a magnificent vaulted room covered with varnished tiles, is located underneath Grand Central Station ➡ 106. Every day hundreds of people visit its counters and the long marble oyster bar to eat fresh fish and seafood, classically presented. Take the chance to try Manhattan or New England Clam Chowder. There is a good list of American wines.

Not forgetting

■ **Typhoon Brewery (61)** 22 East 54th Street (Madison Ave) N.Y. 10022 ☎ (212) 754-9006 ●●● *Thai cuisine and home made beer; very fashionable.* ■ **Fresco by Scotto (62)** 34 East 52nd Street (Madison Ave) N.Y. 10022 ☎ (212) 935-3434 ●●●● *Modern Italian.*

➥ 152 ➥ 154
➥ 156 ➥ 158
➥ 160 ➥ 162

60

58

61

Have lunch in the Oyster Bar and discover the many different types of oyster from Long Island, Maine and Massachussetts.

60

In the area

The west side of Fifth Avenue is dominated by the turbulent worlds of media and finance. ■ Where to stay ➥ 30 ➥ 34 ➥ 36 ➥ 38 ➥ 40 ■ After dark ➥ 88 ➥ 90 ➥ 92 ■ What to see ➥ 116 ➥ 122 ■ Where to shop ➥ 146 ➥ 154 ➥ 156 ➥ 158 ➥ 160 ➥ 162

Where to eat

La Côte Basque (63)

60 West 55th Street N.Y. 10019 ☎ (212) 688-6525 ➠ (212) 758-3361

(between Fifth and Sixth Aves) M *51st St.* ***French*** ●●●●● *Mon.–Thur. noon–2.30pm, 5.30–10.30pm; Fri.–Sat. noon–2.30pm, 5.30–11.30pm; Sun. 5–10pm*

La Côte Basque has long been known for its murals, which re-create the atmosphere of St-Jean-de-Luz. This exquisite French restaurant is run by Jean-Jacques Rachou, whose modern cuisine offers a lighter version of timeless Basque dishes.

The "21" Club (64)

21 West 52nd Street N.Y. 10019 ☎ (212) 582-7200 ➠ (212) 586-5065

(Sixth Ave) M *Lexington Ave.* ***American*** ●●●● *Mon.–Fri. noon–2.30pm, 5.30–10.30pm; Sat. 5.30–11.15pm*

During Prohibition this was a speakeasy (a clandestine drinking club), which quickly established a reputation for its food and its wine cellar. Today the chef offers an updated version of the time-honored house formula: quality produce (meat, game, seafood) accompanied with vintage wines, all served in a stately setting. It is well worth visiting the bar with its remarkable collection of mementos.

JUdson Grill (65)

152 West 52nd Street N.Y. 10019 ☎ (212) 582-5252 ➠ (212) 265-9616

(Seventh Ave) M *Seventh Ave* ***Modern American*** ●●●● *Mon.–Fri. noon–2.30pm, 5.30–11pm; Sat. 5.30–11.30pm*

The restaurant's unusual name comes from the old telephone code: JU(dson) 5. However this huge, friendly restaurant is resolutely modern in style, with expert presentation and an admirable wine list. It is a fashionable venue, and the bar is constantly full.

Le Bernardin (66)

155 West 51st Street N.Y. 10019 ☎ (212) 489-1515 ➠ (212) 265-1615

(Sixth Ave) M *47th St.* ***French*** ●●●●● *Mon.–Thur. noon–2.30pm, 5.30–10pm; Fri. noon–2.30pm, 5.30–11pm; Sat. 5.30–11pm*

This restaurant was opened in the 1980s by Maguy Le Coze and her brother Gilbert. The present chef, Eric Ripert, has taken Gilbert Le Coze's luxuriously minimalist menu and enriched it with the vibrant flavors of Asia and the Mediterranean. Seafood is the specialty.

Not forgetting

■ **The Park Room (67)** Helmsley Park Lane Hotel ➥ 40, 36 Central Park South (Fifth Ave) N.Y. 10019 ☎ (212) 371-4000 ●●● *High ceilings, view over Central Park, and a multicultural menu.* ■ **Christer's (68)** 145 West 55th Street (Seventh Ave) N.Y. 10019 ☎ (212) 974-7224 ●●● *Scandinavian cuisine.* ■ **China Grill (69)** 60 West 53rd Street (Sixth Ave) N.Y. 10019 ☎ (212) 333-7788 ●●● *World cuisine with an Asian influence.*

N
Central Park South
East 60th St.
East 59th St.
West 58th Street
East 58th St.
West 57th Street
East 57th St.
West 56th Street
East 56th St.
West 55th Street
East 55th St.
West 54th Street
East 54th St.
West 53rd Street
East 53rd St.
West 52nd Street
East 52nd St.
West 51st Street
East 51st St.
West 50th Street
East 50th St.
West 49th Street
East 49th St.
Seventh Avenue
Sixth Avenue
Fifth Avenue
Madison Avenue
M 57th St.
M 57th St.
M 5th Av.
M 7th Av.
M 5th Av.
M 47th-50th Sts-Rockefeller Center
M 49th St.
CARNEGIE HALL THEATER
TRUMP TOWER
ROCKEFELLER CENTER
ST. PATRICK'S CATHEDRAL

67

63

65

64

A few years ago this section of West 57th Street was a haven of culture – now it is dominated by theme restaurants (as well as shops ➡ 160) dedicated to musical and cinematic subjects. These hold an irresistible fascination for visitors from all over the world.

Where to eat

Hard Rock Cafe (70)

221 West 57th Street N.Y. 10019 ☎ (212) 489-6565 ➡ (212) 765-5098

(between Broadway and Seventh Ave) M *57th St.* ***Traditional American*** ●● *Sun.–Fri. 11.30am–12.30am; Sat. 11–1.30am*

The Hard Rock Cafe is at the same time a museum, a bar, a general store, and a hamburger chain: it is the model for contemporary "theme" restaurants. American rock 'n' roll is celebrated in the decor – the bar is shaped like a guitar – and displays of classic rock memorabilia, including items from Kurt Cobain, the Beatles, and Michael Jackson. Even if you come here mainly for the décor, you will not be disappointed by the food, which has a good reputation: the hamburgers and the chicken club sandwiches are excellent.

72

71

Jekyll & Hyde Club (71)

1409 Sixth Avenue N.Y. 10019 ☎ (212) 541-9517

(W. 57th St.) M *57th St.* ***Traditional American*** ●● *Mon.–Tue., Thur.–Fri. 11.30–2.30am; Wed., Sat.–Sun. 11–3.30am*

This theatrical house of horror is always packed with crowds of diners avid for cinematic blood, gore, and terror to accompany their food. The largest theme restaurant in New York City, the Jekyll & Hyde Club claims to have more special effects in evidence than any other place in town. It has been designed for adult amusement as well as family outings, and demonstrates the persisting allure of the old horror movies as well as capitalizing on children's more gory tastes and their unquenchable affection for cinematic monsters. Maintaining a more kindly family spirit, the menu also offers special children's portions.

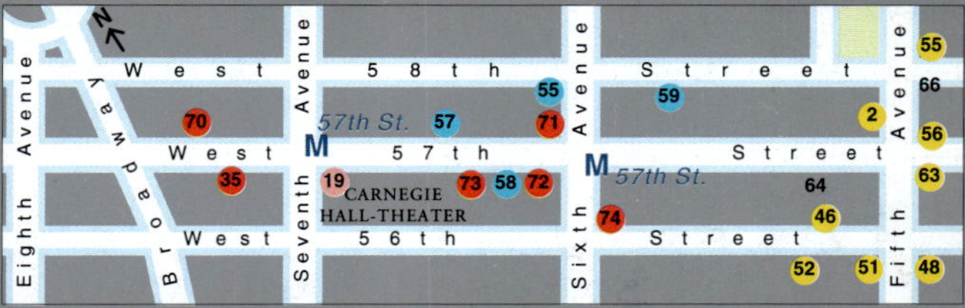

Motown Cafe (72)

104 West 57th Street N.Y. 10019
☎ (212) 581-8030 ➠ (212) 581-9543

(between Sixth and Seventh Aves) M *57th St.* ***Southern American*** ●● *daily 11.30–2am (except Sat. 11–2am)*

This restaurant is a lavish tribute to the famous Detroit record label that launched stars like Smokey Robinson, Diana Ross, and Stevie Wonder. The food is a lighter, popularized variant of soul food: "Smokey's Ribs" are as gentle on the palate as Smokey Robinson's solos are on the ears. Just like the Hard Rock Cafe, the Motown is also a musical museum: stars' shoes and stage costumes are displayed in showcases, alongside bronze statues of Marvin Gaye, the young Michael Jackson, and Martha Reeves. On top of all this, the staff are the friendliest on West 57th Street.

70

71

Not forgetting

■ **Planet Hollywood (73)** 140 West 57th Street (Sixth Ave) N.Y. 10019 ☎ (212) 333-7827 ●● *Salads, pasta, and film souvenirs.*

■ **Harley Davidson Cafe (74)** 1370 Sixth Avenue (W. 56th St.) N.Y. 10019 ☎ (212) 245-6000 ●● *Burgers, beers, and bikes!*

Basic facts

In New York, breakfast is an art form. It may be simple – a bagel with cream cheese, a cranberry muffin, or a danish pastry, with freshly-squeezed juice and a cup of hot coffee. Or it may be more substantial: oatmeal, pancakes with maple syrup and crisp bacon, waffles with fresh fruit salad,

Where to eat

Sarabeth's (75)

423 Amsterdam Avenue N.Y. 10024
☎ (212) 496-6280 ➟ (212) 787-9655

(W. 80th St.) M *79th St.* ***Breakfast*** ●● *Mon.–Fri. 8am–10.30pm; Sat. 9am–11pm; Sun. 9am–9.30pm*

Breakfast fanatics line up like pilgrims outside Sarabeth's, owned by Sarabeth Levine, jam-maker extraordinaire and a baker of genius. Here the breakfast ritual is observed to perfection, from the sweet fruit juices through to the excellent coffee.

Café des Artistes (76)

1 West 67th Street N.Y. 10023 ☎ (212) 877-3500 ➟ (212) 877-7754

(Central Park W.) M *66th St.* ***Brunch*** ●●●● *Mon.–Fri. noon–2.45pm, 5.30pm–12.30am; Sat. 11am–2.45pm, 5.30–12.30am; Sun. 10am–2.45pm, 5.30–11.30pm*

Brunch is the perfect moment to take your seat at the Café des Artistes: at this time of day the famous fresco by Howard Chandler Christy seems to come alive. Follow your sumptuous brunch with a walk in Central Park ➥ 122.

The Regency (77)

The Regency Hotel, 540 Park Avenue N.Y. 10021
☎ (212) 339-4050 ➟ (212) 826-5674

(61st Street) M *Lexington Ave* ***Breakfast*** ●●● ***The Library*** *daily 7–1am;* ***Dining Room*** *daily 7am–10pm*

The restaurant's real name is "540 Park" but everyone calls it The Regency ➥ 42. The Library, with its English-style décor, has become a favorite place for New York's financiers to meet for breakfast. However, the high quality of the food does not entirely make up for the expressionless service.

Bubby's (78)

120 Hudson Street N.Y. 10013 ☎ (212) 219-0666 ➟ (212) 219-0076

(between Franklin and N. Moore Sts) M *Franklin St.* ***Breakfast*** ●● *daily 8am–4pm, 6–11pm*

This ultra-laid-back restaurant in TriBeCa has become something of an institution; it serves breakfast from morning until around midnight. Here you can sample pancakes with walnut and banana or *huevos rancheros*, all perfectly prepared, while the rest of the city is sitting down to dinner.

Not forgetting

■ **Sylvia's (79)** 328 Lenox Avenue (W. 126th St.) N.Y. 10027 ☎ (212) 996-0660 ● *Mecca for soul food fans.* ■ **Le Régence (80)** Plaza Athénée ➥ 42, 37 East 64th Street (Park Ave) N.Y. 10021 ☎ (212) 606-4647 ●●●● *Luxury brunches.* ■ **Danal (81)** 90 East 10th Street (Third Ave) N.Y. 10003 ☎ (212) 982-6930 ●●● *Have brunch in a cozy antique shop.*

or huge omelettes. Brunch is more elegant, often accompanied by a mimosa (champagne and orange juice) or a bloody Mary (vodka, tomato juice and tabasco).

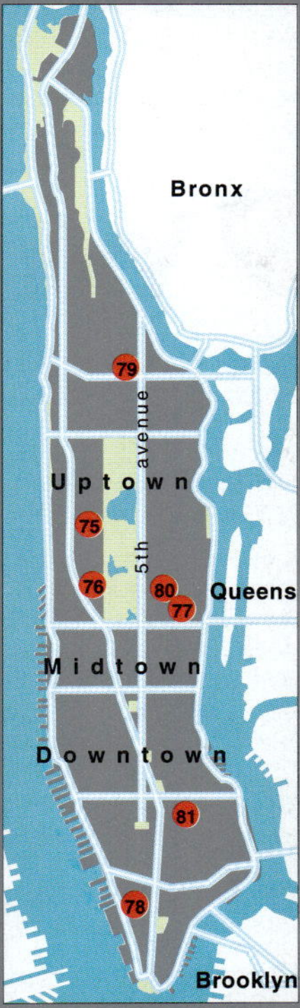

76

80

75

After your breakfast, buy some of Sarabeth Levine's excellent muffins or cookies to enjoy later in the day.

75

77

In the area

Wealth and culture predominate in this conservative area, which has the highest concentration of museums in New York, along the Museum Mile ➡ 120. Once you are beyond Fifth Avenue, heading toward the East River, rents are less expensive, as are the restaurants. ■ Where to stay

Where to eat

The Lobster Club (82)

24 East 80th Street N.Y. 10021 ☎ (212) 249-6500 ➡ (212) 396-0829

(Madison Ave) M *77th St.* ***Modern American*** ●●● *Mon.–Thur. 11.30am–2.45pm, 5.30–10.45pm; Fri.–Sat. 11.30am–2.45pm, 5.30–11pm; Sun. 11.30am–2.45pm, 5.30–9.45pm*

A duplex restaurant close by the Metropolitan Museum of Art ➡ 118, named after the legendary club sandwich invented by Anne Rosenzweig, the restaurant's chef and proprietor. This delicacy, made with fresh Maine lobster and lemon mayonnaise, was already very popular at Arcadia, Ms Rosenzweig's previous restaurant near to Midtown. Many of the dishes are American classics with a new twist, some in low-calorie versions. The desserts are unforgettable.

Daniel (83)

60 East 65th Street N.Y. 10021 ☎ (212) 288-0033 ➡ (212) 737-0612

(Park Ave) M *68th St.* ***French haute cuisine*** ●●●●● *Mon.–Sat. noon-2.30pm, 5.45–11.30pm*

After several years in a quiet residential district on the East Side, Daniel Boulud, the famous chef from Lyons, has returned to the scene of his great New York debut. The former chef of Le Cirque (now Le Cirque 2000 ➡ 66) is today competing with the Park Avenue restaurant that he left to go into business for himself. The dining room is decorated in an austere, tasteful style, with contemporary paintings adding a dash of color here and there.

Aureole (84)

34 East 61st Street N.Y. 10021 ☎ (212) 319-1660

(Madison Ave) M *Lexington Ave* ***Modern American*** ●●●●● *Mon.–Fri. noon–2.30pm, 5.30–11pm; Sat. 5.30–11pm*

A calm, luxurious place with magnificent and original flower arrangements filling every corner with perfume. The chef and proprietor is the highly regarded Charlie Palmer, famous for his skillful way with American ingredients. In order to guarantee the highest quality for these, he makes some of the basic products himself: he has his own dairy, for example, which supplies the butter and cheese used in the restaurant. Aureole is well known for generous portions and a grand style of presentation. The service is unfailingly impeccable.

Not forgetting

■ **L'Absinthe (85)** 227 East 67th Street (Second Ave) N.Y. 10021 ☎ (212) 794-4950 ●●● *French cuisine; Belle-Epoque decor.*

■ **Park Avenue Cafe (86)** 100 East 63rd Street (Park Ave) N.Y. 10021 ☎ (212) 644-1900 ●●●● *Modern American cooking from a witty chef.*

■ **Matthew's (87)** 1030 Third Avenue (E. 61st St.) N.Y. 10021 ☎ (212) 838-4343 ●●●●● *Mediterranean cuisine, just a convenient step or two from Bloomingdale's ➡ 146.*

➥ 40 ➥ 42 ■ After dark ➥ 88 ➥ 92 ■ What to see ➥ 120 ■ Where to shop ➥ 164

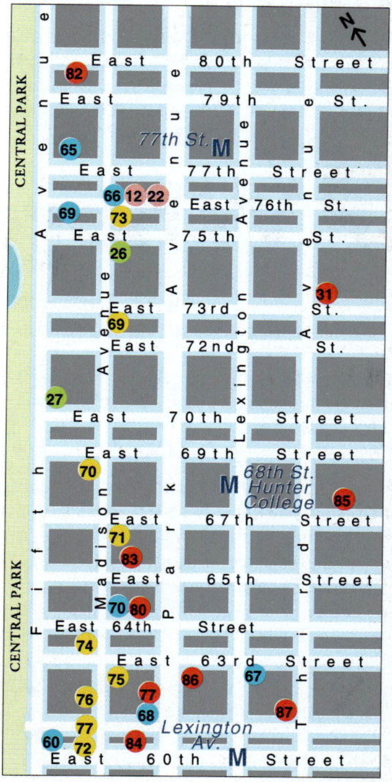

83

82

85

L'Absinthe is named after a famous but noxious liqueur, very fashionable in the early part of the century, and banned in the 1920s.

87

86

In the area
Residents of the Upper West Side often complain of the scarcity of good restaurants, but things are beginning to look up as a number of young, imaginative chefs move into the area. The best restaurants are still grouped within a short walk of Lincoln Center ➡ 102. ■ Where to

Where to eat

Rain (88)

100 West 82nd Street N.Y. 10024 ☎ (212) 501-0776 ➡ (212) 501-9147

(between Amsterdam and Columbus Aves) M *81st St.* ***Asian*** ●●● *Mon.–Thur. noon–3pm, 6–11pm; Fri. noon–4pm, 6pm–midnight; Sat. noon–4pm, 5pm–midnight; Sun. noon–4pm, 5–10pm* ***Main Street Restaurant*** *446 Columbus Ave N.Y. 10024 ☎ (212) 873-5025*

This spacious restaurant, with a distinctively minimalist decor, serves an imaginative menu that borrows judiciously from Thai, Malaysian, and Vietnamese culinary traditions. The noodle and the vegetable dishes are specially recommended. The first courses are mainly low in calories, so finish off in style with an exotic ragout of bananas – or a huge portion of chocolate cake, which makes a delicious contrast to the Asian flavors that have preceded it through the meal.

Gabriel's (89)

11 West 60th Street N.Y. 10023 ☎ (212) 956-4600 ➡ (212) 956-2309

(between Broadway and Columbus Ave) M *59th St.* ***Italian*** ●●● *Mon.–Fri. noon–3pm, 5.30–11pm; Sat. 5.30pm–midnight*

Gabriel Aiello and his chef serve a highly individual version of Italian cuisine, strongly flavored and full of charm. A giant appetite is necessary to follow up a pasta appetizer with one of the main dishes, but it would be almost criminal not to try as many dishes as possible. The location of this restaurant makes it ideal for dining before or after a performance at Lincoln Center ➡ 102.

Picholine (90)

35 West 64th Street N.Y. 10023 ☎ (212) 724-8585 ➡ (212) 875-8979

(between Broadway and Central Park W.) M *66th St.* ***French Mediterranean*** ●●●● *Mon. 5.30–11.45pm; Tue.–Sat. 11.45am–2pm, 5.30–11.45pm; Sun. 5–10.30pm*

Picholine serves strikingly unusual cuisine with a Provençal bias. This style has been perfected by American chef Terrance Brennan, who likes to draw out the rich flavors of those inexpensive ingredients that are so highly valued by French chefs: carrots, turnips, knuckle of beef, aromatic herbs. While taking his inspiration from the Mediterranean, Brennan has also created his own distinctive new dishes, which are always interesting. There is also a splendid cheeseboard accompanied by wonderful home-made rolls with olives. You can be sure of leaving Picholine full and contented. Like Gabriel's, its location is handy before or after a concert or a play at Lincoln Center.

Not forgetting

■ **Mad Fish (91)** 2182 Broadway (between W. 77th and W. 78th Sts) N.Y. 10024 ☎ (212) 787-0202 ●●● *Fresh seafood, modern American cooking.*
■ **Blue Star (92)** 329 Columbus Avenue (between W. 75th and W. 76th Sts) N.Y. 10023 ☎ (212) 579-0505 ●●● *American cooking and a well-stocked bar.*
■ **Café Luxembourg (93)** 200 West 70th Street (between Amsterdam and West End Aves) N.Y. 10023 ☎ (212) 873-7411 ●●● *A chic French bistro, which also serves American dishes.*

stay ➥ 44 ■ After dark ➥ 94
➥ 102 ■ What to see ➥ 122
■ Where to shop ➥ 148
➥ 166

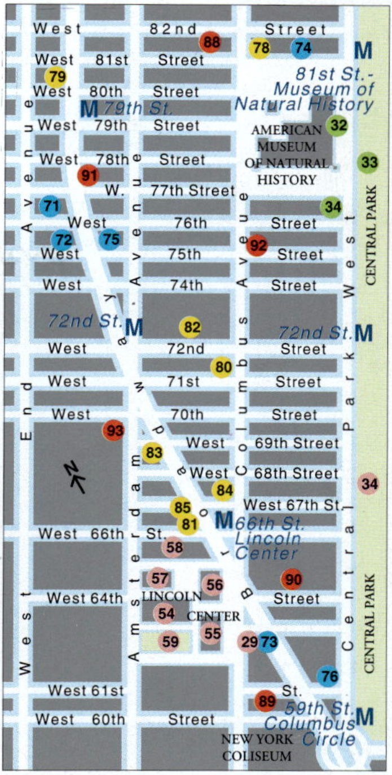

89

89

Upper West Side has recently been adopted by a new, young crowd: this is now a lively district, well worth exploring.

90

Basic facts
It is not for nothing that New York is known as the city that never sleeps. If you are struck by late-night cravings you can be sure there will be a nearby restaurant, coffee shop, delicatessen, or even a steakhouse to satisfy your hunger. In addition to the few suggestions given here, try

Where to eat

Wollensky's Grill (94)

201 East 49th Street N.Y. 10017
☎ (212) 753-1530 ➡ (212) 751-5446

(Third Ave) M *51st St.* ***Traditional American*** ●●● *daily 11am–1.30am*

Looking for a place that's open late, but that is still free of ear-splitting music? You could opt for this annex of Smith & Wollensky, the popular steakhouse, with its pub-style decor and its generous meals, served well after most restaurants of this type have closed their doors. Steaks are available at any time, but after midnight you may be more tempted by the top-quality burgers. In good weather there are tables outside on the sidewalk, where it can be a special pleasure to sit and watch the world go by.

94

Florent (95)

69 Gansevoort Street N.Y. 10014
☎ (212) 989-5779 ➡ (212) 645-2498

(Washington St.) M *14th St.* ***French bistro*** ●● *Sun.–Thur. 9–5am; Fri.–Sat. 24 hrs*

The fashionable place to be in the wee hours, especially if you're out on the town with a crowd of friends. Florent is on the borders of Greenwich Village near to Gansevoort Market, where the wholesalers' trucks begin rumbling in to deliver their goods well before dawn.

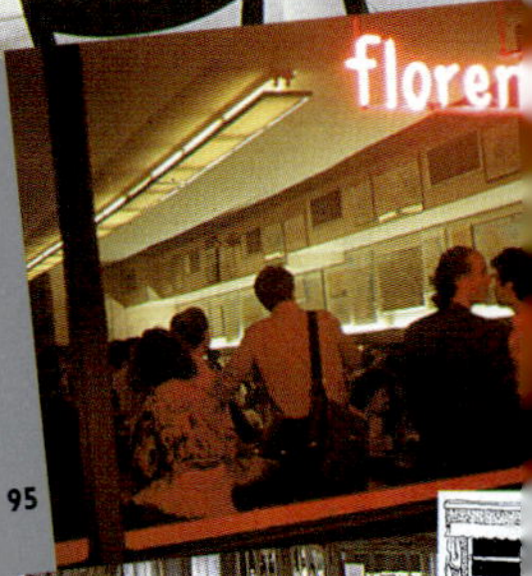

95

97

First (96)

87 First Avenue N.Y. 10003
☎ (212) 674-3823 ➡ (212) 674-8010

(E. 6th St.) M *Astor Pl.* ***Modern American*** ●●● *Mon.–Thur. 6pm–2am; Fri–Sat. 6pm–3am; Sun. 11am–3pm, 4pm–1am*

The 'in' restaurant in East Village, First is as notable for its sense of irony as for its imaginative menu that changes frequently. The chef offers dishes inspired by the 1950s, with a characteristic humorous twist. First is also famous for its bar and the power of its music.

99

Chinatown where many restaurants stay open very late, as do a large number of Korean restaurants on West 32nd Street, between Fifth Avenue and Broadway.

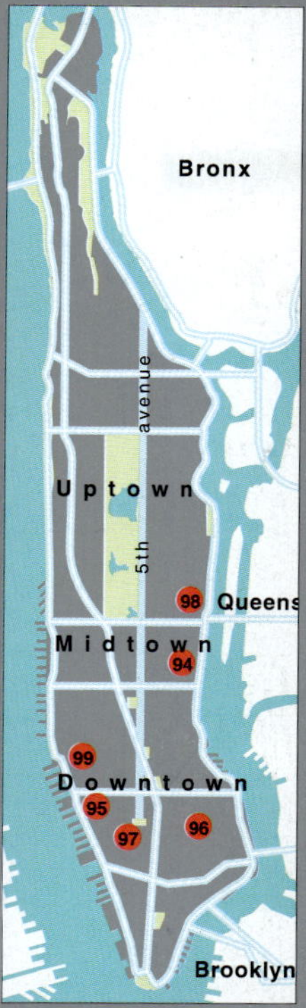

95

99

96

Corner Bistro (97)
331 West 4th Street N.Y. 10014 ☎ (212) 242-9502

(Jane St.) Ⓜ *14th St.* ***Traditional American*** ● *Mon.–Sat. 11–4am; Sun. noon–4am*

A rather threadbare, poetically dingy bar in Greenwich Village, which serves the best burgers in the city. They are juicy, grilled to order, and accompanied by golden fries that have become almost legendary.

97

Not forgetting

■ **Sushihatsu (98)** 1143 First Avenue (between E. 62nd and E. 63rd Sts) N.Y. 10021 ☎ (212) 371-0238 ●●● *Sit at the bar and try the excellent sushi. Open to 3.30am most days.*

■ **Empire Diner (99)** 210 Tenth Avenue (W. 22nd St.) N.Y. 10011 ☎ (212) 243-2736 ●● *This diner* ➥ 60 *is open all around the clock, serving an upmarket version of traditional diner food. A fashionable, noisy place no matter when you choose to visit.*

Entrance charges

Cover charge: entrance charge. ***Minimum charge***: minimum drinks order. ***Music charge***: supplement for watching a show.

After dark

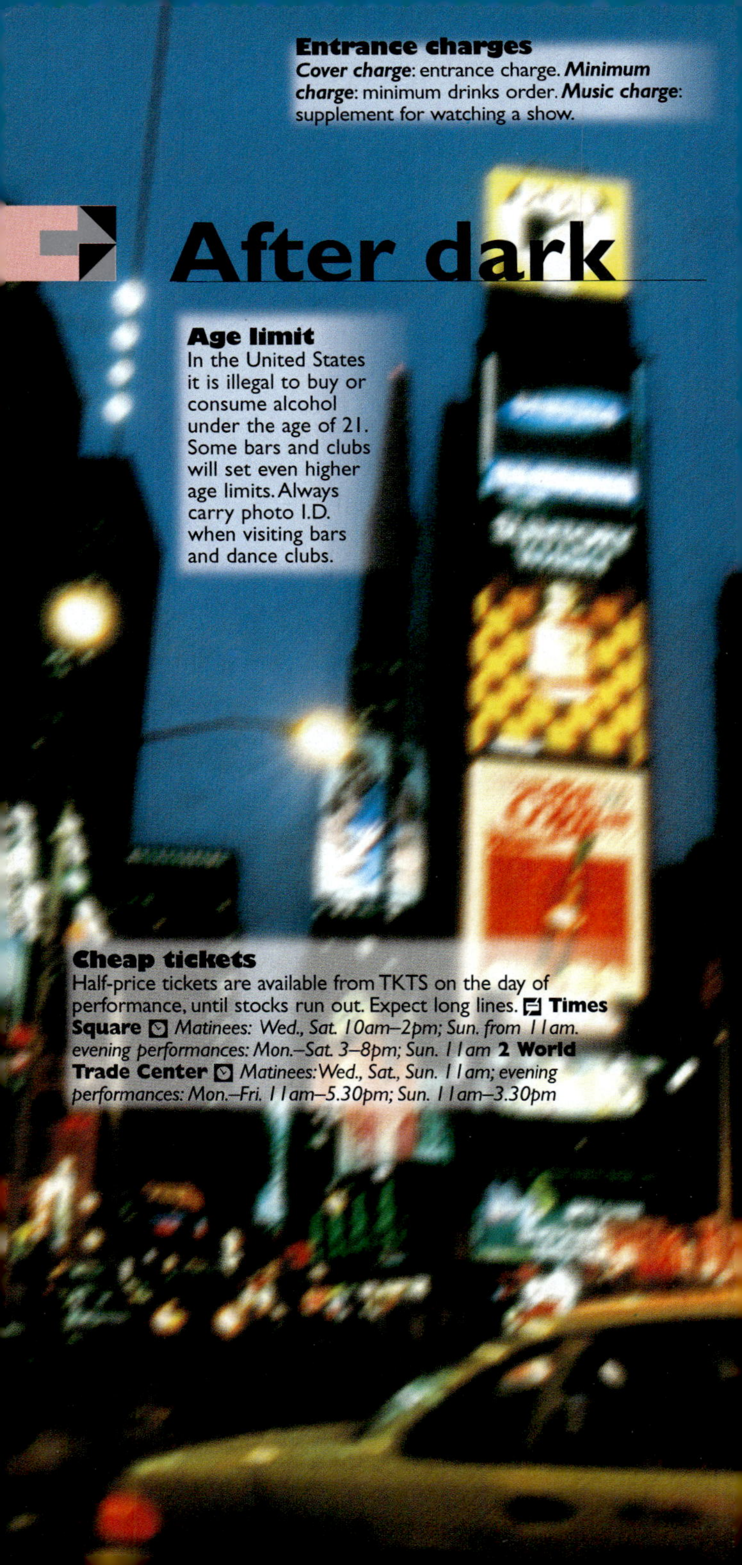

Age limit

In the United States it is illegal to buy or consume alcohol under the age of 21. Some bars and clubs will set even higher age limits. Always carry photo I.D. when visiting bars and dance clubs.

Cheap tickets

Half-price tickets are available from TKTS on the day of performance, until stocks run out. Expect long lines. **Times Square** *Matinees: Wed., Sat. 10am–2pm; Sun. from 11am. evening performances: Mon.–Sat. 3–8pm; Sun. 11am* **2 World Trade Center** *Matinees: Wed., Sat., Sun. 11am; evening performances: Mon.–Fri. 11am–5.30pm; Sun. 11am–3.30pm*

Summer festivals
June Metropolitan Parks Concerts ☎ *(212) 362-6000*
June–August Shakespeare in the Park ☎ *(212) 260-2400*
July N.Y. Philarmonic Parks Concerts ☎ *(212) 875-5709*
August Lincoln Center Out-of-Doors Festival ☎ *(212) 875-5438*
September–October N.Y. Film Festival ☎ *(212) 875-5050*

59 Nights out

THE INSIDER'S FAVORITES

Listings of events in...
Time Out New York, The Village Voice, New York Magazine.

INDEX BY AREA & TYPE

Basic facts

Manhattan offers a bewildering array of bars: large and small, stylish and seedy, noisy and quiet (the latter category in a distinct minority). Some brew their own beers (brewpubs), others offer couches rather than stools, still others sell quality cigars. Most bars stay open until 2am

After dark

Hogs and Heifers (1)

859 Washington Street N.Y. 10014 ☎ (212) 929-0655

(13th St.) M *14th St.* ⌚ *Mon.–Fri. 11–4am; Sat. 1pm–4am; Sun. 2pm–4am* ● *$3.50* *1843 First Avenue (between 95th and 96th Sts)*

For a unique experience, leap into a taxi and head for this extraordinary establishment, frequented by a mixed crowd. The bar has a collection of bras on display, donated by the women (famous and not so famous) who have danced on its tables.

McSorley's Old Ale House (2)

15 East 7th Street N.Y. 10003 ☎ (212) 473-9148

(between Second and Third Aves) M *Astor Pl.* ⌚ *Mon.–Sat. 11–1am; Sun. 1pm–1am* ● *$3*

This traditional drinking establishment (dating from 1854) owes its charm to its decor and its 100%-original floor, complete with sawdust and grime. It was known for brewing its own beer long before brewpubs became popular in the city. It attracts a lot of people from out of town, but it's good to say that you've been there.

Fez (3)

380 Lafayette Street N.Y. 10003 ☎ (212) 533-7000 ➡ (212) 995-0591

(between E. 4th St. and Great Jones) M *Astor Pl.* ⌚ *Sun.–Thur. 6pm–2am; Fri.–Sat. 6pm–4am* ● *$4* ***Shows*** *Thur. 9.30pm, 11.30pm;* ● *$18; Fri.–Wed. $8–20*

This cocktail bar in Time Café, designed in the Moroccan style with a contemporary twist, is famous for its atmosphere and its music. Subdued lighting and soft sofas to sink into combine to make having a drink here a highly relaxing experience.

Zinc Bar (4)

90 W. Houston Street N.Y. 10012 ☎ (212) 477-8337 ➡ (212) 420-1804

(La Guardia Place) M *Bleecker St.* ⌚ *daily 6pm–3am* ● *$4* ***Shows*** *Mon.–Fri. 10pm, midnight, 2am; Sat.–Sun. 11pm, 12.30am, 2am* ● *$5*

A small, underground oasis where New York's jet set comes to relax. A combination of local bar and chic cafe, it attracts an international clientele: still one of the most fashionable places downtown.

Not forgetting

■ **Pravda (5)** 281 Lafayette Street (between Prince and Houston Sts) N.Y. 10012 ☎ (212) 226-4944 *Try some of the bar's 70-odd vodkas with caviar dishes from a vast menu.* ■ **Whisky Bar (6)** The Paramount Hotel ➡ 30, 235 West 46th Street (between Broadway and Eighth Ave) N.Y. 10036 ☎ (212) 819-0404 *Beautiful people, trendy furniture.* ■ **Bowery Bar (7)** 40 East 4th Street (Bowery) N.Y. 10003 ☎ (212) 475-2220 *Not quite as fashionable as it was but still worth a visit.* ■ **Temple Bar (8)** 332 Lafayette Street (between Bleecker and Houston Sts) N.Y. 10012 ☎ (212) 925-4242 *Dress in black and order a vodka martini.*

during the week and 4am on weekends; many offer bar snacks or even meals. The clientele varies according to the time and the place.

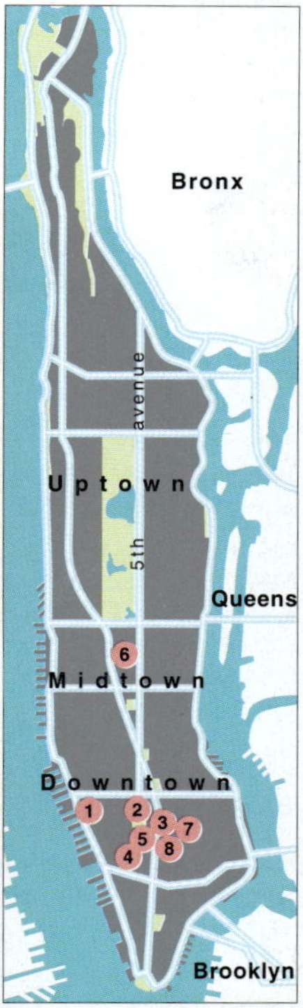

5

9

3

5

2

After 10pm the Zinc Bar fills up with SoHo's fashionable and trendy crowd.

4

Basic facts
When President Roosevelt declared his passion for martinis in the 1930s he unleashed a national obsession with cocktails. These sometimes simple, sometimes exotic mixed drinks came to be seen as the height of sophistication, taking over the hotels, bars and homes of the nation. In the

After dark

Fifty Seven Fifty Seven Bar (9)
Four Seasons Hotel, 57 East 57th Street N.Y. 10022
☎ (212) 758-5700 ➡ (212) 758-5711

(between Madison and Park Aves) *59th St.* ***Martinis and cigars*** *Mon.–Sat. 3pm–1am; Sun. 3pm–midnight*

The bar of the Four Seasons Hotel ➡ 38 is one of the most elegant in New York City. Art by Kimon Nicolaides, furniture by Dakota Jackson, and design by I. M. Pei combine to create a stunning post-modern setting. If you're after the largest choice of martinis and the most impressive place to drink them in, look no further: this is the place for you.

Morgans (10)
Morgans Hotel, 237 Madison Avenue N.Y. 10016 ☎ (212) 726-7600

(between 37th and 38th Sts) *33rd St.* *Mon.–Tue. 5pm–2am; Wed.–Sat. 5pm–4am; Sun. 6pm–1am* ● *$7*

This chic bar is a meeting place for famous faces, set in the building described by the magazine *Vanity Fair* as "the most beautiful hotel in New York" ➡ 24. The interior is stunning. There is no bar, just an enormous table, 21 feet long and brilliantly lit. Waiters emerge from behind a black curtain to bring your order. Morgans is difficult to find: keep an eye out for the doorman signaling its discreet entrance on the east side of Madison Avenue.

The Greatest Bar on Earth (11)
1 World Trade Center N.Y. 10048 ☎ (212) 524-7011

(106th floor) *World Trade Center* *entrance on West St.* *Mon.–Thur. noon–2pm, 4pm–1am; Fri. noon–2pm, 4pm–2am; Sat. noon–2am; Sun. 11am–11pm* ● *cover charge $5 (Thur.–Sat. after 9pm)*

If you are attracted by the idea of quenching your thirst at the top of the world, choose this huge, bustling bar perched on the 106th floor of the World Trade Center. Sitting by its windows, you will feel like you are floating over the city, with an amazing view from the Statue of Liberty to Verrazano Bridge. Each of the three bars has its own specialty: oysters, sushi, or *shabu shabu*. And of course there is the Windows on the World Restaurant ➡ 50, on the same floor. A pianist plays from 5pm, followed by a live band after 9pm.

Not forgetting
■ **Bemelmans Bar (12)** Carlyle Hotel ➡ 42, 981 Madison Ave (between 76th and 77th Sts) N.Y. 10021 ☎ (212) 744-1600 *Cocktails only. Live music after 9.30pm* ■ **The Oak Bar (13)** The Plaza Hotel ➡ 40, 768 Fifth Avenue (between 59th St and Central Park South) N.Y. 10019 ☎ (212) 759-5320 *This very elegant bar with its oak pillars will give you a taste of life at the Plaza.* ■ **The Rainbow Promenade Bar (14)** 30 Rockefeller Plaza (between 49th and 50th Sts) N.Y. 10112 ☎ (212) 632-5000 *From the 64th floor, the best view of Manhattan, in a 1930s setting. Open from 4pm. Jacket required. Restaurant ➡ 48.*

1950s and 1960s the cocktail hour became an institution. Nowadays you can have a cocktail at any time of the evening or night. Here are some of the best places to try them.

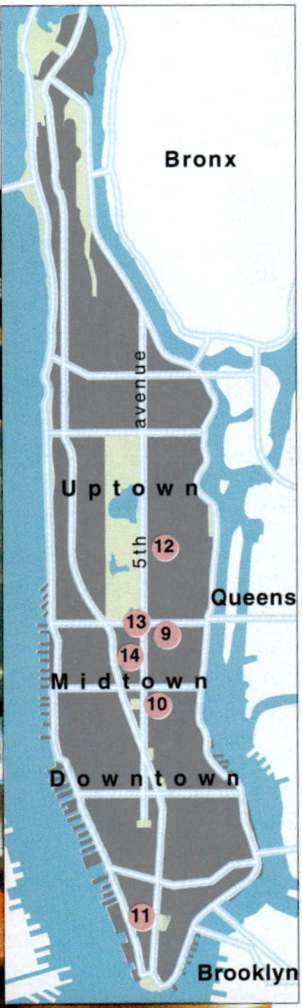

14

9

14

13

10

Basic facts

New York has declared itself the world capital of music and indeed it does offer an extraordinary range of musical styles, from folk music to rock via world music, and of course jazz ➡ 94 and classical. Many famous performers like Bob Dylan, Janice Joplin, Ella Fitzgerald and Patti

After dark

Apollo Theater (15)

253 West 125th Street N.Y. 10027 ☎ (212) 864-0372 ➡ (212) 749-2723

(between Seventh and Eighth Aves) M *125th St.* ***Jazz*** *box office Mon.–Fri. 10am–6pm; (except Wed. 10am–8.30pm)* ***Performances*** *Thur.–Tue. variable; Wed. 7.30pm 'The Original Amateur Night'* ● *$10–18.50*

Go to Harlem to visit this New York legend, which showcases some of the best black music acts. Frank Sinatra's famous line "if I can make it there, I'll make it anywhere" applies with a vengeance on Wednesday's Amateur Night, when young musicians are judged by a discerning audience. Those who pass the test, as Ella Fitzgerald and Billie Holiday did, are sure to be heading for success.

CBGB OMFUG (16)

315 Bowery N.Y. 10003 ☎ (212) 982-4052 ➡ (212) 995-0019

(Bleecker St.) M *Second Ave* ***Alternative Rock*** *daily 7pm–2am* ● *$3–$9*

An institution among New York's music clubs, famous for its ear-splitting daily shows and its surprise guest appearances. A place of pilgrimage for American Punk Rock: it was here that groups like Police, Talking Heads, The Ramones, and Blondie made their debuts.

Bottom Line (17)

15 West 4th Street N.Y. 10012 ☎ (212) 228-6300 ➡ (212) 777-2370

(Mercer St.) M *8th St.* ***Variety*** *Box office daily 10am–11pm*
Performances *7.30pm, 10.30pm* ● *$15–$30, minimum $8*

One of the best venues for live music. The cream of contemporary singer-songwriters in a rather shabby bar. It can get crowded but it is one of the best places in New York to listen to very good music.

Brooklyn Academy of Music (BAM) (18)

30 Lafayette Avenue, Brooklyn N.Y. 11217
☎ (718) 636-4100 ➡ (718) 857-2021

Bus BAM from Midtown, booking compulsory ☎ (718) 636-4100 M *Atlantic Ave* ***Music, opera, ballet, theater*** *Box office Mon.–Fri. 10am–6pm; Sat. noon–6pm* ***Performance*** *times vary* ● *vary*

BAM, founded in 1861, was the first American center for the theatrical arts and remains at the hub of the theatrical world today. Every autumn it organizes a festival of avant-garde music, theater, and choreography, which is enjoyed by public and critics alike.

Not forgetting

■ **Carnegie Hall (19)** 881 Seventh Ave (57th St.) N.Y. 10019 ☎ (212) 247-7800 *Legendary concert hall: opera, popular and classical music.*
■ **Radio City Music Hall (20)** 1260 Sixth Ave (between 50th and 51st Sts) N.Y. 10020 ☎ (212) 247-4777 *Home base of the famous Rockettes.*
■ **SOB's – Sounds of Brazil (21)** 200 Varick Street (W. Houston St.) N.Y. 10014 ☎ (212) 243-4940 *New York mecca for world music.*

Smith started out in the city's clubs. The style and the quality of the music vary from club to club: who knows, maybe you'll discover a star of the future.

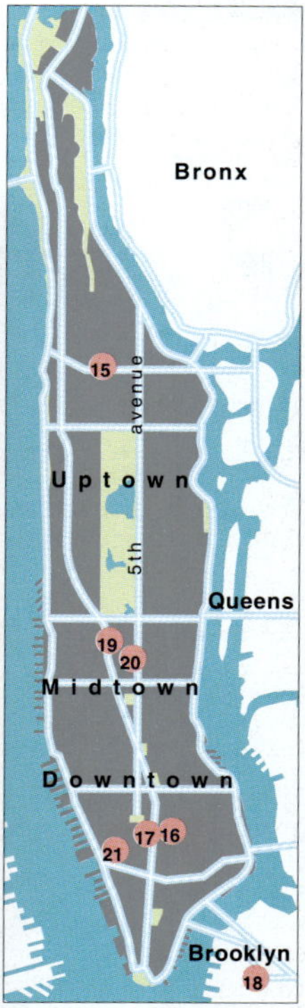

20

19

19

21

20

Basic facts

In New York a cabaret is a place where you can eat and drink while watching a show or listening to music. Comedy clubs offer just what the name promises: some of America's best-known comedians got their start in the clubs of New York. To get into a club or cabaret, you will need to

After dark

Café Carlyle (22)

(Carlyle Hotel), 981 Madison Anenue N.Y. 10021 ☎ (212) 570-7184

(Madison Ave) M *77th St.* P ***Cabaret*** *Mon.–Sat. 6pm–midnight* ● *$50*

Very stylish, very romantic, very intimate. The legendary Bobby Short and Eartha Kitt are regulars here.

Tatou (23)

151 East 50th Street N.Y. 10022 ☎ (212) 753-1144 ➟ (212) 838-5972

(between Lexington and Third Aves) M *53rd St.* ***Cabaret and jazz*** P *dinner Mon.–Sat. 5.30pm–4am* ***Performances*** *11pm–4am* ● *Tue.–Thur. $15; Fri.–Sat. $20*

Intimate and never overcrowded, Tatou has a subdued atmosphere with luxurious decor. Dancing follows supper.

Firebird Café (24)

363 West 46th Street N.Y. 10036 ☎ (212) 586-0244

(between Ninth and Eighth Aves) M *50th St.* P ***Cabaret*** ***Performances*** *Tue.–Thur. 9pm; Fri.-Sat. 9pm, 11pm* ● *$40 minimum 2 drinks* ***FireBird Café*** *or* ***FireBird Restaurant*** *before the performance from 7.30pm*

This luxury club is attached to a Russian restaurant. An elegant and stylish venue that welcomes many of the very best cabaret artists, with Steve Ross frequently topping the bill.

The Oak Room (25)

Algonquin Hotel, 59 West 44th Street N.Y. 10036 ☎ (212) 840-6800

(between Fifth and Sixth Aves) M *42nd St.* P ***Cabaret*** *Performances Mon.–Thur. 9pm; Fri.–Sat. 9pm, 11.30pm* ● *$35* ***Dinner-opera*** *Sun. 8.30pm* ● *$70*

One of the oldest clubs in town, with a rich literary past. Its musical history is just as illustrious: Harry Connick, Jr., Andrea Marcovicci, and many others made their debuts here. Monday night highlights the spoken word, with readings and book signings.

Catch a Rising Star (26)

253 West 28th Street N.Y. 10001 ☎ (212) 462-2824 ➟ (212) 971-0850

(between Seventh and Eighth Aves) M *28th St.* P ***Comedy club*** *Tue.–Sat. 5pm–midnight* ***Performances*** *Tue.–Sat. varies* ● *$5–12.50*

This huge showcase for cabaret and variety was founded in 1973 and re-opened on West 28th Street in 1996. It presents comedians as well as jazz, R&B, and rock groups.

Not forgetting

■ **Dangerfield's (27)** 1118 First Avenue N.Y. 10021 (between 61st and 62nd Sts) ☎ (212) 593-1650 *Las Vegas-style comedy club.* ■ **Caroline's Comedy Club (28)** 1626 Broadway N.Y. 10019 (between 49th and 50th Sts) ☎ (212) 956-0101 *Topical comedy from up-and-coming performers.*

pay an entrance charge or buy a drink, or sometimes both. Whatever venue you choose, ask about the cover charges, music charges, and minimums (minimum charge for drinks).

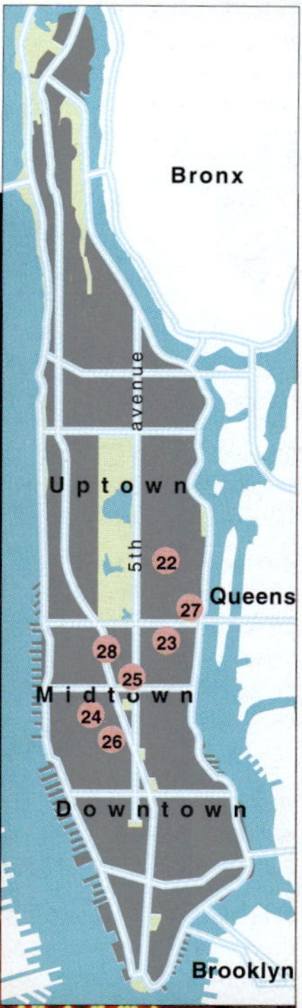

26

Catch
New York City

28

23

24

28

CAROLINES
IS COMEDY

Basic facts

Jazz may have been born in New Orleans, but it grew up in New York. The Big Apple also owes its name to the jazz world: in the 1930s this was regarded as the best place to play, the biggest fruit on the tree. The city has its own intimate style of jazz, heard in the jazz clubs of Harlem,

After dark

Iridium Jazz Club (29)

48 West 63rd Street N.Y. 10023 ☎ (212) 582-2121 ➠ (212) 977-4356

(Columbus Ave) M *66th St.* *Mon.–Sat. 5pm–1am; Sun. 11.30am–11pm* ***Shows*** *Mon.–Thur. 8.30pm, 10.30pm; Fri.–Sat. 8.30pm, 10.30pm, midnight ● $20–30; $10 minimum* ***Merlot*** *Mon.–Sat. 5pm–1am; Sun. 11.30am–11pm*

This club, elected "Best Jazz Club" by *New York Magazine* in 1995 and 1996, has a separate entrance, good acoustics, and numerous seats. The tables are arranged as if in a cafeteria but the performers, including the legendary guitarist Les Paul (who appears every Monday) are excellent. A varied menu is on offer, including snacks, pasta, and Maine lobster.

Village Vanguard (30)

178 Seventh Avenue South N.Y. 10014 ☎ (212) 255-4037

(Waverly Place and West 11th St.) M *14th St.* ***Shows*** *Sun.–Thur. 9.30pm, 11.30pm; Fri.–Sat. 9.30pm, 11.30pm, 1am ● $15 cover; $10 minimum*

The Village Vanguard, some 60 years old, is now showing its age: this is the oldest and perhaps most prestigious jazz club in New York. Don't hesitate to go down into its dark, smoky basement, which musicians such as Miles Davis and John Coltrane loved as much as their audience always has. Strictly no-frills: only drinks are served and food is not available – but the music is the star. It is advisable to book in advance.

Blue Note (31)

131 West 3rd Street N.Y. 10012 ☎ (212) 475-8592 ➠ (212) 529-1038

(between Sixth Ave and MacDougal St.) M *W. 4th St.* P *Sun.–Thur. 7pm–2am; Fri.–Sat. 7pm–4am* ***Shows*** *Thur.–Sat. 9pm, 11.30pm, 1.30am ● music charge about $7–$60; minimum $5* *Sun.–Thur. 7pm–1am; Fri.–Sat. 7pm–2am*

This is probably the most famous of all New York's jazz clubs. A name that is synonymous with classic performances by many of the jazz greats, Blue Note has hosted some unforgettable artists, Ray Charles, B.B. King, Dizzy Gillespie, the incomparable Sarah Vaughan, and Oscar Peterson among them. There is no sign that it is losing ground, either, and the club still attracts figures like George Benson and David Sanborn. Buy tickets ahead.

Not forgetting

■ **Cotton Club (32)** 656 West 125th Street (between Broadway and Riverside Drive) N.Y. 10027 ☎ (212) 663-7980 *Blues, jazz, and gospel. Reservation necessary.*

■ **Birdland (33)** 315 West 44th Street (between Eighth and Ninth Aves) N.Y. 10036 ☎ (212) 581-3080 *Historic night club over two floors. Some nights devoted to Latin American music. Food with a New Orleans flavor.*

■ **Chestnut Room (34)** The Tavern on the Green, Central Park West (67th St.) N.Y. 10023 ☎ (212) 873-3200 *A high-level club with accessible prices.*

■ **The Jazz Standard (35)** 116 East 27th Street (between Park and Lexington Aves) N.Y. 10016 ☎ (212) 576-2232. *The latest of the New York jazz clubs is in a basement. The minimalist-style restaurant above serves good modern American dishes.*

Greenwich Village, and 52nd Street. The last of these was the hub of the jazz scene in the 1930s and 1950s and is currently experiencing a revival.

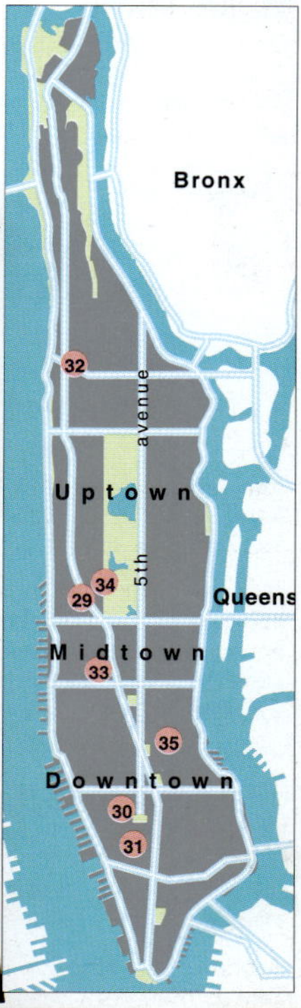

30

34

34

31

33

Blue Note
NEW YORK

At the heart of the Village, the Blue Note still attracts the biggest names in jazz.

Basic facts

No stay in New York would be complete without a trip to Broadway. For nearly a century this has been the epicenter of American theater. To perform, or to be performed, here means success. Bright neon signs advertise productions that have been running for decades, or just for a

After dark

The Lion King (36)

New Amsterdam Theater, 214 West 42nd Street N.Y. 10036
☎ (212) 307-4100

(between Seventh and Eighth Aves) M *42nd St.* *Wed.–Sat. 8pm; matinees Wed., Sat. 2pm, Sun. 1pm and 6.30pm (in summer: Tue.–Sat. 8pm, matinees Wed., Sat. 2pm; Sun. 3pm)* ● *$25–$75*

A spectacular show adapted from the Walt Disney film about a young lion cub. A 'Tony Award' winner whose ingenious costumes and enchanting songs by Elton John will delight children and adults alike. It is staged in New York's most beautiful theater, the former home of the Ziegfeld Follies. There is a Disney shop next door to the theater.

Ragtime (37)

Ford Center for the Performing Arts, 214 West 43rd Street N.Y. 10036 ☎ (212) 307-4100

(between Seventh and Eighth Aves) M *42nd St.* *Tue.–Sat. 8pm; matinees Wed.–Sat. 2pm, Sun. 3pm* ● *$31–$76*

A powerfully emotive musical based on the semi-fictional novel by E.L. Doctorow about three American families, one black, one Jewish and one WASP (White Anglo-Saxon Protestant) in the early 20th century. Although it claims to be 'politically correct', it above all pays tuneful, intelligent and dazzling homage to the generosity of the human soul.

Rent (38)

Nederlander Theater, 208 West 41st Street N.Y. 10036
☎ (212) 307-4100

(between Seventh and Eighth Aves) M *Times Square* *Tue.–Sat. 8pm, Sun. 7pm; matinees Sat.–Sun. 2pm* ● *$35–$80*

The story of Generation X of East Village, told in song. This is both somber (most of the heroes are drug addicts or AIDS sufferers) and uplifting. A rock opera that captures the heart and the imagination, it has received many awards since it opened in 1995. Although there are many local references, you don't have to be a New Yorker to appreciate the show.

Not forgetting

■ **Chicago (39)** Shubert Theater, 225 West 44th Street, N.Y. 10036 ☎ (212) 239-6200 *A musical comedy about sex, love and murder. Superbly choreographed against a jazz setting.* ■ **Cabaret (40)** Kit Kat Club, 124 West 43rd Street (between Sixth and Seventh Aves) N.Y. 10036 ☎ (212) 239-6200 *This trendy club presents an excellent and daring version of the film and stage classic, set in Berlin in the 1930s.* ■ **Cats (41)** Winter Garden Theater, 1634 Broadway (50th St.) N.Y. 10019 ☎ (212) 239-6200 *Feline fantasy first performed in 1982. Children love it.* ■ **Les Misérables (42)** Imperial Theater, 249 West 45th Street (between Broadway and Eighth Ave) N.Y. 10036 ☎ (212) 239-6200 *Poignant adaptation of Victor Hugo's masterpiece by Boulbie and Schonberg.* ■ **Phantom of the Opera (43)** Majestic Theater, 245 West 44th Street (between Broadway and Eighth Ave) N.Y. 10036 ☎ (212) 239-6200 *Show by Andrew Lloyd Webber inspired by Gaston Leroux's play, recounting the passion of a ghost in the Paris opera house for a young singer.*

few months. Although ticket prices are high, Broadway offers the best in international theater.

Broadway (Theater District)

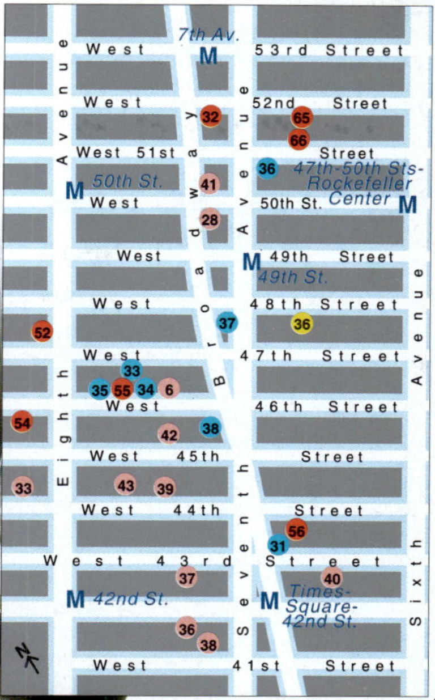

42

43

41

For actors such as Thomas James O'Leary in *Phantom of the Opera*, playing on Broadway is the realization of a life's dream.

41

Basic facts
Off-Broadway is miles from Broadway and Theater District, literally and figuratively. Many of its theaters lead a precarious existence with limited budgets and little publicity. Yet the pay-off for this is the artistic freedom they enjoy. It is a lively, varied theatrical landscape, with new productions

After dark

Stomp (44)

Orpheum Theater,
126 Second Avenue N.Y. 10003
☎ (212) 477-2477

(8th St.) Ⓜ *Astor Place* ***Music, dance*** 🕓 *Tue.–Fri. 8pm; Sat. 7pm, 10.30pm; Sun. 3pm, 7pm* ● *$24.50–$49*

This vibrant show is taking the world by storm: an amazing concert of "percussion" instruments in which the performers use all sorts of metallic and everyday objects to produce a staggering range of noises. Unique and very funny.

Blue Man Group Tubes (45)

Astor Place Theater,
434 Lafayette Street N.Y. 10003
☎ (212) 254-4370

(between 4th and 8th Sts) Ⓜ *Astor Place* ***Theater*** 🕓 *Tue.–Thur. 8pm; Fri.–Sat. 7pm, 10pm; Sun. 4pm, 7pm* ● *$39–$45*

No languages at all are required to follow this avant-garde show, which defies all description. No dialogue or songs: just a large number of objects flying across the stage. Bizarrely, the audience always participates enthusiastically, adding another dimension to the event. See it: it's the only way to make up your own mind!

The Fantasticks (46)

Sullivan Street Playhouse,
181 Sullivan Street N.Y. 10012
☎ (212) 674-3838

(between Bleecker and Houston Sts) Ⓜ *Washington Square* ***Musical*** 🕓 *Tue.–Fri. 8pm; Sat. 3pm, 7pm; Sun. 3pm, 7.30pm* ● *Tue.–Thur. $35; Fri.–Sun. $37.50*

This musical love story, which manages to avoid the usual clichés, has been running longer than any other American musical. It has bequeathed to posterity such unforgettable songs as "Try to remember the kind of September...". Don't expect a luxury production: *The Fantasticks* is performed in a small theater with minimal sets.

Not forgetting

■ **The Joyce Theater (47)** 175 Eighth Avenue (between 18th and 19th Sts.), N.Y. 10011 ☎ (212) 242-0800 *New York's leading dance theater welcomes top American and international dance companies, from the very traditional to the avant-garde. The theater's most regular performers include Pilobolus, Momix and Ballet Tech.*

■ **La Mama E.T.C. (48)** 74A East 4th Street (between Bowery and Second Aves), N.Y. 10003 ☎ (212) 475-7710 *The 'grandmother' of the New York experimental theater movement (E.T.C. stands for Experimental Theater Club), founded in 1962. Every year, some of the most avant-garde American and international directors and playwrights present their work on one of La Mama's two stages: Sam Shepard, Elizabeth Swados, Peter Brook and Andrei Serban to name but a few.*

constantly appearing, although a few shows run year after year. For listings look in the weeklies *Time Out New York*, *Theater Week*, and *New York Magazine*.

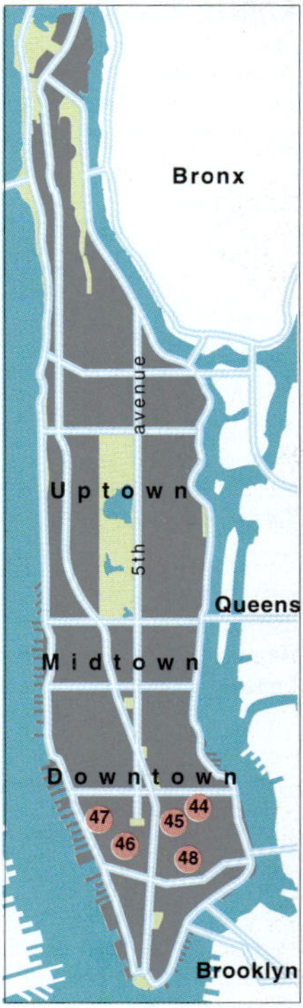

44

46

44

45

Basic facts
From the magical setting of a former theater to the mystical atmosphere of a converted church, from rock music to the latest in urban techno, you can be sure of finding a dance floor that suits you. Every club has a special night: find out about programs and timing beforehand. The best night is

After dark

Le Bar Bat (49)
311 West 57th Street N.Y. 10019 ☎ (212) 307-7228

(between Eighth and Ninth Aves) Columbus Circle ***Dance club*** *Tue.–Sun. 9pm–4am* ***Shows*** *Mon.–Sat. 11pm, 1am, 3am • cover charge $10–$20 Mon.–Fri. 11.30am–3.30pm, 5.30pm–4am; Sat.–Sun. 6pm–4am*

If you want to dance but you're not a fan of body piercing, then this bar-restaurant-dance club is the place for you. The average age of the clientele is around the 30 mark, and so the mood is a little more composed than elsewhere. However, there is nothing subdued about the setting: a cross between a haunted house and a bat-ridden belfry.

Tunnel (50)
220 Twelfth Avenue N.Y. 10001 ☎ (212) 695-4682

(W. 27th St.) 23rd St. Fri. 10pm–6am, Sat. 10pm–9am ***Shows*** *10pm, midnight, 1am • $20*

One of New York's most fashionable clubs. Get your fix of rap and techno in this old railway tunnel, where the brick walls and some sections of rail are still intact. A night at the Tunnel is the perfect introduction to New York's underground, showing the full spectrum of its personalities and styles, in a psychedelic venue.

Bowlmor Lanes (51)
110 University Place N.Y. 10000 ☎ (212) 215-8158

(between 12th and 13th Sts) Union Sq. Mon. from 10pm • $20

Believe it or not, but bowling is Manhattan's latest craze, and combining the game with clubbing is the ultimate. Monday nights see a DJ playing house music, as New York's hippest don bowling shoes and take over the lanes.

Webster Hall (52)
125 East 11th Street N.Y. 10003 ☎ (212) 353-1600 ➠ (212) 353-1642

(between Third and Fourth Aves) 14th St. Thur.–Sat. 10pm–4am • $20

Webster Hall is the "amusement park" of the club world, with each one of its rooms (on different levels) devoted to a particular type of music. You're sure to find something that suits you here! A former Victorian theater, large and diverse enough to attract a mixed crowd, both native and foreign, urban and suburban. Madonna honored the Webster with a visit, holding her famous pajama party here.

Not forgetting

■ **Nell's (53)** 246 West 14th Street (between Seventh and Eighth Avenues) N.Y. 10000 ☎ (212) 675-1567 *A classy alternative. Dress up and enjoy music and dancing on two levels. Three bars and a restaurant.*

Thursday, not least to avoid the suburban crowd that swarms the city on weekends. The action never starts much before midnight and can go on all night at some venues.

52

49

Basic facts

In May 1959, President Dwight D. Eisenhower laid the foundation stone of Lincoln Center, to the sounds of the New York Philharmonic and the Juilliard Chorus conducted by Leonard Bernstein. Today the center employs a workforce of 6000 and puts on 3000 shows each year,

After dark

The Metropolitan Opera (54)
20 Lincoln Center N.Y. 10023 ☎ (212) 362-6000

(64th St.) ***Operas, ballets*** *⏲* ***Opera*** *Sept.–Apr.* ***American Ballet Theater*** *Apr.–June. $24–$150* *on reservation ● ☎ (212) 769-7000*

The opera house is the centerpiece of the Lincoln Center. The present building, designed by Wallace K. Harrison (1966) is very different from traditional opera-house design. The lavish interior has red carpets, marble, gold leaf and a huge staircase framed by two immense Chagall murals, *The Triumph of Music* and *The Sources of Music*. Individual screens on the seatbacks provide simultaneous translations.

New York State Theater (55)
20 Lincoln Center N.Y. 10023 ☎ (212) 870-5570

(between Columbus Ave and West 63rd St.) ⏲ ***New York City Opera*** *fall and winter seasons ● $17–$78* ⏲ ***New York City Ballet*** *In rep.: Jan.–Feb., end Apr.–June; ● $23–$68* ***Nutcracker*** *end Nov.–Dec. ● $11–$70*

This building is home to both the New York City Opera, which has been presenting contemporary and classical works for more than 50 years, and the New York City Ballet, founded by George Balanchine in 1948 and one of the world's leading dance companies. Alongside the classics, it performs Balanchine's unmissable *Nutcracker* every year.

Avery Fisher Hall (56)
10 Lincoln Center N.Y. 10023 ☎ (212) 875-5030

(65th St.) ***New York Philharmonic*** ⏲ ***Concerts*** *Sept.–June,* ***concerts in the parks*** *July ● $16–70*

In this hall, the New York Philharmonic, the oldest orchestra in the United States, founded in 1842, gives 170 classical concerts each year. Special programs include free summer concerts in parks (including memorable concerts in Central Park) and Rush Hour Concerts (in the early evening). Do not miss the *Masque Tragique* of Beethoven by Antonio Bourdelle and the bronze bust of Mahler by Rodin.

Vivian Beaumont Theater (57)
150 West 65th Street N.Y. 10023 ☎ (212) 362-7600

(65th St.) ***Theater, musicals*** ⏲ *variable ● $50–$65*

This theater has a tradition of putting on original plays and musicals. Spalding Gray's *Monster in a Box*, David Mamet's *Speed-the-Plow*, John Guare's *Six Degrees of Separation*, and Mbongeni Ngema's *Sarafina* all premiered here.

Not forgetting

■ **Juilliard School of Music (58)** 60 Lincoln Center Plaza N.Y. 10023 ☎ (212) 875-5000 *Students at this famous school of music, dance, and theater present more than 500 free performances each year.*

■ **Damrosch Park and Guggenheim Bandshell (59)** *Open-air concerts are held here in the summer; in December this is where the Big Apple Circus sets up its tent.*

attracting audiences of around five million people.

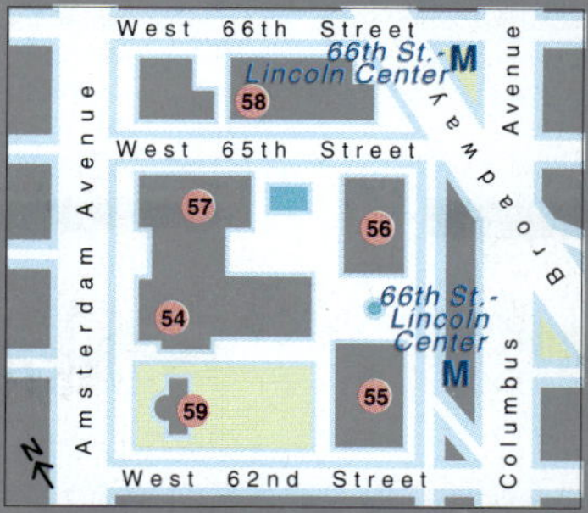

54

54

54

54

Discover the magic behind the scenes and meet the performers on a guided tour of the Lincoln Center. Information on (212) 875-5370.

Personal tours
A native New Yorker will give you an insider's view of the city, free of charge ➡ 14. *Big Apple Greeter ☎ (212) 669-2896*

What to see

Ferry
The best deal in New York is a free ride: cross New York Bay to Staten Island ➡ 138 passing by the Statue of Liberty. *Staten Island Ferry (Battery Park), Whitehall Terminal ☎ (212) 815-2628*
● free

Cable car
Fly across the East River to what was once "Welfare Island," a hospital and prison complex and is now a pleasant residential neighborhood ● $3 *Roosevelt Island Tramway, Second Avenue (60th St.) ☎ (212) 832-4543*

Tours …
on foot
Downtown ($5) *Adventure on a Shoestring* ☎ *(212) 265-2663*
Manhattan ($5) *Big Onion Walking Tours* ☎ *(212) 439-1090*

by water
Three-hour mini-cruise around Manhattan ($17–$20) *Circle Line* ☎ *(212) 563-3200*

by air
Manhattan ($44–$150) *Liberty Helicopters* ☎ *(212) 487-4777*

40 Sights

THE INSIDER'S FAVORITES

Annual events

December 31 New Years Eve celebration in Times Square
End January–early February Chinese New Year (Chinatown)
March 17 St Patrick's Day Parade (on Fifth Ave, from 44th to 86th Sts)
Easter Easter Parade (on Fifth Avenue: from 44th to 59th Sts)
July 4 Fireworks on East River (watch from Battery Park)
October 31 Halloween Parade (Greenwich Village)
4th Thursday in November Macy's Thanksgiving Day Parade (on Broadway, from Central Park West to Herald Square)

INDEX BY TYPE

Basic facts

Visiting Manhattan is like exploring a living museum of architecture and engineering. The Big Apple is crammed with architectural treasures, well-planned parks and engineering feats. There is a surprise around every corner. A distinctive feature of American architecture is the outlandish

What to see

Abigail Adams Smith Museum & Gardens (A)

This site once belonged to the daughter of second US President John Adams; today it has an 18th-century house that is a museum of 19th-century furniture. Near the Queensboro Bridge. *421 East 61st St. (First Ave) ☎ (212) 838-6878 Tue.Sun. 11am–4pm; (Tue. 11am–7pm in June-July); closed August ● $3; students, over-65s $2*

Intrepid Sea Air & Space Museum (B)

Dedicated to the history of sea, air, and space, this museum is housed in three naval vessels: the aircraft carrier *Intrepid*, the destroyer *Edson*, and the submarine *Growler*. Ideal for children. *Hudson River, Pier 86 (West 46th St.) ☎ (212) 245-2533 Apr.–Sept.: Mon.–Fri. 10am–5pm; Sat.–Sun. 10am–6pm Oct.–Mar.: Wed.–Sun. 10am–5pm ● $10*

Gracie Mansion (C)

Gracie Mansion is the last of the 19th-century country houses to survive in New York, and one of the best examples of Federal architecture in the city. It has been the official residence of the mayor since 1942. Tours by appointment. *East End Ave (88th St.) ☎ (212) 570-4751 Wed. 10am, 11am, 1pm, and 2pm ● $4*

Grand Central Station (D)

Built in 1903–13, the station's 42nd-Street façade is classical in style. Be sure to look at the ceiling of the main concourse, which depicts the celestial vault, not as seen from the ground, but as from on high – with 2500 lightbulbs for stars. *42nd St. (Park Ave) Wed. 12.30pm Meet the Municipal Art Society in the Main Concourse*

General Electric Building (E)

Art Deco details at the summit of the building and in the lobby depict forms of energy. *570 Lexington Ave. (51st St.)*

Chrysler Building (F)

Built in 1930, this steel, streamlined skyscraper is one of the symbols of New York. Only the Art Deco lobby is open to visitors. *405 Lexington Ave (42nd St.)*

Flatiron Building (G)

The Flatiron Building was the tallest building in the world when it was constructed in 1902, marking the beginning of the skyscraper era. Its name derives from its shape. *175 Fifth Avenue (22nd St.)*

juxaposition of every style imaginable: from the gable to the dome.

City Hall (H)

New York's city hall (1811) is an architectural jewel, in the Louis-XVI and Georgian styles. Be sure to see the rotunda, the Governor's room, and the courtrooms on the second floor. *City Hall Park (between Broadway and Park Row)*

Washington Square (I)

Chess-players, punks, joggers, old ladies, and children all mix in this small park in Greenwich Village. The triumphal archway marks the centenary of George Washington's investiture in 1789. Carvings on the pillars depict 'Washington at war' and 'Washington in the peace'. *West 4th Street (University Pl.)*

Woolworth Building (J)

Once called the 'cathedral of commerce' by its owner, Frank Woolworth, the founder of the chain of 'five-and-ten' stores. It remained the tallest skyscraper until it was supplanted by the Chrysler Building in 1930. In the lobby look for the caricatures of Woolworth counting his nickels and the architect Cass Gilbert clasping a scale model of the building. *233 Broadway (Park Pl.)*

Brooklyn Bridge (K)

A masterpiece of engineering, constructed between 1869 and 1883. It held the record as the longest and tallest bridge in the world until the end of the 19th century. Take a walk across the bridge to Brooklyn Heights ➡ 132 and enjoy the extraordinary view over lower Manhattan.

In the area

The city of New York is made up of a group of islands, including two small islands to the south of Manhattan: Liberty Island and Ellis Island. For more than 50 years, hopeful immigrants who arrived from Europe by boat had to go through clearance and quarantine on Ellis Island, the

What to see

Ellis Island Immigrant Museum (1)

Ellis Island, New York Harbor N.Y. 10004 ☎ (212) 363-7620

Castle Clinton 9.30am–3.30pm ● $7; over-65s $6; under-17s $3
☎ (212) 269-5755 daily 9.30am–5pm; (summer 9.30am–6pm) ● free
Recorded tours ● $3

With its neo-Renaissance architecture, its spires and its elegant domes, the immigration center on Ellis Island must have seemed extraordinarily majestic to the young Annie Moore, the first future American to disembark on the island in 1892, and to the 17 million immigrants who came after her up to 1954. Yet the experiences retraced by the island's museum, through its exhibitions, documentary films, and dramatic reconstructions, are painful ones. The Baggage Room on the first floor displays a collection of baskets, suitcases, clothes, and other personal effects that illustrate the trials suffered by these travelers. The tour continues in the neighboring room, which presents a huge, comprehensive panorama of the history of immigration in the United States. Upstairs, two semicircular galleries show the lengthy process immigrants had to go through before they could become Americans: medical examinations, literacy tests, and so on. The third floor is the most fascinating in the museum, with a variety of exhibits (both valuable and ordinary) illustrating the immigrants' geographic diversity (a Scottish teapot, an Austrian pipe…) and their hopes (wedding slippers, sewing machines, musical instruments…). A series of photographs shows how the center was vandalized and consigned to oblivion after 1954, while other exhibits recount the renovation of this national symbol (which welcomed the ancestors of an estimated 40% of present-day Americans). It is well worth spending a full day here.

'Isle of Tears,' under the watchful gaze of Liberty standing close by.

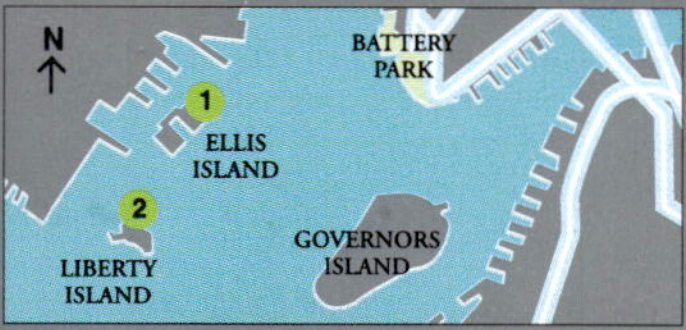

Statue of Liberty (2)

Liberty Island, New York Harbor
N.Y. 10004 ☎ (212) 363-3200

Castle Clinton 9.30am–3.30pm ● *$7; over-65s $6; under-17s $3* ☎ *(212) 269-5755* *daily 9.30am–5pm; (summer 9.30am–6pm)* ● *free* *Recorded tour* ● *$3*

When visitors come to pay homage to the lady of Liberty they generally have only one thing on their mind: climbing up the 345 steps (168 of them inside her 'body') to get up to her crown, 144 feet above ground level (for safety reasons the torch is no longer accessible). It is quite possible to get to the top if you take it steadily, but when you get there the view is not all that interesting. Don't undertake this expedition in the hottest days of summer when the inside of the statue is like a furnace. But if you decide to try, be prepared for a wait of two or three hours (3 million tourists visit Liberty every year). All in all it is a better idea to visit the museum in the base of the statue, which recounts the history of 'Liberty enlightening the world': designed by French sculptor Auguste Bartholdi and architect Gustave Eiffel, the monument had a very turbulent history before it finally ended up on Liberty Island. It was presented by France on October 28, 1886, in order to symbolize the two nations' commitment to liberty, as represented by the date engraved on the stone tablet the figure holds in her left hand: the day of the Declaration of Independence, July 4, 1776 (JULY IV MDCCLXXVI). At the base of the pedestal is a bronze tablet with a poem, 'The New Colossus,' written by Emma Lazarus: 'Give me your tired, your poor, your huddled masses yearning to breathe free.'

In the area

New Amsterdam, as New York was first known, was founded by the Dutch in 1624. The northern limit of the town was marked by a wooden wall built to protect it first from the Native Americans and later from the English. This wall later gave its name to Wall Street. You can sense

What to see

National Museum of the American Indian (3)

1 Bowling Green N.Y. 10004 ☎ (212) 668-6624

(between State and Whitehall Sts) Ⓜ *Bowling Green* 🕒 *daily 10am–5pm; (except Thur. 10am–8pm); closed Dec. 25* ● *free*

This small museum displays a multitude of traditional artifacts that retrace Native American history, spanning more than ten thousand years. The museum, part of the Smithsonian Institute, also works closely with Native American groups today and is meant to be the archive of a living culture. This museum is in a former U.S. Custom House which also attracts visitors who are interested in its architecture. This *Beaux-Arts* masterpiece was built in 1907 and possesses an astounding array of allegorical ornamentation. On either side of the entrance stand four sculptures by Daniel Chester French (the creator of the Lincoln memorial in Washington D.C.) symbolizing the four continents (Asia, Europe, Africa, and America). Inside are murals painted under Works Progress Administration sponsorship in the 1930s, depicting contemporary American life.

Fraunces Tavern (4)

54 Pearl Street N.Y. 10004 ☎ (212) 425-1778

(Broad St.) Ⓜ *Whitehall St.* 🕒 *Mon.–Fri. 10am–4.45pm; Sat.–Sun. noon–4pm* ● *$2.50; over-65s $1; under-6s free* ☎ *(212) 269-0144*

This establishment was called the Queen's Head Tavern when George Washington gave his famous farewell speech here on December 4, 1783. In order to celebrate the colonies' independence, proprietor Samuel Fraunces changed the tavern's name to his own. It was built in 1719 as a private home, was converted to a tavern in 1762, and then restored in the 20th century. Today this fascinating historical site has a restaurant and a museum with period furniture and exhibitions retracing the beginnings of New York and the Revolutionary era in America.

Castle Clinton National Monument (5)

Battery Park N.Y. 10004 ☎ (212) 344-7220

(Broadway) Ⓜ *Bowling Green* 🕒 *daily 8.30am–5pm; closed Dec. 25* ● *free*

This fortification was built in 1811, 300 feet from the shore, as the country faced the prospect of war with England. It was abandoned and then renamed Castle Clinton in 1815 in honor of the then mayor of New York. Later it housed a concert hall and an immigrant clearing center (eight million people passed through its doors); after this it was converted into an aquarium. Today it displays a small exhibition retracing its history. Tickets for the Statue of Liberty are sold here.

Not forgetting

■ **Cunard Building (6)** 25 Broadway (Bowling Green) N.Y. 10004 *The former headquarters of the Cunard shipping company, now a post office. See its superb painted, coffered ceiling.*

■ **India House (7)** 1 Hanover Sq. N.Y. 10004 ☎ (212) 269-2323 *Sandstone mansion in the Italian style housing a collection of art works and naval objects as well as a businessmen's club.* 🕒 Mon.–Fri. 9am–4.45pm

the city's maritime past as you walk along the seafront in Battery Park.

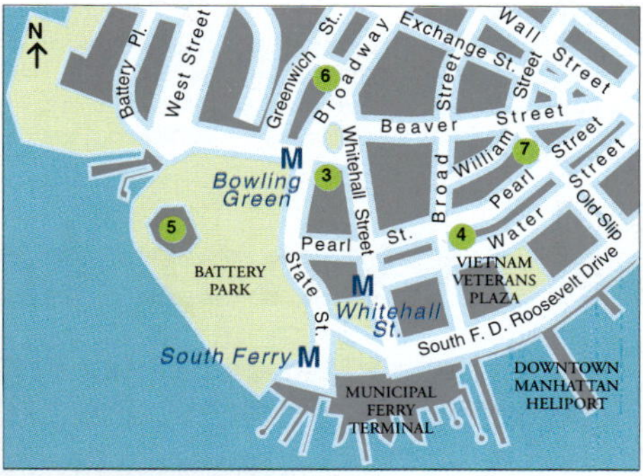

6

3

3

Decoration of eagles' feathers created by a Ponca artist from Oklahoma and worn for ceremonial dances.

5

4

In the area

The Financial District, one of the hubs of the modern international financial world, came into being in 1792, when the stock exchange was founded – under a plane tree! ■ Where to stay ➡ 18 ■ Where to eat ➡ 50 ➡ 52 ■ After dark ➡ 88 ■ Where to shop ➡ 168

What to see

World Trade Center (WTC) (8)
2 World Trade Center N.Y. 10047 ☎ (212) 323-2340

*(between West and Church Sts) Ⓜ Cortlandt St. ⏲ **WTC 2 Observatory** (Top of the Tower) daily: Sep.–May 9.30am–9.30pm / June–Aug. 9.30am–11.30pm ● $12; over 65s $9; 6–12 years $6; under 6 free ▭ ▦ 🍴 **WTC 1** Windows on the World ➡ 50 🍸 Greatest Bar on Earth ➡ 88*

The WTC business center is famous above all for its "Twin Towers," 1350 feet high. An impressive elevator ride propels you to the observation deck on the 106th floor in 58 seconds. In clear weather, you can see for 35 miles. For even more heightened sensations go up to the 110th floor, to the highest man-made platform in the world.

South Street Seaport Museum (9)
12 Fulton Street N.Y. 10038 ☎ (212) 784-8600

Ⓜ Fulton St. ⏲ Apr.–Sep.: daily. 10am–6pm (except Thur. 10am–8pm) Oct.–Mar.: Wed.–Mon. 10am–5pm ● $6; over-65s $5; children $3 ▣ 1st and 3rd Thur. 4pm ● $10 (reservations ☎ (212) 669-9416) ▦ ♿ access to boats 🍴 Harbour Lights ➡ 52

This lively port once welcomed ships from all over the world: memories of its golden age live on in the charm of this 11-block-long museum, with buildings, ships, and galleries. Its fish market is still the largest wholesale market in the country. There are also lots of lively cafes where you can have a drink or a meal.

Trinity Church and cemetery (10)
74 Trinity Place N.Y. 10006 ☎ (212) 602-0872

(Wall St.) Ⓜ Wall St. ⏲ Mon.–Fri. 7am–6pm; Sat. 8am–4pm; Sun. 7am–4pm ▣ Mon.–Fri. 2pm ♫ free concerts Thur. 1pm

This church in the Gothic Revival style was built in 1846 and was the tallest building in the city until the end of the 19th century: ships once used it as a seamark. The cemetery is a Who's Who of colonial America.

New York Stock Exchange (11)
20 Broad Street N.Y. 10005 ☎ (212) 656-5165

(Wall St.) Ⓜ Wall St. ⏲ Mon.–Fri. 9.45am–4.30pm ● free

The neoclassical façade of the building, which dates from 1903, conceals the vast trading floor, where hundreds of stockbrokers go about their business. A fascinating spectacle: watch it from the visitors' gallery.

Not forgetting

■ **St Paul's Chapel (12)** Broadway (Fulton St.) N.Y. 10007 ☎ (212) 602-0874 *The oldest church in New York (1766).*
■ **Federal Reserve Bank (13)** 33 Liberty Street (between William and Nassau Sts) N.Y. 10008 ☎ (212) 720-6130 *This neo-Renaissance building holds 40% of the world's gold. ⏲ by appointment.*
■ **Federal Hall (14)** 26 Wall Street (Nassau St.) N.Y. 10005 ☎ (212) 825-6888 *The museum retraces the foundation and history of the United States.*

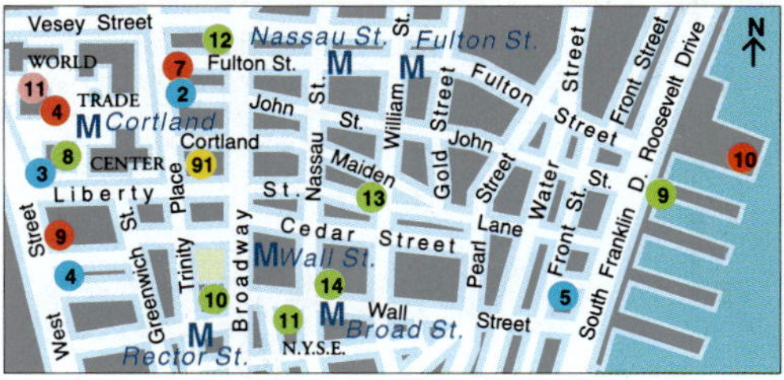

12

In summer, Wall Street workers eat their lunch in the shade of the trees in the peaceful cemeteries of St Paul's Chapel and Trinity Church.

11

In the area

This diverse district, served by two stations, Grand Central Station ➡ 106 and Pennsylvania Station, connects the city with the suburbs and the rest of America. ■ Where to stay ➡ 22 ➡ 24 ➡ 26 ➡ 28 ■ Where to eat ➡ 50 ➡ 70 ■ After dark ➡ 88 ➡ 92

What to see

United Nations (15)
First Avenue N.Y. 10017 ☎ (212) 963-1234

(entrance on 46th St.) M *Grand Central* ⏲ *daily 9.15am–4.45pm; closed on weekends in Jan.–Feb., Jan. 1, Dec. 25* ● *$7.50; over-62s $5.50; 6–12s $3.50 under-5s not admitted* Delegates Dining Room *Mon.–Fri. 11.30am–2.30pm (reservations ☎ (212) 963-7625)*

The multicolored flags of the member states mark the border between New York territory and the international enclave of the U.N. Plaza. The complex was designed just after World War II by a team of 11 architects, including the great Le Corbusier and Niemeyer. The halls of the General Assembly and the Security Council are closed to the public, but the fascinating guided tour, presented by guides from around the world, will explain the workings of this world parliament.

New York Public Library (16)
476 Fifth Avenue N.Y. 10018 ☎ (212) 930-0800

(between 40th and 42nd Sts) M *42nd St.* ⏲ *Mon., Thur.–Sat. 10am–6pm; Tue., Wed. 11am–7.30pm* ● *free* *Bryant Park Grill* ➡ *50*

Two lions (dubbed "Patience" and "Fortitude" by the then mayor Fiorella La Guardia) flank the entrance of this palatial white marble building, built in 1911 in the *beaux-arts* style. The double staircase leads to the library, the fifth largest research library in the world. There are free guided tours as well as exhibitions on a wide variety of subjects, from the great books of this century to the city's waste disposal systems.

Pierpont Morgan Library (17)
29 East 36th Street N.Y. 10016 ☎ (212) 685-0008

(Madison Ave) M *33rd St.* ⏲ *Tue.–Fri. 10.30am–5pm; Sat. 10.30am–6pm; Sun. noon–6pm* ● *$6; over-60s $4; under-12s free* *Tue.–Fri. noon*

J.P. Morgan was more than just the great financier of his time (he saved the city from bankruptcy three times): he was also an unrivaled collector, passionate about rare books, manuscripts, and objets d'art. He had this *beaux-arts* building constructed in 1902 to house his collection. The library opened its doors to the public in 1924. The old library displays the historic books and an annex houses temporary exhibitions.

Empire State Building (18)
350 Fifth Avenue N.Y. 10118 ☎ (212) 736-3100

(34th St.) M *34th St.* ⏲ *daily 9.30am–midnight* ● *$4.50; over-65s, under-12s $2.25, under-5s free*

Once the tallest skyscraper in the world (1250 feet) this is an enduring symbol of New York and an essential tourist attraction. The art deco building, which opened in 1931, has captivated not only King Kong but also millions of tourists, who have ascended its 86 floors to get to the observation platform and then 16 more floors to get to its glass-covered observatory. At special times the 30 top floors are lit up in different colors: orange at Halloween, green for St Patrick's Day…

■ Where to shop ➡ 146 ➡ 152 ➡ 154 ➡ 168

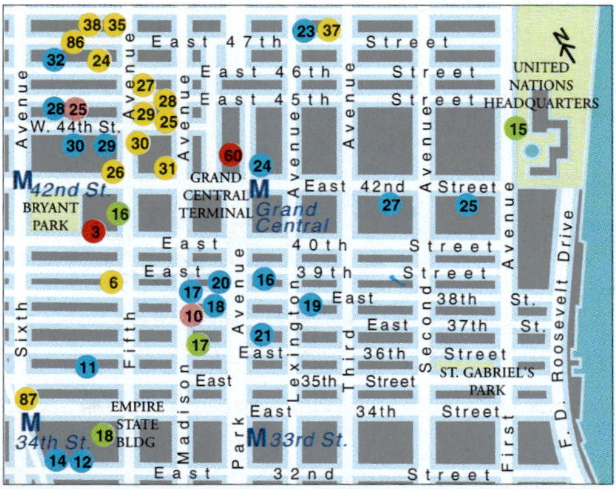

18

A copy of the Gutenberg Bible (c. 1455) is one of the treasures on display in the Pierpont Morgan Library.

17

16

15

In the area

For New Yorkers, Midtown is the center of the world: the stronghold of industry, the media, theater, and culture, as well as the luxury shops of Fifth Avenue and New York's top hotels. ■ Where to stay ➡ 34 ■ Where to eat ➡ 48 ➡ 66 ➡ 70 ➡ 72 ■ After dark ➡ 88 ➡ 90

What to see

Museum of Modern Art (MoMA) (19)
11 West 53rd Street N.Y. 10019 ☎ (212) 708-9480

(between Fifth and Sixth Aves) M 50th St. Sat.–Tue. 10.30am–6pm; Thur.–Fri. 10.30am–8.30pm; closed Thanksgiving, Dec. 25 ● $9.50 (Thur. voluntary contribution 5.30–8.30pm); over-65s $6.50, under-16s free reservations ☎ (212) 708-9710

Where can you have cup of tea next to a Rodin, see a film or a lecture on contemporary architecture, look at *La Danse* by Matisse, find out about the history of photography, or enjoy free jazz concerts on a Friday evening? At the Museum of Modern Art, as famous for its permanent collection of painting, sculpture, drawings, photography, design, and film as it is for its temporary exhibitions, all dating from the last half of the 19th century. MoMA presents one of the most comprehensive overviews of modern art. The building itself, designed in 1921, is a memorable modernist construction, and the sculpture garden, designed by Philip Johnson, is ideal on a sunny day.

Rockefeller Center (20)
47th–52nd Streets N.Y. 10020 ☎ (212) 632-3975

(between Fifth and Sixth Aves) M Rockefeller Center The Promenade *➡ 88* *Rainbow Room* *➡ 48* *Radio City Hall* *➡ 90*

The 19 skyscrapers of Rockefeller Center, built between 1932 and 1973, draw more than 200,000 visitors and employees every day. Key attractions are the performances at Radio City Musical Hall ➡ 90 and the guided tour of the NBC Studio (you can stroll past the windows of the studio from which *The Today Show*, NBC's famous news program, is broadcast). Sculpture and murals are integrated with the architecture: look out for the frescos of the General Electric Building, the Atlas of the International Building, and the Prometheus at the center of Lower Plaza. In the winter watch the ice skaters on the plaza, or take a spin yourself.

St Patrick's Cathedral (21)
Fifth Avenue N.Y. 10022 ☎ (212) 753-2261

(between 50th and 51st Sts) M 51st St. daily 8.30am–8.45pm

This Gothic cathedral with 2400 seats, the work of James Renwick Jr, was dedicated in 1879, 21 years after the first stone was laid. This is New York's most famous Catholic church, the seat of the powerful Cardinal O'Connor and the setting for the funerals of many dignitaries, as well as firemen who have died on the job. The Lady Chapel behind the altar, made of Vermont marble, is a real gem. It displays the arms of Leon XIII and a rose window depicting the mysteries of the Rosary.

Not forgetting

■ **Villard Houses (22)** 455 Madison Avenue (between 50th and 51st Sts) N.Y. 10022 ☎ (212) 935-3960 *Replica of a Renaissance palazzo built by railroad magnate Henry Villard. Now occupied by the restaurant Le Cirque 2000* *➡ 67* *Mon.–Wed., Fri.–Sat. 11am–5pm* ■ **Museum of Television and Radio (23)** 24 West 52nd Street N.Y. 10020 ☎ (212) 621-6800 *Tue.–Sun. noon–6pm (except Thur. noon–8pm)*

➥ 92
■ Where to shop ➥147
154 ➥ 156

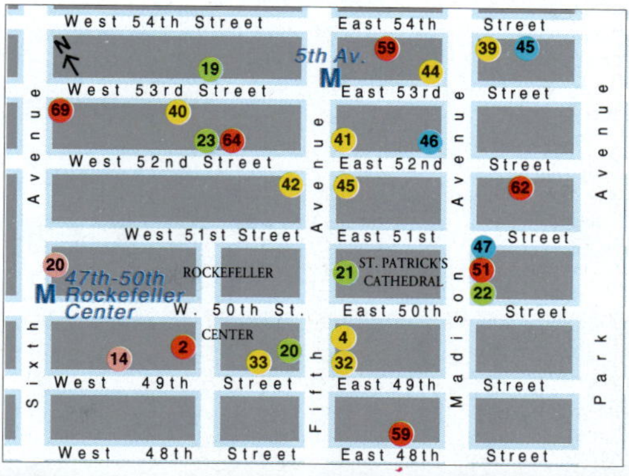

20

21

November onward, the tallest Christmas tree in the world stands over the ice rink of the Rockefeller Center.

19

22

Basic facts

It is impossible not to be dazzled by the wide-ranging international collection of art and artifacts held by New York's Metropolitan Museum of Art. From costume to musical instruments, pre-Columbian art to 20th century sculpture, the museum has something among its three million

What to see

C

B

A

Metropolitan Museum of Art (24)

1000 Fifth Avenue N.Y. 10028 ☎ (212) 535-7710

(82nd St.) M 86th St. P Sun., Tue.–Thur. 9.30am–5.15pm; Fri.–Sat. 9.30am–8.45pm ● $8; over-65s $4; under-12s free; closed Thanksgiving, Dec. 25, Jan. 1. Twin ticket The Cloisters ● same prices The Cloisters *➥ 126*

One visit is not enough to experience the Met's fabulous collections. Rather than going through all the museum superficially, it is better to choose a single period, style or region to focus on. In the summer, to finish off this rich dose of culture, you can relax on the garden terrace decorated with 20th-century sculptures and have a cup of coffee while enjoying the view over Central Park ➥ 122.

The European Collection

Here you can see the masterpieces of the French, Italian, Flemish, and Dutch schools. The collection includes such outstanding works as the portrait of Juan de Pareja (1650) by Velázquez (A) and of Don Manuel Osorio Manrique de Zuñiga (1788) by Goya (B). The most unforgettable section of the European collection covers the 19th century, which occupies a total of 21 rooms. Here you can admire David's *The Death of Socrates*, Van Gogh's *L'Arlésienne: Madame Joseph-Michel Ginoux* (1888) (C), as well as Impressionist and Post-Impressionist paintings, including 37 works by Monet, 21 by Cézanne, and a number by Manet, Turner, and Degas. Rodin's *Burghers of Calais* (1884–95) takes center stage in the European Sculpture Court.

exhibits to interest every visitor. It is truly an encyclopedia of art.

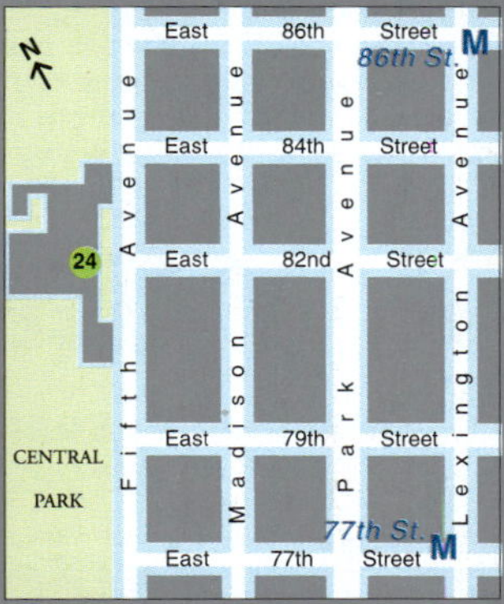

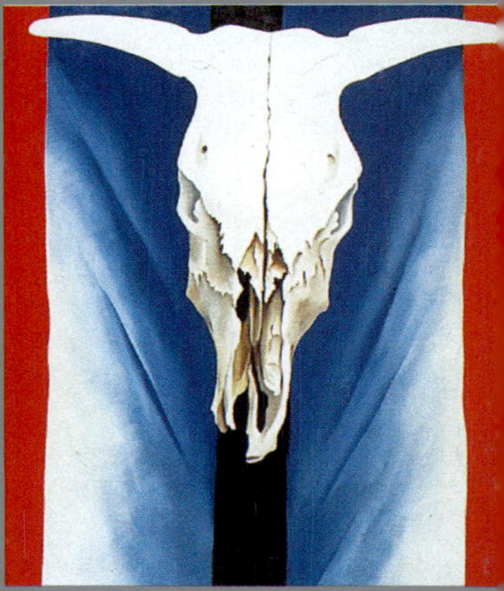
D

The Egyptian Collection

The 35,000 exhibits are presented chronologically, from the pre-dynastic period (3100 BC) to the 8th century. The best pieces are the tomb of Perneb (Old Kingdom), the jewelry from the Middle and New Kingdoms and the Temple of Dendur. The latter building, a gift of the Egyptian government, was built around 15 BC; it was completely reconstructed (including terrace, courts, and foundation walls) in The Sackler Wing, a large contemporary glass building created specially for this purpose.

The American Wing

This wing presents one of the best and most comprehensive collections of American art. The collection of paintings covers nearly all periods from the end of the 18th century up to the start of the 20th century: be sure to see the masterful *Washington Crossing the Delaware* (1851) by Emanuel Gottlieb Leutze. The sculpture collection is just as impressive, with especially good coverage of the neoclassical and *Beaux-Arts* periods, and the decorative arts collection extends from the late 17th to the early 20th centuries. Rooms devoted to different periods offer an insight into the American lifestyle, including the splendid "Living Room of the Little House", designed by Frank Lloyd Wright around 1914. Works by modern artists including *Red, White and Blue* by Georgia O'Keeffe (D). Works by Edward Hopper, Willem de Kooning, Jackson Pollock, Marcel Breuer, and Isamu Noguchi are exhibited in the Lila Acheson Wallace Wing, which opened in 1987 to house the impressive collection of 20th-century art.

In the area

The area around Fifth Avenue between 70th and 104th Streets, known as the Museum Mile, is home to more than 50 of the city's finest museums. And for a break from this feast of culture, pop over to Madison Avenue for some luxury window-shopping.

What to see

Solomon R. Guggenheim Museum (25)
1071 Fifth Avenue N.Y. 10128 ☎ (212) 423-3500

(89th St.) M *86th St.* *Sun.–Wed. 10am–6pm; Fri.–Sat. 10am–8pm* ● *$12 (Fri. 6–8pm voluntary contribution); students, over-65s $7; under-12s free* *575 Broadway N.Y. 10012* ☎ *(212) 423-3800*

It is worth visiting the Guggenheim Museum just for the architecture. Since it was opened in 1959, Frank Lloyd Wright's unique building has been one of the most controversial in New York. Although popular with the general public, the circular design has been criticised as being 'unsuitable' for displaying works of art. Take the escalator to the top and view the permanent and temporary displays as you make your way down the long spiral ramp. The beautiful collections of modern art, including works by Camille Pissarro, Édouard Manet and Paul Klee, are housed in the new annex, the Towers Galleries.

Whitney Museum of American Art (26)
945 Madison Avenue N.Y. 10021 ☎ (212) 570-3676

(75th St.) M *77th St.* *Wed., Fri.–Sun. 11am–6pm; Thur. 1–8pm; closed Independence Day, Thanksgiving, Dec. 25, Jan. 1* ● *$8 (Thur. 6–8pm free); over-62s $7; under-12s free* *Sarabeth's* ➡ *76* *120 Park Ave*

The Whitney Museum, created by American architect Marcel Breuer, is a forbidding granite building. Behind this harsh façade is the world's largest collection of American works, with paintings, sculptures, graphic works, films and videos produced after 1900. The museum was founded in 1931 by Gertrude Vanderbilt Whitney (a sculptress and enlightened patron of the arts) and moved several times before settling here in 1966. It has always taken a resolutely non-conformist stance.

The Frick Collection (27)
1 East 70th Street N.Y. 10021 ☎ (212) 288-0700

(Fifth Ave) M *68th St.* *Tue.–Sat. 10am–6pm; Sun. 1–6pm; closed Jan. 1, July 4, Thanksgiving, Dec. 24–25* ● *$5; over-65s $3;*

In 1914 steel magnate Henry Frick had this mansion built with a view to its being converted into a museum after his death. With its pink marble staircase and its French and Italian Renaissance furniture, the Frick residence is itself one of the masterpieces on display. The walls are covered with paintings by Gainsborough, Rembrandt, and El Greco, to name just a few of the most famous, but the highlights are three rare pieces by Vermeer, including the *Officer and Young Woman Smiling* (c. 1657).

Not forgetting

■ **El Museo del Barrio (28)** 1230 Fifth Ave (104th St) N.Y. 10029 ☎ (212) 831-7272 *Wed.–Sun. 11am–5pm* ■ **Museum of the City of New York (29)** 1220 Fifth Ave (103rd St.) N.Y. 10029 ☎ (212) 534-1672 *Wed.–Sat. 10am–5pm; Sun. noon–5pm*
■ **International Center of Photography (30)** 1130 Fifth Ave (94th St.) N.Y. 10128 ☎ *(212) 860-1777* *Tue. 11am–8pm; Wed.–Sun. 11am–6pm*
■ **The Jewish Museum (31)** 1109 Fifth Ave (92nd St.) N.Y. 10128 ☎ (212) 423-3230 *Sun.–Mon., Wed.–Thur. 11am–5.45pm; Tue. 11am–8pm*

■ Where to stay ➥ 42 ■ Where to eat ➥ 78 ■ After dark ➥ 88 ➥ 92 ■ Where to shop ➥ 164

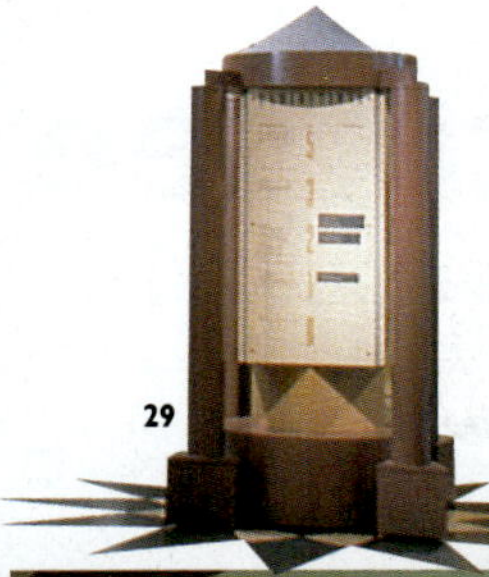

29

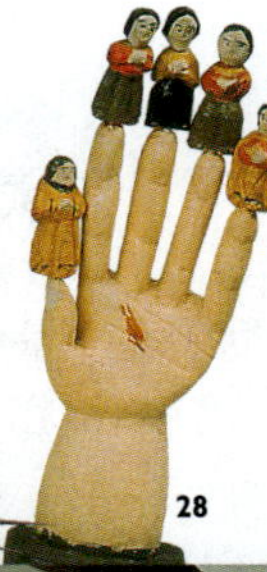

28

25

Natural light through the glass cupola illuminates the works exhibited along the Guggenheim's spiral ramp.

27

26

MUSEUM OF
MC
THE CITY OF
NY
NEW YORK

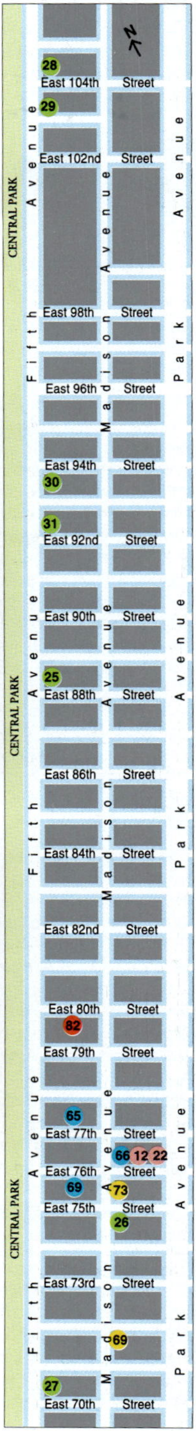

In the area

The charms of Upper West Side include two open spaces, Riverside Park and Central Park, an unrivaled selection of restaurants, a number of respected museums, and a clutch of fashionable bars ■ Where to stay ➡ 44 ■ Where to eat ➡ 80 ■ Where to shop ➡ 166

What to see

American Museum of Natural History (32)

Central Park West N.Y. 10024 ☎ (212) 769-5100

(between 77th and 81st Sts) M 81st St. Sun.–Thur. 10am–5.45pm; Fri.–Sat. 10am–8.45pm; closed Thanksgiving, Dec. 25 ● $8; over-65s $6; children $4.50 Whale's Lair Garden Cafe Diner Saurus

The biggest natural history museum in the world? Look no further: stars, meteorites, minerals, forests, dinosaurs, invertebrates, humans, mammals, reptiles, fish, shellfish, and birds, all have their place here. The collections, including dioramas on animal habitats and a lifesize reproduction of a blue whale, retrace the evolution of life on earth. The newly renovated dinosaur hall is always popular with children and adults alike. The museum has undergone a number of alterations since the first stone was laid in 1874, but its majestic *beaux-arts* entrance (1936), with a statue of Theodore Roosevelt in front of it, is easily spotted from Central Park. Do not miss the biodiversity hall. Also, keep an eye out for the statues of Daniel Boone, John James Audubon and the explorers Lewis and Clark above the entrance. The Hayden Planetarium in the north wing will be closed until the year 2000.

Central Park (33)

59th Street-110th Street, Fifth Avenue-Central Park West N.Y. 10021 ☎ (212) 360-3444 / (212) 794-6564

(Information: The Dairy, entrance on 64th St.) M 59th, 72nd, 81st or 96th Sts; cycle and boat hire at Loeb Boathouse Tavern on the Green ➡ 94

This oasis of green at the heart of the city offers facilities for all the outdoor activities you can imagine: skating on the Wollman ice rink in winter, free plays by Shakespeare, and concerts organized by Lincoln Center ➡ 102. Notable sights include the Belvedere Castle (79th St. Transverse), Bethesda Fountain (opposite the Mall), the delightful Central Park Zoo (Fifth Ave and 65th St.), and the moving memorial to John Lennon at Strawberry Fields (Central Park West and 73rd St.). The park's 843 acres are divided into a number of distinct zones: the Sheep Meadow is the most peaceful; the lake is a favorite with lovers, cyclists, and rowers; ball-players choose the Great Lawn, joggers the path around the Reservoir, and bird-lovers the quiet area of the Ramble, also a focal point of New York's gay scene.

New York Historical Society (34)

2 West 77th Street N.Y. 10024 ☎ (212) 873-3400

(Central Park West) M 81st St. Tues.–Sun. 11am–5pm ● $5; over-65s, children $3

The eclectic collection of New York City's oldest museum has something for everyone. Nowhere else could you find watercolors depicting The Birds of America by naturalist John James Audubon, alongside more than 150 Tiffany lamps, an elegant portrait of George Washington by Gilbert Stuart, and a curious picture of the colonial governor Lord Cornbury in female dress. This is in addition to photos, paintings, and postcards of New York going back as far as the 17th century.

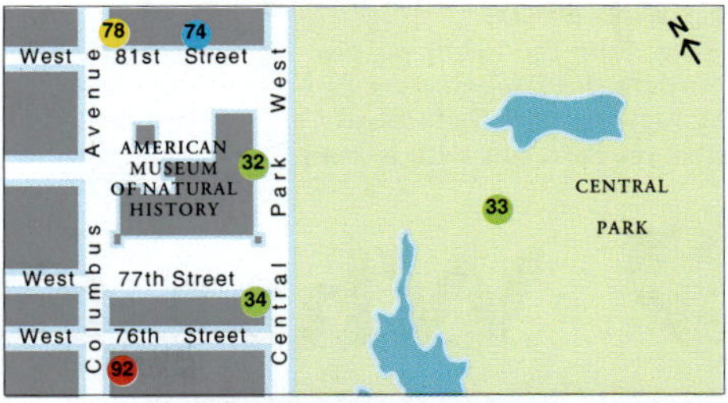

34

32

32

33

32

Tyrannosaurus rex (left), *Apatosaurus* (right) and *Allosaurus* (center) at close quarters in the Dinosaur room.

In the area

Away from the hectic pace of life on Wall Street and in Midtown, the borders of Manhattan are often overlooked not only by tourists but also by New Yorkers themselves. Yet here you can find quiet, peaceful places that are resonant with history. Stroll along the Hudson River in

What to see

Morris-Jumel House (35)
65 Jumel Terrace N.Y. 10032 ☎ (212) 923-8008

(between 160th and 162nd Sts) M *163rd St.* ⏲ *Wed.–Sun. 10am–4pm; closed Jan. 1, Independence Day, Thanksgiving, Dec. 25 ● $3; over-65s $2; under-12s free*

The oldest residential building on the island is a Georgian country house with a breathtaking view over the Bronx, Queens, and Manhattan. It was built in 1765 for Lieutenant Colonel Roger Morris and was used as a temporary headquarters by his superior George Washington in 1776. In the early 19th century it was acquired by Frenchman Stephen Jumel, a wealthy wine merchant who furnished it with souvenirs brought over from France, some of which are said to have belonged to Napoleon. The museum, founded by the Daughters of the American Revolution in 1907, concentrated at first on the revolutionary period. The acquisition of furniture and decorative works belonging to Stephen and Eliza Jumel extended its focus to include daily life in New York in the 18th century. Today each one of the house's 13 rooms preserves a different aspect of its rich past. Here you can see what may be the earliest octagonal room in America, hand-painted Chinese wallpaper, and mahogany-framed Chippendale mirrors. The surrounding area, Jumel Terrace Historic District, is also worth a look.

Cathedral of St John the Divine (36)
1047 Amsterdam Avenue N.Y. 10025 ☎ (212) 316-7540

(112th St.) M *106th St.* ⏲ *Mon.–Sat. 7am–6pm; Sun. 7am–7.30pm ● $3 (suggested donation)* *Tue.–Sat. 11am; Sun. 1pm; for information on concerts and other events ☎ (212) 662-2133* *daily 9.00–5.00*

This building is so impressive that it is difficult to believe it is still under construction, even though craftworkers can be seen at work. The church was started in 1892 following a design by Heinz and LaFargue, and continued until it was interrupted by World War II. Work was not resumed until 1982, and then in the Gothic style. When it is completed it will be the largest Gothic cathedral in the world, covering a larger surface area than Chartres and Notre-Dame de Paris combined. Its rose window, 40 feet in diameter, contains some 10,000 pieces of glass. In addition to its functions as an episcopalian place of worship, the Cathedral of St John also acts as a cultural center, hosting concerts, lectures, and exhibitions. There are some precious tapestries on display, including the Barbarini tapestries in the crossing, which were woven on the papal looms.

Not forgetting

■ **General Grant National Memorial (37)** Riverside Drive (122nd St.) ☎ (212) 666-1640 *This tomb contains the remains of Ulysses S. Grant (1822–85), commander in chief of the army during the Civil War and President of the United States from 1868 to 1877. His wife is buried with him.*
■ **Riverside Church (38)** 490 Riverside Drive (120th St.) N.Y. 10027 ☎ (212) 870-6700 *Gothic-style church inspired by Chartres cathedral, commissioned by John D. Rockefeller. The peal of 74 bells, named after Laura Spelman Rockefeller (mother of John), is the largest in the world.* ⏲ *Mon.–Sat. 9am–5pm; bells: Sun. noon, 4pm*

Riverside Park, among the historic houses, and imagine what the island was like in former times. ■ Where to eat ➥ 48 ■ After dark ➥ 94

36

37

36

Sign of the times: a capital on the porch of St John showing an apocalyptic vision of Manhattan.

35

'If those who succumb to the charm of this place let themselves be inspired by the peace, the calm and the beauty it radiates and leave strengthened in courage and hope...then its builders will not have labored in vain.' This was John D. Rockefeller's wish when the Cloisters

What to see

The Cloisters (39)
Fort Tryon Park N.Y. 10040
☎ (212) 923-3700

M 190th St. Mar.–Oct.: Tue.–Sun. 9.30am–5.15pm / Nov.–Feb.: Tue.–Sun. 9.30am–4.45pm; closed Thanksgiving, Dec. 25, Jan. 1 ● $8; over-65s $4; under-12s free; ***Twin ticket*** *Metropolitan Museum of Art Tue.–Fri. 3pm Metropolitan Museum of Art* ➡ *118*

This romantic medieval retreat overlooks the Hudson River and the cliffs of New Jersey. The building may not have existed during the lifetime of St Thomas Aquinas, but that doesn't stop it looking authentic. In fact the Cloisters were made of five French monasteries that were faithfully reconstructed and incorporated into one building in this pleasant New York City park. The place was created in 1938, with the help of oil magnate John D. Rockefeller Jr. He donated the plot, financed the works, and furnished the building with an impressive collection of medieval art. His donations, along with a collection acquired in 1925, formed the starting point of the museum, which is dedicated to European art and architecture of the Middle Ages. A covered walkway bordered with colonnades, around a huge courtyard, leads to the various cloisters and chapels that house the museum's collections (metal works, sculptures, tapestries, stained-glass windows, panel paintings, manuscripts, and decorative works in the Romanesque and Gothic styles), covering the period between 1000 and 1520. Take a walk through the peaceful gardens, where the herb garden includes varieties once cultivated in medieval kitchen gardens and where the flowers featured are the same as those in the world-famous Unicorn Tapestries (on display in the museum). You may hear the sounds of a concert of sacred music from The Chapel of Fuentidueña, whose Romanesque apse (once part of the church of St Martin of Fuentidueña) is on permanent loan from Spain. The Gothic Chapel houses recumbent statues with idealized faces, including that of the knight Jean d'Alluye, who took part in the Crusades.

were built. It is still a special place today.

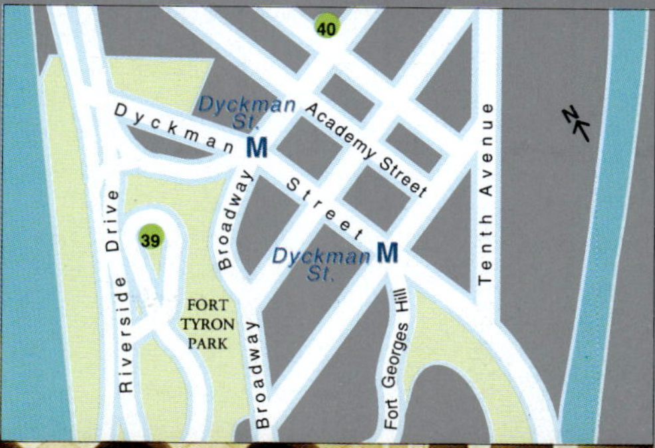

Dyckman Farmhouse (40)

4881 Broadway N.Y. 10034 ☎ (212) 304-9422

(204th St.) Ⓜ *207th St.* 🕓 *Tue.–Sun. 11am–4pm* ● *free*

It is a miracle that this historic farmhouse, the last of the original wooden buildings in Manhattan, is still standing. It belonged to a family of Dutch settlers, the Dyckmans, who moved to the northern tip of the island in 1661. They built the present-day farmhouse in 1784 after the English had burnt down their original farm during the American Revolution (1775–82). The building was restored by their descendants in 1915 and converted into a museum a year later. Today the displays re-create rural life in the colonial era. All the exhibits are original: the furniture, the china, and the kitchen utensils. A herb garden and a military hut complete the picture: a remarkable contrast to modern-day Gotham.

Further afield

Beaches

Coney Island Beach (Brooklyn)
M *lines B, D, F, station Stillwell Ave*

Brighton Beach (Brooklyn)
M *lines D, Q, station Brighton Beach*

Rockaway Beach (Queens)
M *line H, station Rockaway Park*

Calendar of events
1st Saturday in summer Mermaid Parade *Surf Avenue, Coney Island*
July 4 Hot-dog eating contest at Nathan's Famous *1310 Surf Avenue, Brooklyn* ☎ *(718) 946-2202*
Labor Day West Indian American Day Carnival *Brooklyn Museum* ➡ *132*
Two weeks either side of Labor Day US Open ➡ 140 *Flushing Meadows, Queens*

27 Days out

THE INSIDER'S FAVORITES

Tour of N.Y. mansions

Take Route 9 north out of town and discover these magnificent houses, built by notable New York families early in the century along the lush green valley of the Hudson River. They are now open to the public.

Van Cortlandt Manor
Croton-on-Hudson ☎ *(914) 271-8981*
Franklin D. Roosevelt Home
Hyde Park ☎ *(914) 229-2501*
Vanderbilt Mansion
Hyde Park ☎ *(914) 229-7770*

Tour of vineyards

Take Route 25 to visit the North Fork vineyards (the northeastern tip of Long Island). Tastings of chardonnay, cabernet sauvignon, merlot, pinot noir, riesling, and gewürztraminer all year round.

Peconic Bay Vineyards
Cutchogue ☎ *(516) 734-7361*
Pindar Vineyard
Peconic ☎ *(516) 734-6200*
Lenz Vineyard Peconic
Peconic ☎ *(516) 734-6010*

INDEX BY TYPE

In the area

Beyond the skyscrapers of Manhattan, discover the other boroughs of New York City: Brooklyn, Queens, the Bronx, and Staten Island. In the past some areas may have suffered from a bad reputation (much of which is no longer justified today), but they are full of interesting sights.

Further afield

7

10

12

16

Brooklyn Heights (1)

M *2 or 3, station Clark St.; 4 or 5 station Borough Hall*
Bus *25 or 41, stop Clark St.*

Brooklyn Museum (2) & Brooklyn Botanic Garden (4)

M *2 or 3, station Eastern Pkwy; D or Q, station Prospect Park St.*
Bus *B 41, B 69 or B 71, stop Eastern Parkway*

Park Slope (3)

M *F, station 7th Ave-Park Slope*
Bus *B 63, B 67, or B 75, stops 5th, 6th or 7th Aves*

N. Y. Transit Museum (5)

M *A, C, or G, station Hoyt - Schermerhorn Sts.*

New York Aquarium (6) & Coney Island Amusement Area (7)

M *F or D, station 8th St. B, D, F, or N, station Stillwell Ave-Coney Island*

Isamu Noguchi Garden Museum (8)

M *N, station Broadway (15 mins walk)*
Bus *Sat.–Sun.: every 30 mins from 11.30am, from Park Avenue/ 70th St.*

American Museum of the Moving Image (9)

M *R or G, station 36th St.*

N. Y. Hall of Science (10)

M *7, station 111th St.*

Jamaica Bay Wildlife Refuge (11)

M *A, station Broad Channel*
Bus *Q 53, stop Wildlife Refuge; Q 21, stops Broad Channel*

Wave Hill (12)

M *1 or 9, station 231st St. then bus Bx 7 or Bx 10, stop 252nd St.*
Train *Metro-North at Grand Central Terminal, station Riverdale*

Bartow-Pell Mansion (13) & City Island (14)

M *6, station Pelham Bay Park, then bus Bx45 to the gates (except Sun.)*
Bus *Bx 29, stop City Island*

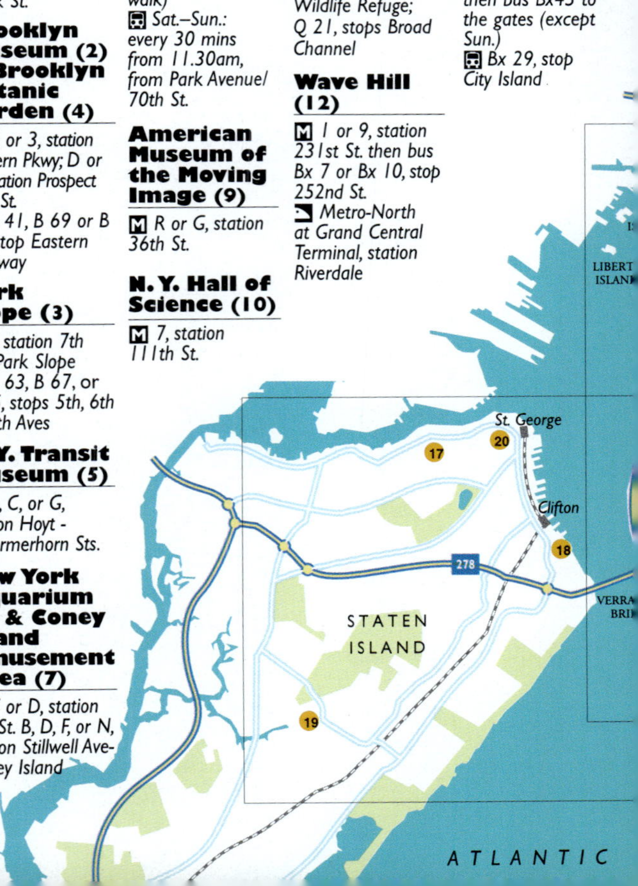

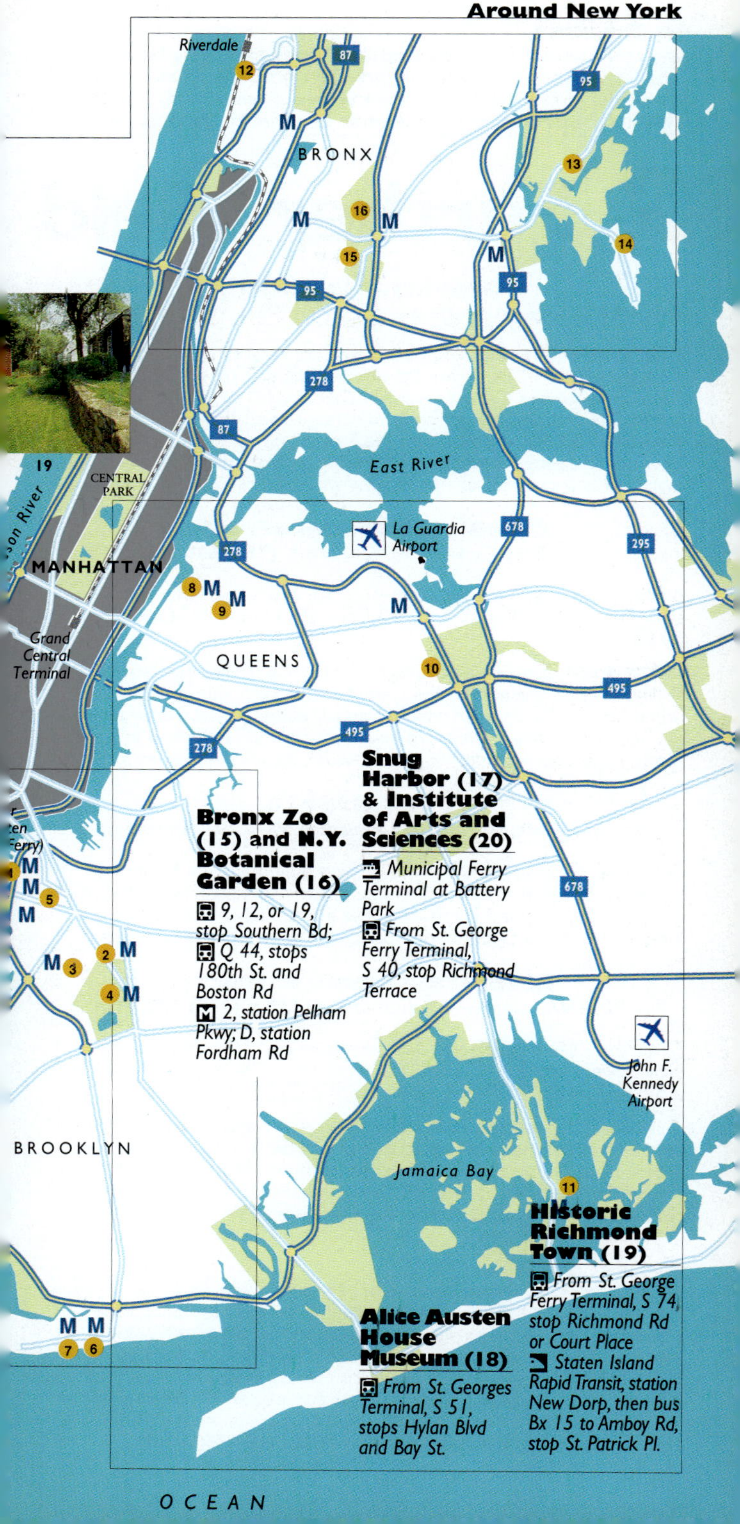

Bronx Zoo (15) and N.Y. Botanical Garden (16)

9, 12, or 19, stop Southern Bd; Q 44, stops 180th St. and Boston Rd

M 2, station Pelham Pkwy; D, station Fordham Rd

Snug Harbor (17) & Institute of Arts and Sciences (20)

Municipal Ferry Terminal at Battery Park

From St. George Ferry Terminal, S 40, stop Richmond Terrace

Historic Richmond Town (19)

From St. George Ferry Terminal, S 74, stop Richmond Rd or Court Place

Staten Island Rapid Transit, station New Dorp, then bus Bx 15 to Amboy Rd, stop St. Patrick Pl.

Alice Austen House Museum (18)

From St. Georges Terminal, S 51, stops Hylan Blvd and Bay St.

In the area

The area where Barbara Streisand and Woody Allen were born is the most densely populated of New York City's boroughs. Brooklyn was founded in 1645 by Dutch settlers and only united with Manhattan in 1898. Its treasures include the majestic Brooklyn Heights and the

Further afield

Brooklyn Heights (1)

Brooklyn Bridge, Atlantic Ave, Cadman Plaza W., The Promenade

Walk over the Brooklyn Bridge and explore an area with a rich literary heritage: Arthur Miller wrote *Death of a Salesman* (1949) at 31 Grace Court, and Truman Capote wrote *In Cold Blood* (1965) at 70 Willow Street. The architecture is rich in towers, turrets, and wrought-iron grills: the best examples are on Montague Street, a lively shopping street. There is a striking view of Lower Manhattan from the Promenade, its skyscrapers a contrast to the Heights' more human scale.

Brooklyn Museum of Art (2)

200 East Parkway N.Y. 11238 ☎ (718) 638-5000

(Washington Ave) Wed.–Fri. 10am–5pm; Sat. 11am-7pm, Sun. 11am-6pm; closed Thanksgiving, Dec. 25, Jan. 1 ● $4; over-65s $1.50; under-12s free

This landmark *beaux-arts* building has some 1.5 million exhibits: it is the seventh largest museum in the United States, with an international reputation for its Egyptian and African collections. Also worth seeing is the Schenck House, a Brooklyn house built for Jan Martense in the 17th century and reconstructed in the museum, stone by stone, in 1952.

Park Slope (3)

Flatbush Ave, 15th Street, Prospect Park, Seventh Avenue

The Slope, the heart of old Brooklyn, was built along the border of Prospect Park in the 1870s. Each one of the 1600 Victorian brownstones is slightly different, and there are some outstanding buildings, like the Montauk Club (25 Eighth Ave), a palace in the Venetian-Gothic style.

Brooklyn Botanic Garden (4)

1000 Washington Avenue N.Y. 11238 ☎ (718) 622-4433

Apr.–Sep.: Tue.–Fri. 8am–6pm, Sat.–Sun. 10am–6pm / Oct.–Mar: Tue.–Fri. 8am–4.30pm, Sat.–Sun. 10am–4.30pm; closed Mon., Thanksgiving, Dec. 25, Jan. 1 ● $3; over-65s $1.50; 6–16s 50¢.; Tue.–Fri. free

This peaceful garden, established in 1910, grows more than 12,000 plant species, from bonsai trees to aquatic plants. Be sure to see the Shakespeare Garden where all the plants mentioned in the bard's plays are represented. The Steinhardt Conservatory is a glazed oasis with specimens from tropical, temperate, and desert environments.

Not forgetting

■ **New York Transit Museum (5)** 130 Livingstone St. N.Y. 11201 ☎ (718) 243-8601 *A disused subway station houses the museum of urban transport. Tue.–Fri. 10am–4pm; Sat.–Sun. noon–5pm* ■ **New York Aquarium (6)** West 8th St., Coney Island (Surf Ave) N.Y. 11224 ☎ (718) 265-3474 *Magic world of the sea, from the beluga to the giant tortoise.* daily *10am–6pm* ■ **Coney Island Amusement Area (7)** From W. 10th St. to W. 16th St. and from Surf Avenue to Boardwalk N.Y. 11224 *Huge amusement park: hot dogs, Astroland, the Cyclone roller coaster.*

pleasures of Coney Island.
■ Where to eat ➡ 50

7

4

2

At the New York Aquarium, Sea Cliffs allows visitors to observe the life of marine mammals like these walruses above and below the water.

6

4

In the area

The largest borough in New York, Queens is less like an urban district than a collection of small towns. Simon and Garfunkel, former residents of Forest Hills, dedicated a song, *The 59th St. Bridge Song*, to the Queensboro bridge. Queens hosted the World Fairs of

Further afield

Isamu Noguchi Garden Museum (8)

32-37 Vernon Boulevard N.Y. 11106 ☎ (718) 204-7088

(33rd Rd) Apr.-Nov.: Wed.–Fri. 10am–5pm; Sat.–Sun. 11am–6pm ● $4; over-65s $2 every day 2pm

Isamu Noguchi believes the way you relate to a work of art depends on where it is exhibited, and so he designed the whole of this museum and arranged every one of his 300 sculptures himself. At the heart of the exhibition is the garden where the sculptures – in granite, basalt, wood and metal – are in perfect harmony with nature, in accordance with their creator's philosophy.

American Museum of the Moving Image (A.M.M.I.) (9)

35th Avenue, Astoria N.Y. 11106 ☎ (718) 784-4520

(36th St.) Tue.–Fri. noon–5pm; Sat.–Sun. 11am–6pm; closed Thanksgiving, Dec. 25, Jan. 1 ● $8; over-65s $5; 5–18 years $4

This museum shares a building with the famous Astoria Studio, which opened in 1920. From the earliest cameras to the latest make-up effects, including costumes and posters covering the history of cinema, the exhibition presents a panorama of the television and film industry. Many of the exhibits are hands-on: visitors can try out editing equipment and make their own short films. A must for fans of the small and big screens.

New York Hall of Science (10)

47-01 111th Street, Flushing Meadows Corona Park N.Y. 11368 ☎ (718) 699-0005

(48th Ave) Mon.-Wed. 9.30am-2pm; Thur.-Fri. 9.30am-5pm; Sat.-Sun. 11am-5pm; closed Labor Day, Thanksgiving, Dec. 25, Jan. 1 ● $6 (Thur.–Fri. 2–5pm free); under-16s, over-65s $4

Science can be intimidating, but New York's only interactive center for science and technology knows how to make it fun. This showcase for science and innovation is housed in a pavilion built for the 1964 World Fair. Among its 175 displays, many of which are interactive, you can explore the universe of sound in *Sound Sensations*, plunge into the secret world of microbes in *Hidden Kingdoms*, and discover the world of physics in *Realm of the Atom*, a unique 3-D reproduction of a hydrogen atom.

Jamaica Bay Wildlife Refuge (11)

Cross Bay Boulevard N.Y. 11234 ☎ (718) 318-4340

daily 8.30am–5pm ● free

More than 325 species of birds including egrets, sandpipers, and gray herons, have been observed in this internationally respected urban nature sanctuary. A huge variety of amphibians, from the tree frog to *pterousus glaucus*, butterflies, and plants complete the idyllic picture. Well-marked trails will take you (with or without guide) wandering over hills, passing by pools and sandy banks, with a view of the Manhattan skyline as a surreal backdrop.

1939 and 1964. The giant Unisphere still stands at the center of Flushing Meadows, Corona Park.

9

10

In A.M.M.I., the exhibit "Behind the Screen" will show you all there is to know about making a film, from basic editing to special effects.

9

8

In the area

The South Bronx's reputation for crime has overshadowed some of the attractions in the rest of the borough. Besides the famous Yankee Stadium ➡ 140, the Bronx has a number of little-known treasures, such as the landscape gardens of Wave Hill, the marinas and the Nautical Museum on

Further afield

Wave Hill (12)

625 West 252nd Street N.Y. 10471-2899 ☎ (718) 549-3200

mid-Oct.–mid-May: Tue.–Sun. 9am–4.30pm / mid-May–mid-Oct.: Tues.–Sun. 9am–5.30pm ● $4 (mid-Nov.-mid-Mar Tue., Sat. morning free); over-65s $2; under-6s free

After the non-stop buzz of Manhattan, Wave Hill is an oasis of beauty and peace. This huge estate overlooking the Hudson River has magnificent gardens with more than 3000 different types of plant and tranquil pathways along the river. Wave Hill House holds concerts in Armor Hall; Glyndor House has an interesting gallery.

Bartow-Pell Mansion (13)

895 Shore Road N.Y. 10464 ☎ (718) 885-1461

***Museum** Wed., Sat., Sun. noon–4pm, closed Thanksgiving, Dec. 25, Jan. 1, Easter, and 3 weeks before Labor Day ● $2.50 (first Sun. each month free); over-65s $1.25; under-12s free **Gardens** Tue.–Sun. 8.30am–4.30pm ● free*

This house in the Classic Revival style will transport you back to the 19th century. It was built in 1842 and decorated in the American Empire style, featuring Greek Revival details and an impressive circular staircase.

City Island (14)

Chamber of Commerce N.Y. 10464 ☎ (718) 885-9100

This island was once the home of New York's shipbuilding industry: today the Nautical Museum explores its fascinating past. Breathe in the fishing-village atmosphere as you stroll the length of the island (only 1.5 miles) and investigate its pretty side streets.

Bronx Zoo (15)

Bronx River Parkway & Fordham Road N.Y. 10460 ☎ (718) 367-1010

Apr.-Oct.: Mon.–Fri. 10am–5pm; Sat.–Sun. 10am–5.30pm / Nov.-Mar.: daily 10am-4.30pm ● $7.75 (Wed. free); over-65s, under–12s $4

The largest urban zoo in the country, and very proud of its 600 species. The zoo will transport you to a *Wild Asia* populated by tigers, elephants, and rhinoceroses, or to the *Jungle World*, a tropical forest under glass. The real kings of the jungle here are the children, who can take a camel ride or fly over the zoo on the "Skyfari."

New York Botanical Garden (16)

200th Street N.Y. 10458-5126 ☎ (718) 817-8700

Tue.–Sun.: Apr.–Oct. 10am–6pm / Nov.–Mar. 10am–4pm ● $3; under-12s $1

Forests, parks and formal gardens in a magnificent 250-acre estate.

Not forgetting

■ **Le Refuge Inn** 620 City Island Avenue NY 10464 ☎ (718) 885-2478 ●● *This bed and breakfast overlooking the marina serves excellent French food.*

City Island. And do not forget its world-famous Zoo and Botanical Gardens.

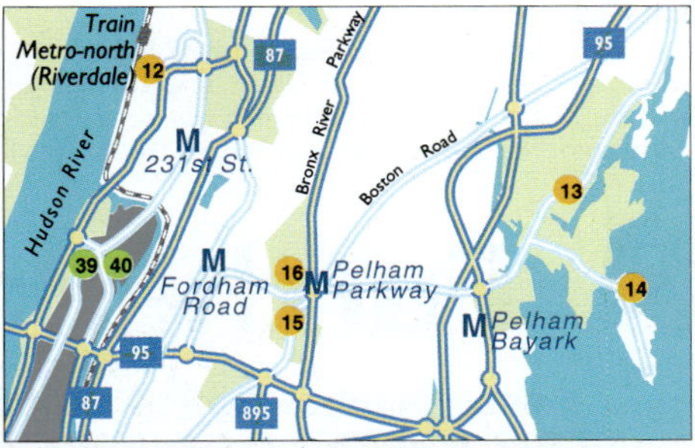

15

12

The magnificent Victorian glasshouse of the N.Y. Botanical Garden is home to an exotic collection of tropical and desert plants.

16

12

14

In the area

Taking the ferry across to Staten Island is an excursion in itself, taking you from Castle Clinton ➡ 110 across the Upper Bay, past Ellis Island, and the Statue of Liberty. Before it was connected to Brooklyn by the Verrazano-Narrows Bridge in 1964 Staten Island was sparsely populated

Further afield

Snug Harbor Cultural Center (17)

1000 Richmond Terrace N.Y. 10301 ☎ (718) 448-2500

Park daily 8.00 to nightfall ***Museums*** *Wed.–Sun. noon–5pm* ***Children's Museum*** ● *$4; parents free*

This group of 28 buildings, completed in 1918, housed the first hospital and retirement home for the nation's sailors. The center was restored and opened to the public in 1976; today it is home to a number of organizations including a Children's Museum, art galleries, and an open-air amphitheater where concerts are held in the summer. The 34-acre estate has magnificent botanical gardens. From Snug Harbor you can watch the boats crossing Kill Van Kull and Upper Bay.

Alice Austen House Museum (18)

2 Hylan Boulevard N.Y. 10305 ☎ (718) 816-4506

(Bay St.) Thur.–Sun. noon–5pm; closed Jan.–Feb., Labor Day, Thanksgiving, Dec. 25, ● *$2; under 12s free*

Alice Austen (1866-1952), an amateur photographer, lived in Clear Comfort, this delightful Victorian cottage overlooking The Narrows, for many years. It was here that she learned and perfected her art. Her works were overlooked during her lifetime; today they are recognized as a unique record of New York life and especially the rural world of Staten Island.

Historic Richmondtown (19)

441 Clarke Avenue, La Tourette Park N.Y. 10306 ☎ (718) 351-1611

Sep.–June: Wed.–Sun. 1–5pm / July–Aug.: Wed.–Fri. 10am–5pm, Sat.–Sun. 1–5pm ● *$4; over-65s, under-18s $2.50; under-6s free*

Workers and volunteers dressed in period costume will guide you through this carefully restored village with houses dating from the 17th through early 20th century. Most of the buildings belonged to the original hamlet, others were reconstructed here to save them from demolition. Highlights include the oldest school in the country, built in 1695, and a large building in the Greek Revival style, dating from 1837.

Staten Island Institute of Arts and Sciences (20)

75 Stuyvesant Place N.Y. 10301-1998 ☎ (718) 727-1135

Museum *Mon.–Sat. 9am–5pm; Sun. 1–5pm* ● *$2.50; children, over-65s $1.50;* ***Ferry Collection*** *Mon.–Sun. 8am–3pm* ● *$1; under-12s 25¢*

SIIAS, founded in 1881, is one of the oldest museums in New York. Its exhibits include the decorative arts, geological specimens, and an interesting overview of the island's history, including a large display on its world-famous ferry.

Not forgetting

■ **Kenny Rogers Roasters** 1409 Hylan Boulevard (Reed Ave) N.Y. 10305 ☎ (718) 351-9300 ● *Excellent steakhouse with very reasonable prices, owned by the country-and-western singer.*

and almost rural in character. Even today it is the least urban of New York's boroughs.

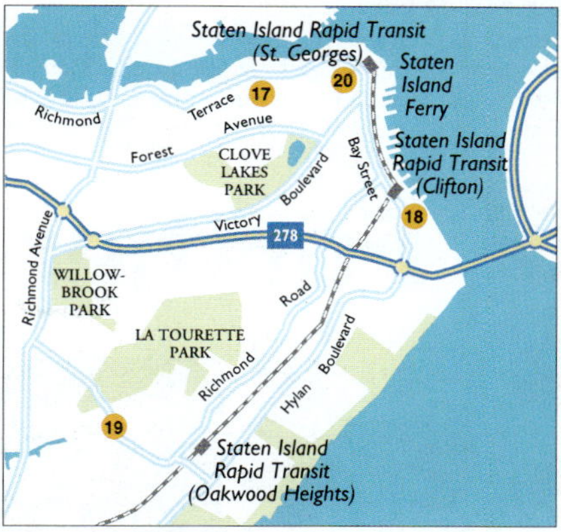

20

20

20

More than 500,000 different types of insect and 25,000 plant varieties are exhibited in the Family Gallery of the SIIAS: the displays are designed to be fun.

19

Basic facts

Sports are close to all New Yorkers' hearts. The city has two professional baseball teams, two football teams, one basketball team, and one ice-hockey team. If you can't get a ticket, watch the game live at the All Star Cafe (*1540 Broadway, Times Square*). The restaurant's owners include

Further afield

21

23

21

25

Baseball

Shea Stadium and Yankee Stadium ("the stadium Babe Ruth built") are the two largest stadiums in the United States. They are the homes, respectively, of the *Mets*, and of the *Yankees*, winners of the 1996 World Series. Guided tours of the stadiums will give you a flavor of the national sport, which started in Manhattan in 1845.

Season: Apr.–Oct.

Shea Stadium (22) *126th Street, Flushing, Queens N.Y. 11368-1699*
☎ (718) 507-8499
M 7 (Roosevelt Ave)

Yankee Stadium (21)
E. 161st Street, Bronx N.Y. 10452
☎ (718) 293-6000
(718) 293-4300
Ticket master
☎ (212) 307-1212
M C, D, 4 (161st St.)

Football

You are unlikely to see the *Giants* while you are in New York because tickets often sell out months in advance. However you could try to see a match with the *Jets*, New York's second team. Today the two teams share the same stadium: Giants Stadium in New Jersey.

Season: Nov.–Dec.

Giants Stadium (23) *Meadowlands, East Rutherford N.J. 07073*
☎ (201) 935-3900
N.J. Giants
☎ (201) 935-8222
Jets
☎ (516) 560-8200

Basketball

The *New York Knicks* are the only New York basketball team: if you are very lucky, you might get to see them play live from October through April at Madison Square Garden. Be warned: basketball is the sport of the moment in New York and Knicks tickets sell out immediately. For a different take on the game, go to see the Harlem Globetrotters, famous for their trickster ball-handling, choreographed to the song, *Sweet Georgia Brown*.

Season: Oct.–Apr.

Madison Square Garden (24)
Seventh Avenue (33rd St.)
☎ (212) 465-6741
M 34th St.

Tennis

From mid-August through mid-September the *US Open Tennis Tournament* is held at Flushing Meadows in Queens, birthplace of tennis star John McEnroe.

National Tennis Center (25)
Flushing Meadows-Corona Park, Flushing N.Y. 11368

quarterback Joe Montana, and tennis player Andre Agassi.

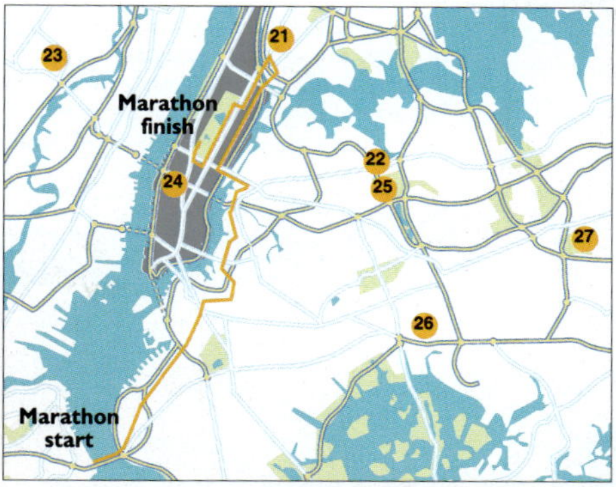

25

☎ *(718) 760-6200*
Ⓜ 7 *(Shea Stadium)*
In November the 16 seeded players in the WTA rankings compete in the **Women's Tennis Association Tour Championship** (formerly the Virginia Slims) at Madison Square Garden (see above).

Ice hockey

With its own cult following, ice hockey is a game well suited to the New York City temperament: fast, furious, and no holds barred. The *New York Rangers* are the city's top team, having won the Stanley Cup in 1994; their home stadium is at Madison Square Garden (see above). The New York Islanders play in Nassau Coliseum on Long Island (☎718 217-5477), and the New Jersey Devils in the Meadowlands (see above).
⏲ *Season: Oct.–Apr.*

Boxing

When you go to see a boxing match at Madison Square Garden ➡ 140 it can be as interesting to look out for the celebrities in the audience as to watch the fight going on in the ring. Hollywood stars are a particular attraction for celebrity spotters.

Horse-racing

Races are held every day except Tuesday from mid-October to May at Aqueduct Race Track. From June to July and from September to mid-October races are held at Belmont Park Race Track. During July and August they take place at Saratoga near Albany.

Aqueduct Race Track (26)
Rockaway Boulevard, Ozone Park, Queens 11417
☎ *(718) 641-4700*

Belmont Park Race Track (27)
Hempstead Turnpike, Elmont, Long Island 11003
☎ *(718) 641-4700*

Marathon

On the first Sunday in November every year, some 25,000 people come from all over the world and gather on the Verrazano bridge for the start of the New York marathon. The course (marked in orange on the map) begins on Staten Island, passes through the five boroughs, and ends at Tavern on the Green ➡ 94 in Central Park. To take part you need to register six months in advance. Some travel agents are authorized to sell packages including registration for the race.

Sales

Twice yearly, at Christmas and in July, but also for various public holidays:
President's Day 3rd Monday in February
Memorial Day last Monday in May
Columbus Day 2nd Monday in October

Where to shop

Opening hours

Generally 9am to 6pm. Stores stay open later for Christmas shopping. The Lower East Side and the Diamond District close early on Fridays for the Sabbath and on Jewish holidays. Opening hours are slightly later in Chelsea, SoHo, and Greenwich Village (11am to 9pm).

Sizes: men

Shirts

UK and US jacket, trousers and shirt sizes are the same.

Shoes

US 8½ = UK 8
US 9½ = UK 9
US 10½ = UK 10

Sizes: women

Clothes sizes

US 8 = UK 10
US 10 = UK 12
US 12 = UK 14

Shoes

US 7½ = UK 4
US 8½ = UK 5
US 9½ = UK 6

Flea markets

Trawled by fashion designers for inspiration and smart shoppers for vintage clothes, records, and antiques.

The Annex Antiques Fair & Flea Market *Sixth Avenue and 26th Street* *Sat.–Sun.* • *$1* **Metropolitan Arts & Antiques** *110 West 19th Street* *(212) 463-0200* *Sat.–Sun. 6.30am–6.30pm* **The Garage** *112 West 25th Street* *(212) 647-0707* *Sat.–Sun. 6.30am–6.30pm*

91 Stores

THE INSIDER'S FAVORITES

INDEX BY TYPE

Basic facts

You can buy anything you want in New York, and looking around the stores in the 'capital of shopping' is a fascinating experience. Here is a selection of American classics, old and new, with the focus on products that are typical of New York.

Where to shop

Jeans (A)

You cannot leave without your "501"! The price varies between *$34.99* (Canal Jeans ➡ 148) and *$52* (Levi's Original Store ➡ 162). Purchase limited to six pairs per person. It is worth checking out the full range of styles for men and women.

Brooks Brothers (B)

Arguably the best shirts in the world: white and blue Oxfords, made by Brooks Brothers since 1818. ● from *$49.50* ➡ 152

C

B

D

Warner Bros. Studio Store (C)

In the middle of this mad cartoon world you are sure to find the perfect souvenir for young and old alike: Bugs Bunny as the Statue of Liberty, perhaps?
● *$18* ➡ 160

Caswell-Massey (D)

Try the eau-de-cologne No.6 (*Number Six*), George Washington's favorite.
● *$22, 3 oz bottle; $44, 8 oz bottle*
➡ 154

Kiehl's (E)

In the heart of East Village, this long-established pharmacy is idolized by women throughout the world. Wonderful hand-made perfumes, beauty and bath products for men and women. Kiehl's products are also sold at Barney's ➡ 164.
109 Third Avenue N.Y. 10003 (between 13th and 14th Sts)
☎ *(212) 677-3171*
● *moisturizing face cream $11.50 for men and women*

Tiffany (F)

For jewelry, accessories for the home, and above all for the famous eggshell blue box in which your gift will be wrapped, (from $30) ➥ 162.

Baseball (G)

A must: the "NY" cap of the Yankees baseball team, winners of the 1996 World Series.
● *caps $16.99 and $23.99*
➥ 160

New York Firefighter's Friend (H)

New Yorkers show their support for the fire department by buying goods bearing the symbol of the F.D.N.Y.
● *t-shirts $15–$25* ➥ 148

Nat Sherman (J)

Nat Sherman ➥ 152 is famous for its excellent selection of cigars (*Manhattan TriBeCa*, band 31C, $115 for a box of 25). The LNS cigars are specially for women (A2, band 31C, $245 for a box of 21). Try Sherman's own cigarettes, too, made with mild Virginia tobacco ($3.75–4.75).

Elizabeth Arden (I)

Fifth Avenue is the latest scent to be launched: don't leave New York without it! ● *$32.50 for a 2 oz spray*

Bagel (K)

What could be more typical of New York than this kind of bread, covered with sesame seeds or poppy seeds? New Yorkers eat them at any time of the day or night, with various fillings, including classic cream cheese and lox (smoked salmon). Try out bialys, too: a type of bagel with onions.
H & H Bagels *639 West 46th Street (Twelfth Ave) N.Y. 10036*
☎ *(212) 595-8000* ● *75¢* each

Timberland (L)

Sturdy walking shoes are essential for exploring the city. Check out the selection of the famous style at Timberland.
● *$70–$175* ➥ 164

Basic facts

New York's department stores are among the most famous in the world. They are like self-contained empires, offering a huge range of products at very competitive prices. These showcases for American and international industry are also the arbiters of taste. Don't be put off by their size: the

Where to shop

Bloomingdale's (1)

1000 Third Avenue N.Y. 10022

☎ (212) 705-2000 ➟ (212) 705-2076

(59th St.) M *Lexington Ave* *Mon.–Fri. 10am–8.30pm; Sat. 10am–7pm; Sun. 11am–7pm* *Tax deducted, international shipment* *Reception desk*

It may not be as big a name as it was in the 1980s, but "Bloomie's" is still the shopping mecca of New York and its "Big Brown Bag" is one to carry proudly. If you want it you can find it here. Displays include the very best of designers for men and women, an inexhaustible range of perfumes and cosmetics, and a dazzling array of bedlinen and articles for the home. Customer service is a priority: they even have a special department catering to international visitors ☎ (212) 705-2098

4

5

Bergdorf Goodman (2)

754 Fifth Avenue N.Y. 10019

☎ (212) 753-7300 ➟ (212) 872-8956

(57th St.) M *Fifth Ave* *Mon.–Wed., Fri. 10am–7pm; Thur. 10am–8pm; Sat. 10am–6pm* *Tax deducted, international shipment* *Men's store 745 Fifth Ave ☎ (212) 753-7300*

You don't have to be a millionaire to do your shopping at Bergdorf Goodman, but it certainly helps! The top New York store for women sells the very best of American and international design including Bill Blass, Oscar de la Renta, Mary McFadden, Marc Jacobs, and Isaac Mizrahi. Jeweler Barry Kieselstein-Cord and Judith Leiber, the leading American leather goods designer, have their own boutique on the ground floor. Be sure to visit the antiques and gift departments on the sixth floor. There is an equally luxurious store for men across the street.

top stores are noted for the level of personal service they provide to customers. Many have reception desks to guide you to the right department, where staff are invariably helpful.

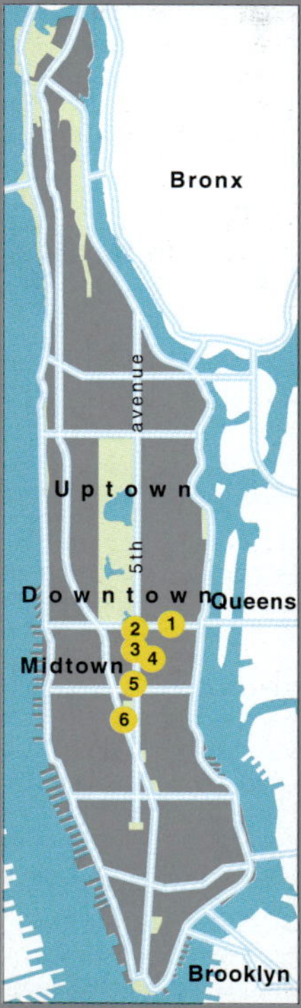

Henri Bendel (3)

712 Fifth Avenue N.Y. 10019
☎ (212) 247-1100 ➟ (212) 397-8519

(between 55th and 56th Sts) Mon.–Wed., Fri.–Sat. 10am–7pm; Thur. 10am–8pm; Sun. noon–6pm Tax deducted, international shipment

This small, elegant store caters for shoppers mad about the latest American designers, the most original tableware, Franck McIntosh and of course the unmistakable white and brown shopping bag, a true symbol of style. You don't have to be a customer to admire the Lalique window on the façade.

1

3

5

Not forgetting

■ **Saks Fifth Avenue (4)** 611 Fifth Avenue (49th St.) N.Y. 10022 ☎ (212) 753-4000 *The last word in luxury, sober and elegant, with a thoughtful selection of styles by the great names of fashion.* ■ **Macy's (5)** Herald Square, 151 West 34th Street N.Y. 10001 ☎ (212) 695-4400 *Famous for its Thanksgiving Day Parade, Macy's prides itself on being the biggest department store in the world; pennywise shoppers flock to the sales here.*

■ **Lord & Taylor (6)** 424 Fifth Avenue (between 38th and 39th Sts) N.Y. 10018 ☎ (212) 391-3344 *The oldest department store in the country (1826) and a standard-bearer for American brands. Another specialty: it stocks women's fashions in the full range of sizes.*

In the area

Go shopping between Bleecker and Broome Streets to experience the very best of Downtown: the sophistication of SoHo (SOuth of HOuston Street), the vitality of NoHo (NOrth of HOuston Street) and the offbeat fashions of the East Village to the east of Broadway. Even the appearance

Where to shop

Lost City Arts (7)

275 Lafayette Street N.Y. 10012 ☎ (212) 941-8025 ➠ (212) 219-2570

(between Houston and Prince Sts) M *Prince St.* ***Antiques*** *Mon.–Fri. 10am–6pm; Sat.-Sun. noon–6pm* *International shipment*

See New York in detail: this store sells street signs from the 1930s, gargoyles, friezes, and other architectural ornaments salvaged from demolished buildings. Among the larger pieces you might be tempted by a gas pump, a piece of 1950s furniture, a clock with advertising logo, or a Coca Cola vending machine. Or if your budget won't stretch that far, settle for an old picture postcard at $3!

Dean & Deluca (8)

560 Broadway N.Y. 10012 ☎ (212) 431-1691 ➠ (212) 334-1683

(Prince St.) M *Prince St.* ***Fine grocery*** *Mon.–Sat. 10am–8pm; Sun. 10am–7pm* *Cafe: 1 Rockefeller Plaza N.Y. 10020 ☎ (212) 664-1363*

Dean & Deluca is New York's top grocery store. The displays are dazzlingly opulent, with a huge range of the very freshest products, and similarly extravagant prices. Cookies of the enduring symbols of New York City – a yellow cab, the Empire State Building, the Statue of Liberty – are on sale at $13.50 each. There is also a small cafe in the Rockfeller Plaza branch for those tempted to stop for a snack.

Canal Jean Co. (9)

504 Broadway N.Y. 10012 ☎ (212) 226-3663 ➠ (212) 226-8084

(between Spring and Broome Sts) M *Spring St.* ***Jeans, accessories*** *Sun.-Thur. 9.30am-8pm; Fri.-Sat. 9.30am-9pm /*

A huge emporium throbbing to the sound of rock music, overflowing with clothes for the fashion-conscious of both sexes: from underwear to coats, including jeans at $34.99. Be sure to look at the army surplus section, the second-hand section offering polyester disco shirts and the excellent Schott jackets in leather and nylon. Among other brands, Canal Jean sells Levi Strauss, CK, Everlast, and Reebok.

Not forgetting

■ **Kate's Paperie (10)** 561 Broadway (Spring and Prince Sts.) N.Y. 10012 ☎ (212) 941-9816 *Paper paradise, with paper goods and accessories.* ■ **Atrium (11)** 644 Broadway (Bleecker St.) N.Y. 10012 ☎ (212) 473-9200 *Streetwear popularized by the "hip-hoppers" and other rappers.* ■ **Urban Outfitters (12)** 628 Broadway (between Houston and Bleecker Sts) N.Y. 10012 ☎ (212) 475-0009 *Basics and high fashion, both vintage and new.* ■ **Pottery Barn (13)** 600 Broadway (Houston St.) N.Y. 10012 ☎ (212) 505-6377 *Articles for the home that are practical and stylish, at attractive prices, presented in a stunning loft.* ■ **Pop Shop (14)** 292 Lafayette Street (between Houston and Prince Sts) N.Y. 10012 ☎ (212) 219-2784 *Striking graffiti by the late Keith Haring, reproduced on t-shirts, watches, etc.* ■ **N.Y. Firefighter's Friend (15)** 263 Lafayette Street (between Prince and Spring Sts) N.Y. 10012 ☎ (212) 226-3142 *The friends of the firefighters, the city's heroes, sell firemen's clothing, and t-shirts and other articles with the NYFD logo.*

of chain stores such as Pottery Barn has not made this area any less unconventional. ■ Where to eat ➥ 58 ■ After dark ➥ 86

11

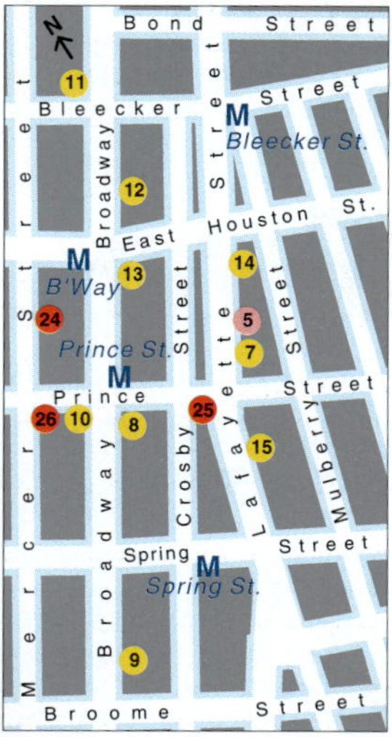

7

9

Lost City Arts: an irresistible emporium that takes you back into New York's Art-Deco past.

9

11

In the area

SoHo is New York's artistic crucible, the place where trends and reputations are made. Its shops, among the city's most stylish, are targeted at an adventurous clientele. Its galleries, often tucked away on the second floor, are famous throughout the world. Don't arrive to shop

Where to shop

J. Crew (16)

99 Prince Street N.Y. 10012 ☎ (212) 966-2739 ➡ (212) 966-4638

(Mercer St.) Ⓜ *Prince St.* ***Men's and women's fashions*** *Mon.–Wed. 10am–8pm; Thur.–Sat 10am–9pm; Sun. noon–7pm* ☎ *(212) 385-3500*

This well-respected mail-order company underwent a transformation when it opened this very attractive store with its minimalist decor: the preppy look of New England was given a New York twist. The basic products remain the same but the "Downtown" influence is there if you look closely. Focuses on practicality (men's coordinates), humor (boxer shorts with aircraft motifs), and retro glamor (little black dresses à la Audrey Hepburn).

Todd Oldham Store (17)

123 Wooster Street N.Y. 10012 ☎ (212) 219-3531

(between Prince and Spring Sts) Ⓜ *Prince St.* ***Men's fashions, accessories*** *Mon.–Sat. 11am–7pm; Sun. noon–6pm* *International shipment*

Todd Oldham is a young, iconoclastic designer who is mad about garish prints, psychedelic colors, sequins and fun fur, nylon and polyester. He is the personification of "hippy chic" but his outfits are of designer quality. The store is a vision of kitsch, with its sugar-candy color tiled floor, and acres of painted velvet forming a backdrop to the designs: mosaic vases, cushions, costume jewelry, perfumes, and of course the clothes.

Anthropologie (18)

375 West Broadway N.Y. 10012 ☎ (212) 343-7070 ➡ (212) 343-2589

(between Spring and Broome Sts) Ⓜ *Spring St.* ***Men's and women's fashions, articles for the home, accessories*** *Mon.–Sat. 11am–8pm; Sun. 11am–6pm* *International shipment*

A mix of high-fashion garments for both sexes, as well as decorative items for the home and the garden, on offer in a huge store. Crisp underwear, silk shirts, glassware, and candles, attractively displayed on chairs, tables, and old suitcases, creating very intimate settings. The decor is vintage SoHo: ceiling of beaten pewter, cast-iron pillars and polished wooden floors.

Not forgetting

■ **Portico Bed & Bath (19)** 139 Spring Street (Wooster St.) N.Y. 10012 ☎ (212) 941-7722 *Articles for the home, stylish and expensive.* ■ **The Enchanted Forest (20)** 85 Mercer Street (Broome St.) N.Y. 10012 ☎ (212) 925-6677 *Furry animals, books, and handmade toys in a fairytale setting.* ■ **Nicole Miller (21)** 134 Prince Street (between Wooster St. and W. Broadway) N.Y. 10012 ☎ (212) 343-1362 *Bright and unusual clothes for women; silk ties and jackets for men with prints of fruit, vegetables, and luxury cars.* ■ **Anna Sui Store (22)** 113 Greene Street (between Prince and Spring Sts) N.Y. 10012 ☎ (212) 941-8406 *Morticia Addams meets Cruella in this black and purple boutique, selling offbeat and gothic women's clothing.*
■ **Ad Hoc Softwares (23)** 410 West Broadway (Spring St.) N.Y. 10012 ☎ (212) 925-2652 *Top-of-the-range accessories for elegant interiors: bedlinen, nightwear, china, even pet-food bowls.*

too early in the morning: SoHo doesn't begin to wake up until around 11am.
■ Where to eat ➡ 58

19

18

SoHo's fascination lies partly in its contrasts: 19th-century cast-iron façades and avant-garde interiors.

18

19

16

In the area

This hectic commercial district around Grand Central Station ➡ 106 has a very professional air about it. This is the stronghold of the Fortune 500 companies, of law firms dedicated to protecting old family fortunes, of exclusive clubs. Tycoons and young turks who work and play in this

Where to shop

McCreedy & Schreiber (24)

37 W. 46th Street N.Y. 10036 ☎ (212) 719 1552 ➠ (212) 997-1080

(between Fifth and Sixth Aves) M *47th St.* ***Shoes*** *Mon.–Sat. 9am–7pm; Sun. 11am–5pm* *International shipment* *213 E. 59th St.* ☎ *(212) 759-9241*

McCreedy & Schreiber is the shoe mecca for the well-dressed man. The store offers a huge range of luxury American shoes: Allen Edmonds brogues, Sperry Topsider deck shoes, Timberland walking shoes, Bass mocassins. Handmade shoes are another specialty: Lucchese boots can be made to order in special leathers. Women must be content with Timberland and Se bago.

Brooks Brothers (25)

346 Madison Avenue N.Y. 10017 ☎ (212) 682-8800 ➠ (212) 309-7273

(44th St.) M *Grand Central* ***Men's fashions*** *Mon.–Sat. 9am–7pm; Sun. noon–6pm* *International shipment* *1 Church St.* ☎ *(212) 267-2400*

Since 1818, Brooks Brothers has been dressing America's eminent citizens: businessmen, politicians (Abraham Lincoln was assassinated in a Brooks suit), and members of the upper class. The store invented the preppy look well before it was commercialized by Ralph Lauren and Tommy Hilfiger. The timeless blue or white Oxford shirt with its button-down collar is still a Brooks Brothers trademark. Today there are also departments for women and children.

Nat Sherman (26)

500 Fifth Avenue N.Y. 10110 ☎ (212) 764-5134

(42nd St.) M *Fifth Ave* ***Tobacco, cigars*** *Mon.–Fri. 9am–7pm; Fri.–Sat. 10am–5.30pm; Sun. 11am–5pm* *International shipment*
@ *www.natsherman.com*

Nat Sherman, the most famous tobacco shop in New York, is renowned for its traditional American blends, its cigarettes made with Virginia tobacco, its smoker's accessories, and its rows of cigar boxes (cigars are available in 17 band sizes and 40 lengths). Stocks are stored in a humidifier next to the luxurious smoking room on the first floor. Subscribers can receive Nat Sherman products anywhere in the world.

Not forgetting

■ **Nobody Beats the Wiz (27)** 555 Fifth Avenue (between 45th and 46th Sts) N.Y. 10017 ☎ (212) 557-7770 *Electronics and games superstore known for choice and competitive prices.* ■ **Paul Stuart Inc. (28)** Madison Avenue (45th St.) N.Y. 10017 ☎ (212) 682-0320 *Traditional, and expensive, elegance for men and women: witty, colorful clothes in simple styles for town and country.* ■ **J. Press (29)** 7 East 44th Street (between Fifth and Madison Aves) N.Y. 10017 ☎ (212) 687-7642 *Tweeds, flannels, and shetland sweaters for men.* ■ **Today's Man (30)** 529 Fifth Avenue (44th St.) N.Y. 10017 ☎ (212) 557-3111 *Fashions for men at discount prices.* ■ **Worth & Worth (31)** 331 Madison Avenue (43rd St.) N.Y. 10017 ☎ (212) 867-6058 *Handmade hats for men only: trilbies, bowlers, schapskas, panamas. No baseball caps!*

area have a range of tailors and classic retailers to choose from.
■ Where to stay ➥ 28
■ After dark ➥ 92

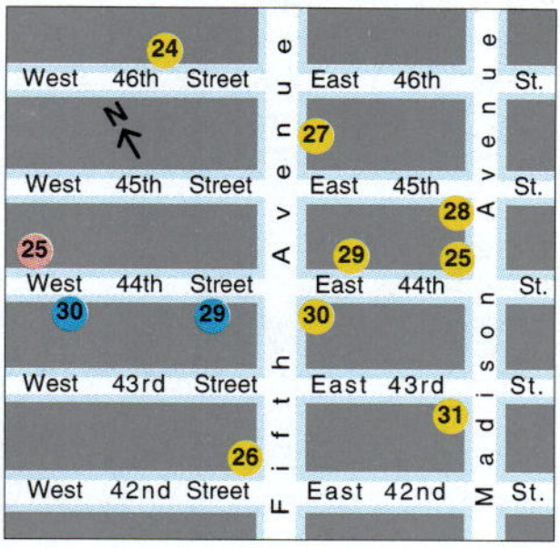

31

24

Worth & Worth Allegro hat, from $185; Brooks Brothers shirts and ties from $49.50 and $39.50.

26

25

28

26

In the area

Television studios, record companies, publishers and the press all occupy the splendid art deco Rockefeller Center. This is a kingdom of pleasure, with luxury stores to match. ■ Where to stay ➡ 26 ➡ 32 ➡ 34 ■ Where to eat ➡ 48 ➡ 70 ■ After dark ➡ 88 ➡ 90 ➡ 92 ■ What to see ➡ 116

Where to shop

Alan Flusser Custom Shop (32)

611 Fifth Avenue N.Y. 10022 ☎ (212) 888-7100 ➡ (212) 940-4699

(between 49th and 50th Sts) M *53rd St.* ***Men's fashions, made-to-measure*** *Mon.–Sat. 10am–6pm* *International shipment*

American designer Alan Flusser follows in the London tradition of men's tailors with made-to-measure elegance: softly styled suits, overcoats in luxury fabrics. Expect to pay around $295 for a shirt and $2200 for a suit. The store is on the fifth floor of Saks ➡ 147, with a lovely view over the Rockefeller Center.

Metropolitan Museum of Art Shop (33)

15 West 49th Street N.Y. 10020 ☎ (212) 332-1360 ➡ (212) 332-1390

(between Fifth and Sixth Aves) M *Rockefeller Center* ***Articles for the home, antiques, books*** *daily 10am-7pm* *International shipment*

The famous collections of the Metropolitan Museum ➡ 118 cover 5000 years of art works from all over the world. Brilliant reproductions of gold jewelry, sculptures, china, glass, and textiles are arranged over three floors in Rockefeller Center. Top-quality, exclusive products.

Caswell-Massey (34)

518 Lexington Avenue N.Y. 10017 ☎ (212) 755-2254 ➡ (212) 888-4915

(48th St.) M *53th St.* ***Cosmetics*** *Mon.–Fri. 9am–7pm; Sat. 10am–6pm* *International shipment* @ *dreamshop.com/caswellmassey* ☎ *(212) 219-3661*

The oldest pharmacy and perfumer in the United States (founded 1752). George Washington, one of the first customers, bought his supplies of eau-de-cologne *Number Six* here (it is still sold today). A stunning range of bath and beauty products in a variety of exotic perfumes.

OshKosh B'Gosh (35)

586 Fifth Avenue N.Y. 10036 ☎ (212) 827-0098 ➡ (212) 575-1219

(between 47th and 48th Sts) M *47th St.* ***Children's clothes*** *Mon.–Sat. 10am–7pm; Sun. noon–5pm*

The only OshKosh B'Gosh store in Manhattan to sell the full collection by this famous manufacturer: clothes and shoes for boys and girls from three months to seven years, all elegant, practical and hard-wearing. There is also a small selection of garments catering for seven to fourteen-year-olds. The store's miniature train decor will delight young and old alike.

Not forgetting

■ **Manny's Music (36)** 156 West 48th St. (between Sixth and Seventh Aves) N.Y. 10036 ☎ (212) 819-0576 *Instruments and professional recording equipment and a rock'n'roll museum.* ■ **The World of Golf (37)** 147 East 47th St. (between Lexington and Third Aves) N.Y. 10017 ☎ (212) 755-9398 *Complete range for golf lovers.* ■ **Gotham Book Mart & Gallery (38)** 41 West 47th St. (between Fifth and Sixth Aves) N.Y. 10036 ☎ (212) 719-4448 *This legendary bookshop still resonates with the spirit of the Beat Generation.*

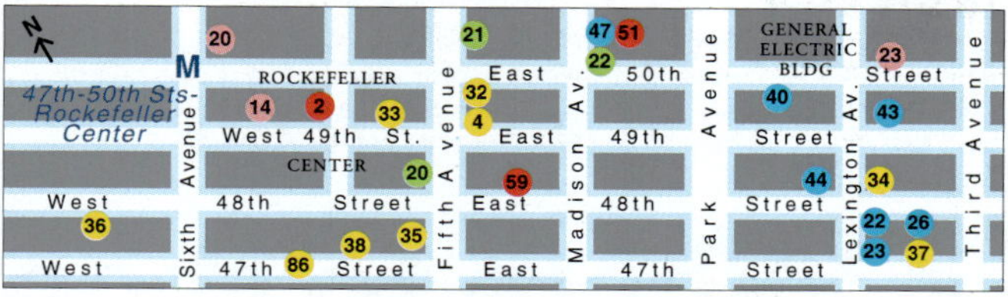

34

"Wise men fish here": the motto of the Gotham Book Mart, where you can discover the most obscure books and editions.

38

33

37

In the area

Today Banana Republic and Liz Claiborne have their stores in the district where the Vanderbilts and the Rockefellers used to live. The beautiful Italian Renaissance-style building occupied by Cartier evokes this elegant past ■ Where to stay ➡ 34 ■ Where to eat ➡ 70 ➡ 72

Where to shop

The Gap (39)

527 Madison Avenue N.Y. 10022 ☎ (212) 688-1260

(54th St.) M *53rd St.* ***Men's and Women's fashions, accessories, cosmetics*** ⏲ *Mon.–Fri. 9am–8pm; Sat. 10am–8pm; Sun. 11am–5pm* ▤ ◆ ***Gap Kids / Baby Gap*** *545 Madison Avenue N.Y. 10022* ☎ *(212) 980-2570*

The Gap specializes in basic items of clothing made with natural fibers at affordable prices. You may like its preppy-style seasonal collections, or the khaki tones of its classics, or its jeans in a range of ten styles. This flagship store also sells its own range of beauty products.

MoMA Design Store (40)

44 West 53rd Street N.Y. 10019 ☎ (212) 767-1050 ➡ (212) 586-7001

(between Fifth and Sixth Aves) M *53rd* ***Articles for the home*** ⏲ *Sat.–Thur. 10am–6pm; Fri. 10am–8pm* ▤

Facing the Museum of Modern Art ➡ 116, this store brings together the best design creations of the century. Everything here is both beautiful and practical. Products range from the useful (electrical adapters for globetrotters) to the ingenious (the best ice-cream scoop ever invented). Also sells furniture in designs by Frank Lloyd Wright, Rennie Mackintosh, and many others.

Banana Republic (41)

655 Fifth Avenue N.Y. 10022 ☎ (212) 644-6678 ➡ (212) 644-6939

(52nd St.) M *53rd St.* ***Men's and Women's fashions, accessories, shoes, perfumes*** ⏲ *Mon.–Wed., Fri., Sat. 10am–8pm; Thur. 10am–8.30pm; Sun. 11am–7pm* ▤ ◆ ☎ *(212) 644-6678*

This magnificent building houses the flagship store of the Banana Republic chain, owned by The Gap. This brand is more fashion-conscious and upmarket than The Gap, but the quality is equally high. A large marble staircase leads to the areas reserved for men's and women's fashions. The clothes are well organized, making this an easy and irresistible place to shop.

Not forgetting

■ **The Liz Claiborne Store (42)** 650 Fifth Avenue (52nd St.) N.Y. 10022 ☎ (212) 956-6505 *Liz Claiborne is the queen of women's casualwear at reasonable prices. Her collection, arranged by color, is spread over this elegant two-story building. Shoes, tights, belts, and handbags complete the inimitable Claiborne look.* ■ **Harrison James (43)** 5 West 54th Street (between Fifth and Sixth Aves) N.Y. 10019 ☎ (212) 541-6870 *Clothes and accessories for men, made-to-measure or off-the-peg, in an early-20th century building that includes two restaurants, a cigar-smoking room, and a traditional barber.* ■ **Eileen Fisher (44)** 521 Madison Avenue (between 53rd and 54th Sts) N.Y. 10022 ☎ (212) 759-9888 *Elegant and accessible women's fashions with fluid lines, subdued colors and comfortable shapes.* ■ **H. Stern (45)** 645 Fifth Avenue (between 51st and 52nd Sts) N.Y. 10022 ☎ (212) 688-0300 *Precious and semi-precious stones beautifully set by an internationally renowned jeweler.*

■ What to see
➥ 116

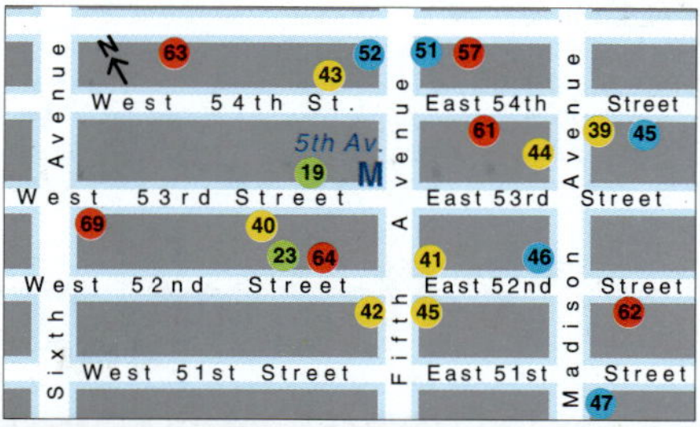

40

THE MoMA DESIGN STORE

40

Bookmark by Frank Lloyd Wright, $15. Black Eileen Fisher dress $184. Gold and diamond ring by H. Stern, from $12,000.

45

44

In the area

For years, this neighborhood has been home to the most expensive, and tantalizing shops in New York City. Tempting sights will overwhelm you as you pass by elegant window displays. ■ Where to stay ➡ 34 ➡ 36 ■ Where to eat ➡ 70 ➡ 72 ■ Where to shop ➡ 146

Where to shop

OMO Norma Kamali (46)

11 West 56th Street N.Y. 10019 ☎ (212) 957-9797 ➡ (212) 581-8016

(between Fifth and Sixth Aves) Ⓜ *57th St.* ***Women's fashions*** *Mon.–Sat. 10am–6pm* *International shipment*

Norma Kamali is one of the most independent-minded designers in America. She is a master of drapery, creating dresses that hang with provocative elegance. Her store is a concrete labyrinth with hidden staircases and unexpected views, revealing her own strong personality.

Belgian Shoes (47)

60 East 56th Street N.Y. 10022 ☎ (212) 755-7372 ➡ (212) 755-7627

(between Madison and Park Aves) Ⓜ *53rd St.* ***Shoes*** *Mon.–Fri. 9am–4.15pm* *International shipment.*

Wearing Belgian Shoes mocassins is one of the most comfortable ways of proclaiming your social status. These shoes, made for men and women, are lightweight; they are handmade in Belgium and sold exclusively by this boutique. They are available in leather or fabric, in a range of around 50 colors. Die-hard fans buy them by the dozen.

Steuben (48)

717 Fifth Avenue N.Y. 10022 ☎ (212) 752-1441 ➡ (212) 753-1354

(56th St.) Ⓜ *57th St.* ***Articles for the home*** *Mon.–Wed., Fri.–Sat. 10am–6pm; Thur. 10am–7pm*

Steuben makes the most beautiful crystal in the United States. Every object in the showroom is presented with care worthy of a great museum. Among the most remarkable and expensive pieces (at $30,000) is a glass sculpture of the Empire State Building.

Bijan (49)

699 Fifth Avenue N.Y. 10022 ☎ (212) 758-7500 ➡ (212) 207-8124

(54th St.) Ⓜ *53rd St.* ***Men's fashions, accessories*** *Mon.–Sat. 10am–6pm*

This Californian store prefers a confident display of style to the discreet charms of Fifth Avenue. It specializes in luxury articles for men with a sense of adventure. This is the place for you if your idea of the height of elegance is a top hat lined with chinchilla. A small tip: to get the red-carpet treatment, make an appointment.

Not forgetting

■ **T. Anthony (50)** 445 Park Avenue (56th St.) N.Y. 10022 ☎ (212) 750-9797 *Luggage for first-class travelers.* ■ **Harry Winston (51)** 718 Fifth Avenue (56th St.) N.Y. 10019 ☎ (212) 245-2000 *The jeweler who is supposed to have made Marilyn Monroe sing "Diamonds are a girl's best friend."*

■ **Felissimo (52)** 10 West 56th St. (between Fifth and Sixth Aves) N.Y. 10019 ☎ (212) 247-5656 *Sumptuous gifts for body and soul in a very "zen" setting, with a tearoom on the top floor.* ■ **Elizabeth Arden Salon (53)** 691 Fifth Avenue (between 54th and 55th Sts) N.Y. 10022 ☎ (212) 546-0200 *Cosmetics, perfumes, and luxurious beauty treatments.*

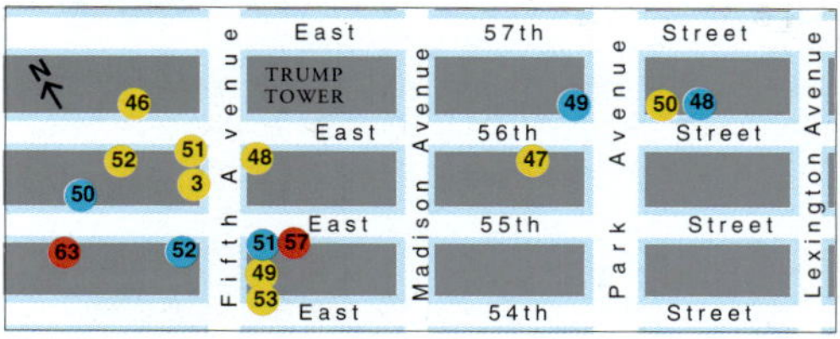

53

52

48

Behind this famous red door is the Elizabeth Arden world of beauty. Expect to pay $77.45 for a facial massage.

47

49

In the area

In less than five years the area around Fifth Avenue and 57th Street, once the province of venerable establishments like Tiffany ➡ 162, has become the stronghold of the entertainment industry. Witness the boom in theme restaurants ➡ 74. Customers have become younger, and the

Where to shop

56

55

59

Yankee Clubhouse (54)

110 East 59th Street N.Y. 10022 ☎ (212) 758-7844

(between Park and Lexington Aves) Ⓜ *59th St.* ***Sportswear*** *Mon.–Fri. 9am–6.30pm; Sat. 9am–6pm; Sun. 11.30am–5pm* *International shipment*

The New York Yankees, winners of the 1996 World Series, are much loved in their home town. Their Clubhouse sells baseball caps, official team jackets and shirts, and other souvenirs.

F.A.O. Schwarz (55)

767 Fifth Avenue N.Y. 10153 ☎ (212) 644-9400 ➡ (212) 826-1826

(58th St.) Ⓜ *Fifth Ave.* ***Toys*** *Mon.–Wed. 10am–6pm; Thur.–Sat. 10am–7pm; Sun. 11am–6pm* *International shipment*

The biggest and most enjoyable toyshop in New York. Two sprawling floors crammed with soft toys, games, and an unrivaled collection of dolls, including a Barbie Statue of Liberty.

Warner Bros. Studio Store (56)

1 East 57th Street N.Y. 10022 ☎ (212) 754-0300 ➡ (212) 754-0387

(Fifth Ave) Ⓜ *Fifth Ave* ***Men's, women's, children's clothes, accessories, housewares, gadgets*** *Mon.–Sat. 10.30am–7pm; Sun. 11am-6pm*

The Looney Tunes brigade (Bugs Bunny, Daffy Duck and the rest) have taken up residence in this cartoon-crazy store. Enjoy the interactive displays and a computer-animated 3D film.

district is livelier than ever.
■ Where to stay ➥ 34 ➥ 36 ➥ 38 ➥ 40 ■ Where to eat ➥ 70 ■ After dark ➥ 88

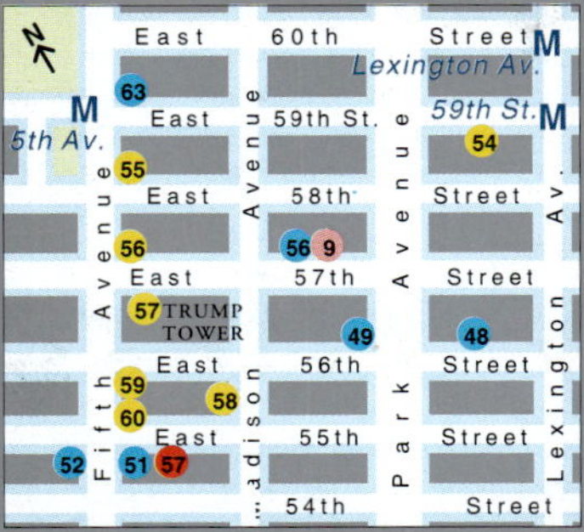

56

56

57

57

Niketown New York City (57)

6 East 57th Street N.Y. 10022 ☎ (212) 891-6453 ➟ (212) 891-6444

(between Fifth and Madison Aves) Ⓜ *Fifth Ave.* ***Sportswear*** ⏲ *Mon.–Fri. 10am–8pm; Sat. 10am–7pm; Sun. 11am–6pm* ▭

A magnificent modern temple dedicated to Nike, where devotees can indulge their passion for sports and sports gear to the full. The floors are arranged around a vast atrium. Sporting events are projected onto giant screens in the atrium.

Sony Style (58)

550 Madison Avenue N.Y. 10022 ☎ (212) 833-8800

(between 55th and 56th Sts) Ⓜ *59th St.* ***Hi-fi, video, electronics*** ⏲ *Mon.–Sat. 10am–7pm; Sun. noon–6pm* ▭ ▭

See the complete range of Sony products in a high-tech setting. On the ground floor is the *Screening Room*, audio and video areas where the latest systems are unveiled.

Not forgetting

■ **Coca-Cola Fifth Avenue (59)** 711 Fifth Avenue (between 55th and 56th Sts) N.Y. 10022 ☎ (212) 418-9260 *Products with the famous logo.*
■ **The Disney Store (60)** 711 Fifth Avenue (55th St.) N.Y. 10022 ☎ (212) 702-0702 *Clothes and other goods based on Walt Disney films.*

In the area

Some of the city's most attractive stores are located in this part of Midtown. Although this area was once the preserve of the very wealthy, today it has shops that appeal to everyone. ■ Where to stay ➡ 34 ➡ 38 ➡ 40 ■ After dark ➡ 88

Where to shop

Geoffrey Beene on the Plaza (61)

783 Fifth Avenue N.Y. 10022 ☎ (212) 935-0470 ➡ (212) 888-3140

(between 59th and 60th Sts) M *Fifth Ave* ***Women's fashions, articles for the home*** *Mon.–Fri. 10am–6pm; Sat. 10am–5pm* *International shipment*

Geoffrey Beene is the American designer of women's fashions who is closest to the world of Parisian couture. His little jewel of a shop, made famous by high-profile customers such as Glenn Close and Paloma Picasso, displays his talent and sophistication.

The Original Levi's Store (62)

3 East 57th Street N.Y. 10022 ☎ (212) 838-2188 ➡ (212) 838-0335

(between Fifth and Madison Aves) M *Fifth Ave* ***Jeans*** *Mon.–Sat. 10am–8pm; Sun. noon–6pm* *International shipment* *750 Lexington Ave ☎ (212) 826-5957*

Jeans are a universal fashion phenomenon, and Levi's is one of the biggest names. Levi's Personal Pair jeans is a special service provided for women: your personal made-to-measure jeans are supplied within three weeks. Purchases through this service are limited to six pairs of jeans per customer.

Tiffany & Co. (63)

727 Fifth Avenue N.Y. 10022 ☎ (212) 755-8000

(57th St.) M *Fifth Ave* ***Accessories, jewelry, gifts*** *Mon.–Wed., Fri.–Sat. 10am–6pm; Thur. 10am–7pm*

Tiffany's, the grand old lady of Fifth Avenue, will fulfil all your dreams and desires, from the platinum and diamond engagement ring to a set of china or a bottle of the store's own perfume. All purchases, from the cheapest (around $35) to the most expensive (no known limit) are packed in the famous eggshell-blue gift boxes.

Border Books and Music (64)

461 Park Avenue N.Y. 10022 ☎ (212) 980-6785 ➡ (212) 980-0529

(57th St.) M *59th St.* ***Books, CDs and videos*** *Mon.–Fri. 9am–10pm; Sat. 10am–8pm; Sun. 11am-8pm*

The four floors of this large store are packed with the latest books, CDs and videos, plus a cafe and more than 2000 magazines in ten languages from over fifteen countries. Specialty: signed copies of the latest titles.

Not forgetting

■ **Crate & Barrel (65)** 650 Madison Ave (59th St.) N.Y. 10022 ☎ (212) 308-0011 *Articles for the home, well designed and affordable.* ■ **Revlon Employee Store (66)** 767 Fifth Avenue (59th St.) N.Y. 10153 ☎ (212) 486-8857 *Perfumes and cosmetics discounted up to 50%. Open to everyone.* ■ **Hammacher Schlemmer (67)** 147 East 57th Street (between Lexington and Third Aves) N.Y. 10022 ☎ (212) 421-9000 *Amusing and useful gadgets, toys for grown-ups.* ■ **Victoria's Secret (68)** 34 East 57th Street (Madison Ave) N.Y. 10022 ☎ (212) 758-5592 *Beautiful lingerie.*

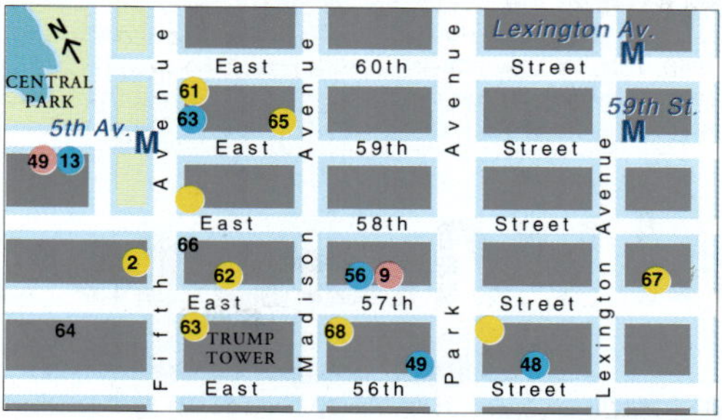

67

Hammacher Schlemmer is a gadget-lover's paradise: laser torch ($39.95); baseball ball signed by Joe Di Maggio ($349.95); submarine scooter ($8450).

62

66

65

In the area

It took only a few years for a crowd of boutiques, many of them European, to colonize this section of Madison Avenue. American fashion was quick to respond, with impressive contributions from the most innovative New York designers – including Ralph Lauren and Calvin Klein.

Where to shop

Polo Ralph Lauren (69)

867 Madison Avenue N.Y. 10021 ☎ (212) 606-2100 ➟ (212) 606-2132

(72nd St.) Ⓜ *68th St.* ***Men's, women's, children's fashions, articles for the home, accessories*** *Mon.–Wed., Fri.–Sat. 10am–6pm; Thur. 10am–8pm* *International shipment* ***Polo Sport*** *888 Madison Ave N.Y. 10021 ☎ (212) 434-8000*

Ralph Lauren is not content with designing clothes: he sells a whole lifestyle. His infatuation with the America of the Great Gatsby has found its supreme expression in this magnificent listed building, the Rhinelander Mansion. A must.

MacKenzie-Childs (70)

824 Madison Avenue N.Y. 10021 ☎ (212) 570-6050 ➟ (212) 570-2485

(69th St.) Ⓜ *68th St.* ***Articles for the home*** *Mon.–Sat. 10am–6pm* *International shipment*

Richard and Victoria MacKenzie-Childs use two town houses as an unforgettable setting for their designs. Their unique, witty objects are presented in rooms with imaginative, even fantastical décors, such as the delightful drawing room on the first floor.

Gallery of Wearable Art (71)

34 East 67th Street N.Y. 10021 ☎ (212) 570-2252 ➟ (212) 744-3083

(between Madison and Park Aves) Ⓜ *68th St.* ***Women's fashions*** *Tue.–Sat. 10am–6pm*

This tiny design studio specializes in one-off or limited edition garments: coats, evening and bridal gowns, and formal jackets for women who want to turn heads.

Calvin Klein (72)

654 Madison Avenue N.Y. 10021 ☎ (212) 292-9000 ➟ (212) 292-9001

(60th St.) Ⓜ *60th St.* ***Men's and women's fashions*** *Mon.–Wed., Fri.–Sat. 10am–6pm; Thur. 10am–8pm; Sun. noon–6pm* *International shipment*

Calvin Klein has created a store that is as minimalist as his fashion designs, presented here in a positively spartan setting. Clothes and accessories from the master's top-of-the-range collections, spiced up with the addition of jeans and provocative underwear.

Not forgetting

■ **Zitomer (73)** 969 Madison Ave (between 75th and 76th Sts) N.Y. 10021 ☎ (212) 737-5560 *A genuine pharmacy, which also sells cosmetics.* ■ **Coach (74)** 710 Madison Ave (63rd St.) N.Y. 10021 ☎ (212) 319-1772 *Top-quality leather goods.* ■ **Timberland (75)** 709 Madison Avenue (63rd St.) N.Y. 10021 ☎ (212) 754-0434 *Outdoor shoes and clothes.* ■ **Sherry-Lehmann (76)** 679 Madison Ave (between 61st and 62nd Sts) N.Y. 10021 ☎ (212) 838-7500 *Exclusive choice of wines, including vintage wines from Long Island and New York State.* ■ **Barneys New York (77)** 660 Madison Ave (61st Sts) N.Y. 10021 ☎ (212) 826-8900 *Distributors of Kiehl's cosmetics* ➡ 144

■ Where to stay ➥ 40 ➥ 42 ■ Where to eat ➥ 76 ➥ 78 ■ After dark ➥ 88 ➥ 92 ■ What to see ➥ 120

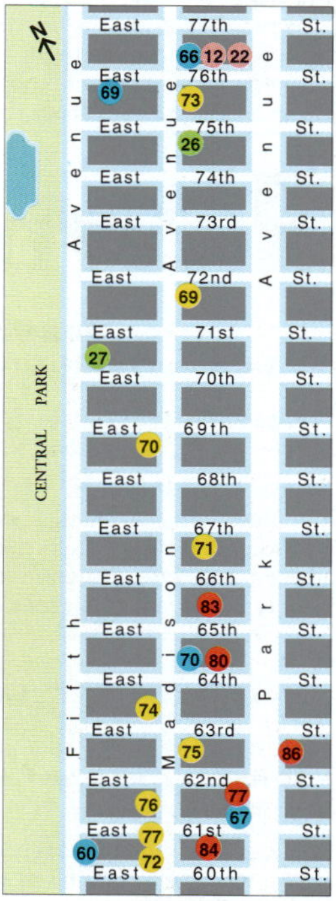

71

2

The 'château' that forms the backdrop for Ralph Lauren's collections has retained the atmosphere of a private residence, with its paneled rooms and fireplaces.

69

In the area

This residential area is bordered by Lincoln Center ➡ 102 to the south, and the American Museum of Natural History ➡ 122 to the north. In between is an agreeable mix of shops and restaurants, with Central Park close by as a retreat from the fray. ■ Where to stay ➡ 44

Where to shop

Maxilla & Mandible (78)

451 Columbus Ave N.Y. 10024 ☎ (212) 724-6173 ➡ (212) 721-1073

(between 81st and 82nd Sts) M *81st St.* ***Antiques*** *Mon.–Sat. 11am–7pm; Sun. 1–5pm* *International shipment*

No visit to the American Museum of Natural History would be complete without taking a detour through this fascinating store. A genuine curiosity shop in the Victorian style, there is an expert staff to advise you on its authentic biological and geological specimens, fossils, insects, skulls, and skeletons.

Zabar's (79)

2245 Broadway N.Y. 10024 ☎ (212) 787-2000 ➡ (212) 580-4477

(80th St.) M *79th St.* ***Fine grocery, articles for the home*** *Grocery store: Mon.–Fri. 8am–7.30pm; Sat. 8am–8pm; Sun. 9am–6pm / Household goods: Mon.–Sat. 9am–7pm; Sun. 9am–6pm* *International shipment*

This legendary delicatessen is too delicious to resist, with a heavenly cheese counter, all kinds of salmon, an unpretentious cafe, and a department selling housewares. A visit here is essential if you're intending to picnic in Central Park ➡ 122.

Betsey Johnson (80)

248 Columbus Ave N.Y. 10023 ☎ (212) 362-3364 ➡ (212) 362-3751

(between 71st and 72nd Sts) M *72nd St.* ***Women's fashions*** *Mon.–Sat. 11am–7pm; Sun. noon–7pm* ☎ *(212) 319-3364*

This designer creates figure-hugging, brightly colored, and garishly printed clothes for extroverts, preferably with waif-like figures! A very 'Downtown' style: fashionable and irreverent.

Tower Records (81)

1961 Broadway N.Y. 10023 ☎ (212) 799-2500 ➡ (212) 799-2559

(66th St.) M *66th St.* ***Stereos, music*** *daily 9am–midnight* *692 Broadway N.Y. 10003* ☎ *(212) 505-1500 (E. 4th St.)* @ *www.towerrecords.com*

A must for lovers of music and videos. More than 500,000 CDs, videos, laser discs, books, and magazines spread over three floors with a large number of listening systems where you can hear the latest releases. Close to Lincoln Center ➡ 102, the store has excellent classical music and jazz departments.

Not forgetting

■ **Blades, Board, and Skate (82)** 120 West 72nd Street (Columbus Ave) N.Y. 10023 ☎ (212) 787-3911 *Specialist in Rollerblades, to buy or to rent.*
■ **Ann Taylor (83)** 2015 Broadway (69th St.) N.Y. 10023 ☎ (212) 873-7344 *Elegant clothes for active women.*
■ **Planet Reebok (84)** 160 Columbus Avenue (between 67th and 68th Sts) N.Y. 10023 ☎ (212) 595-1480 *Reebok shoes and clothing.*
■ **Eddie Bauer (85)** 1976 Broadway (66th St.) N.Y. 10023 ☎ (212) 877-7629 *Outdoor clothes for explorers in the urban jungle.*

Where to eat ➥ 76 ➥ 80
After dark ➥ 94 ➥ 102
What to see ➥ 122

83

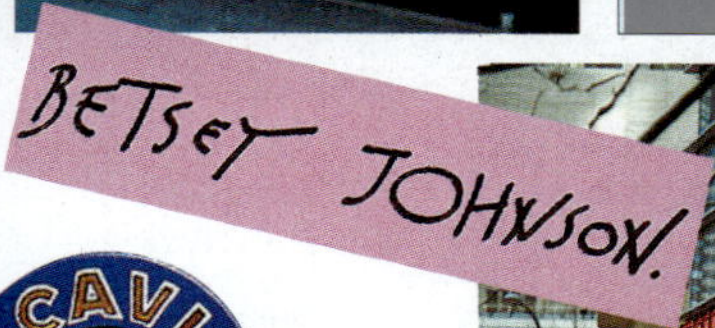

81

79

For a 'dejeuner sur l'herbe' in Central Park, Zabar's is the ideal spot to choose a basket of the most delectable provisions.

80

New Yorkers' golden rule is 'never pay retail': for them, shopping is a sport, and they are ace players. Some areas of Manhattan are noted for 'bargain shopping' and they attract a huge and diverse clientele: even millionaires can't resist a bargain. Elsewhere, stores do offer end-of-season

Where to shop

86 87 88 91

Diamond District (86)

47th Street (between Fifth and Sixth Aves)
Millions of dollars change hands each day on this small section of 47th Street. The block itself may not look like anything special, but here you are at the center of the market for diamonds, other gemstones, and precious metals, sold at wholesale prices. The street is lined with market halls, each housing a number of independent jewelers. One of them, at no. *55*, has 115 brokers spread over three floors. Window-shop by all means but be warned: the traders know how to draw in their customers!

Herald Square and Garment District (87)

Broadway (between Sixth and Eighth Aves)
Favorite stomping ground for bargain hunters. On Seventh Avenue (renamed Fashion Avenue) and Broadway, around **Macy's** ➡ 146 is a vast array of stores offering merchandise at prices that beggar belief.
Toys "Я" Us *(33rd St.)* Toy superstore.
Daffy's *(34th St.)* Off-label boutique specializing in designer fashions.
HMV Records *(57 W. 34th St.)* Hi-fi and equipment specialists.
Kmart *(250 W. 34th St.)* Major discount store.
Manhattan Mall (100 W. 33rd St.) More than 90 stores, including the department store *Stern*, on nine floors.

Ladies' Mile (88)

Sixth Avenue (between 17th and 23rd Sts)
This street was given the name 'Ladies' Mile' in the 19th century because it was the most elegant shopping street in the city. Now Sixth Avenue is again a mecca for shoppers. Three discount stores have moved into the former **Siegel-Cooper Dry Goods Store** *(632 Sixth Ave)* **Bed, Bath and Beyond** Specializes in housewares; **Filene's Basement** and **TJ Maxx** are two off-label boutiques. Next-door, **Old Navy Clothing Co.** *(610 Sixth Ave.)* is owned by The Gap and sells lower-price lines. Nearby are **Barnes & Noble**, discount books and music, **Today's Man**, men's clothing, and **Burlington Coat Factory**, cost-price coats and other clothes.
Loehmann's *(101 Seventh Ave)* is legendary with elegant women for its designer clothes at amazing prices. Stock changes every day.

reductions outside the official sales periods (January and June). Sales are advertised in the Sunday *New York Times*: if you are lucky, you can get as much as 90% off.

86

90

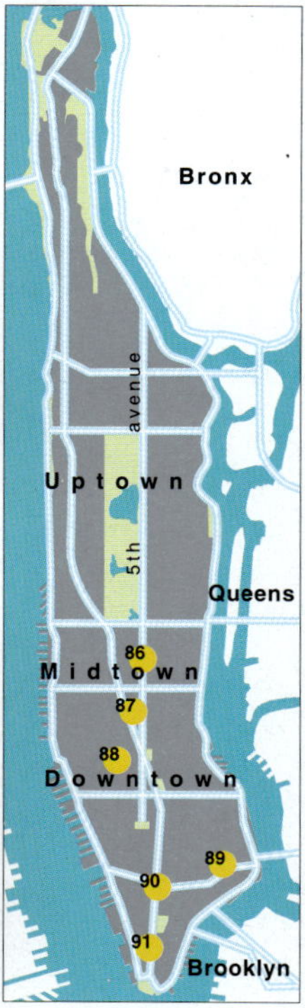

Orchard Street (89)

Visitors Center
261 Broome Street N.Y. 10002
☎ *(212) 226-9010*
⏲ *daily (except Sat.) 9am–5pm*
The Lower East Side has been the heart of New York's Jewish community since the 19th century. Today Orchard Street is still a lively local market, with more than 300 shops selling leather jackets and bags, designer clothes, accessories, and household linen at cost price.
Shopping tours meet in front of Katz's Deli, 205 East Houston St. (Ludlow St.)
⏲ *Sun. 11am (Apr.–Dec.)*

Canal Street (90)

(between W. Broadway and Bowery)
Canal Street is New York life in miniature. Not for the novice! This section of Chinatown is exclusively for hardened shoppers: you have to have a very keen eye and a good deal of confidence to choose wisely from the jewelry (mainly watches and gold jewelry) and the electronic equipment on offer. You can have a great deal of fun on Canal Street, as long as you keep your head. Remember: that delightful, and irresistibly cheap, fake-designer watch you have just bought may never actually tell the time. There are many fruit and vegetable stalls, too: a far less risky proposition. **Kam Man** (*200 Canal St., between Mott and Mulberry Sts*) An extraordinary supermarket selling exotic herbs and products from China.

Century 21 Department Store (91)

22 Cortlandt Street (between Broadway and Church St.) N.Y. 10007
☎ *(212) 227-9092*
This famous department store, opposite the World Trade Center ➡ 112, opens earlier than any other in Manhattan, and attracts canny New Yorkers on the lookout for the latest models by great designers (Donna Karan, Calvin Klein, Dolce & Gabbana, Hugo Boss, Versace) with phenomenal reductions, sometimes as much as 75% off the retail price. The only drawback is that the full range of sizes and styles may not be available. On the other hand, new stock arrives daily so it's worth a return visit if you have a special item in mind.
⏲ *Mon.–Wed. 7.45am–7.30pm; Thur. 7.45am–8.30pm; Fri. 7.45am–8pm; Sat. 10am–7.30pm; Sun. 11am–6pm*

Finding your way

Addresses

New Yorkers usually mention the junction nearest the address. For example: Fifth Avenue and 42nd Street.

Division of Manhattan

Fifth Avenue and Central Park split Manhattan into the east and west sides. The streets run east to west. With the exception of the Financial District and Greenwich Village, streets are numbered from 1st to 215th moving from south to north. Numbering, to the east or west, begins at Fifth Avenue. Avenues run from north to south. They are numbered from south to north ➥ 12.

7 Maps

How to find the street that is nearest to an avenue address

Take off the last figure; divide by 2 and add the key figure given below. The result is the street number.

Example 500 Fifth Avenue. Take off the last 0, divide 50 by 2, add the result (25) to the key figure (17). The nearest street is 42nd Street.

Avenue A	3
Avenue B	3
Avenue C	3
Avenue D	3
First Avenue	3
Second Avenue	3
Third Avenue	10
Fourth Avenue	8
Fifth Avenue (to 200)	13
Fifth Avenue (200–400)	16
Fifth Avenue (400–600)	17
Fifth Avenue (600–1500)	45
Fifth Avenue (1500–2000)	24
Sixth Avenue take off	30
Seventh Avenue (south of Central Park)	12
Seventh Avenue (beyond 110th Street)	20
Eighth Avenue (south of Central Park)	10
Ninth Avenue	13
Tenth Avenue	14
Eleventh Avenue	15
Lexington Avenue	22
Madison Avenue	26
Park Avenue	35
Columbus Avenue	60
Amsterdam Avenue	60
Broadway (beyond 23rd Street) take off	30

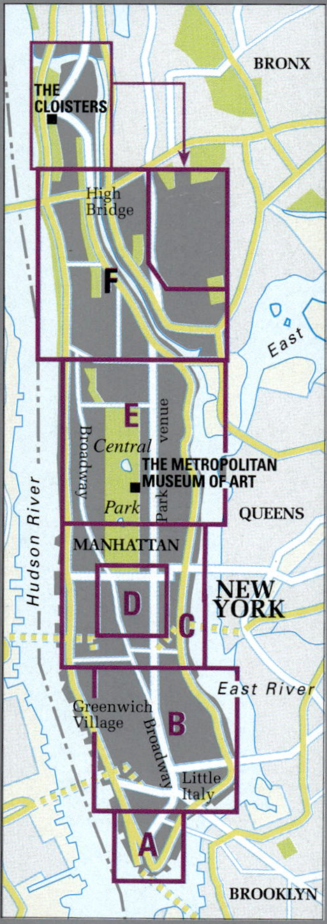

Each street name is followed by a bold letter indicating which map to refer to, and a grid reference.

Index

Bus network

MANHATTAN BUS MAP
New York City Transit
March 1997
©1997 New York City Transit Authority
Unauthorized duplication prohibited
Key
All Day Service (Every day 7am – 10pm)
Part Time Service
Direction of Service (two-way service has no arrows)
Full Time Terminal
Part Time Terminal
Bx19 to Botanical Gardens via Southern Blvd
Bx33 to Port Morris/Walnut Av -132 St
Bx15 from Fordham Plaza
Bx15 to Fordham Plaza via Third Av
60 to LaGuardia Airport
Q102 to Astoria Astoria Blvd - 8th St Operated by Queens Surface Corp
Q32 to Jackson Heights 81 St - Northern Blvd
Q60 to Jamaica 109 Av - 157 St Operated by Green Bus Lines
Q101 to Astoria 19 Av - Hazen St Operated by Queens Surface Corp
B39 to Washington Plaza, Williamsburg connection with B24,B40,B44, B46, B47,B60, B61,Q54, Q59
B51 to Fulton Mall, Downtown Brooklyn
BRONX
QUEENS
BROOKLYN
HUDSON RIVER
EAST RIVER
TRIBOROUGH BRIDGE
QUEENSBORO BRIDGE
WILLIAMSBURG BRIDGE
MANHATTAN BRIDGE
BROOKLYN BRIDGE
RANDALLS ISLAND
WARD'S ISLAND
CENTRAL PARK
RIVERSIDE PARK
RIVERBANK STATE PARK
MORNINGSIDE PARK
MARCUS GARVEY PARK
JEFFERSON PARK
CARL SCHURZ PARK
COLUMBUS CIRCLE
TIMES SQUARE
GRAND CENTRAL TERM
UNITED NATIONS
PORT AUTHORITY BUS TERMINAL
JAVITS CENTER
PENN STATION
MADISON SQUARE GARDEN
CHELSEA PIERS
GRAMERCY PARK
UNION SQUARE PARK
STUYVESANT TOWN
WATERSIDE PLAZA
WASHINGTON SQUARE PARK
EAST RIVER PARK
HUDSON RIVER PARK
CITY HALL
WORLD TRADE CENTER
SOUTH STREET SEAPORT
BATTERY PARK

Subway map

MANHATTAN SUBWAY MAP
New York City Transit
March 1997
©1997 New York City Transit Authority
Unauthorized duplication prohibited
BRONX
QUEENS
BROOKLYN
HUDSON RIVER
EAST RIVER
RANDALLS ISLAND
WARD'S ISLAND
ROOSEVELT ISLAND
CENTRAL PARK
RIVERSIDE PARK
JEFFERSON PARK
MARCUS GARVEY PARK
BATTERY PARK
EAST RIVER PARK
HARLEM
EAST HARLEM
MORNING SIDE PARK
UPPER WEST SIDE
UPPER EAST SIDE
WEST SIDE
MIDTOWN
MURRAY HILL
GRAMERCY PARK
CHELSEA
GREENWICH VILLAGE
EAST VILLAGE
TOMPKINS SQUARE PARK
SOHO
LITTLE ITALY
CHINATOWN
TRIBECA
LOWER EAST SIDE
148 St Lenox Terminal
145 Street 9 rush hours, 1 other times
145 Street A·B·C·D
145 Street 3
149 Street Grand Concourse 2·4·5
138 Street Grand Concourse 4·5
137 Street City College 1·9
135 Street B·C
135 Street 2·3
125 Street 1·9
125 Street A·B·C·D
125 Street 2·3
125 Street 4·5·6
116 Street Columbia Univ 1·9
116 Street B·C
116 Street 2·3
116 Street 6
Cathedral Pkwy (110 Street) 1·9
Cathedral Pkwy (110 Street) B·C
Central Park N (110 Street) 2·3
110 Street 6
103 Street 1·9
103 Street B·C
103 Street 6
96 Street 1·2·3·9
96 Street B·C
96 Street 6
86 Street 1·9
86 Street B·C
86 Street 4·5·6
81 Street B·C
79 Street 1·9
77 Street 6
72 Street 1·2·3·9
72 Street B·C
68 Street 6
66 Street Lincoln Center 1·9
Lexington Av B·Q
Roosevelt Island B·Q
5 Av N·R
Lexington Av N·R
59 Street 4·5·6
59 Street Columbus Circle A·B·C·D·1·9
57 St N·R
57 St B·Q
7 Av B·D·E
5 Av E·F
Lexington-3 Avs E·F
51 St 6
50 Street C·E
50 St 1·9
49 St N·R
47-50 Streets Rockefeller Center B·D·F·Q
42 St Times Sq N·R S 1·2 3 7 9
42 Street A·C·E
5 Av 7
42 St B·D·F·Q
42 Street Grand Central S 4·5·6·7
34 Street Penn Station A·C·E
34 St Penn Station 1·2·3·9
34 Street B·D·F·N Q·R
33 Street 6
LIRR/NJ TRANSIT AMTRAK
PATH
METRO NORTH
28 St 1·9
28 St N·R
28 Street 6
23 Street C·E
23 St 1·9
23 St F
23 St N·R
23 Street 6
18 St 1·9
14 Street A·C·E
8 Av L
6 Av
14 St 1·2·3·9
14 St F
14 St-Union Sq L·N·R·4·5·6
3 Av L
1 Av
Christopher St Sheridan Sq 1·9
West 4 St Washington Sq A·B·C·D·E·F·Q
8 St-NYU N·R
Astor Place 6
Broadway-Lafayette St B·D·F·Q
Bleecker St 6
2 Av F
Houston St 1·9
Prince St N·R
Spring St C·E
Spring St 6
Bowery J·M
Delancey St F
Essex St J·M·Z
Grand St B·D·Q
Canal St 1·9
Canal St A·C·E
Canal St J·M·N·R·Z·6
East Broadway F
Franklin St 1·9
Chambers St A·C
Chambers St 1·2·3·9
Park Place 2·3
City Hall N·R
Chambers St J M Z
Brooklyn Bridge-City Hall 4·5 6
World Trade Ctr C E
Broadway-Nassau St A·C
Cortlandt St 1·9
Cortlandt St N·R
Fulton St J·M·Z·2·3·4·5
Rector St 1·9
Rector St N·R
Wall St 4·5
Wall St 2·3
Broad St J M Z
Bowling Green 4 5
Whitehall St South Ferry N·R
South Ferry 1 9
KEY
Terminal
Local Stop
Express Stop
Express and Local Stop
Route Name
Free Transfer
Station Name
Brooklyn Bridge
Terminal
Full Time Service
Part Time Service (6am – midnight)

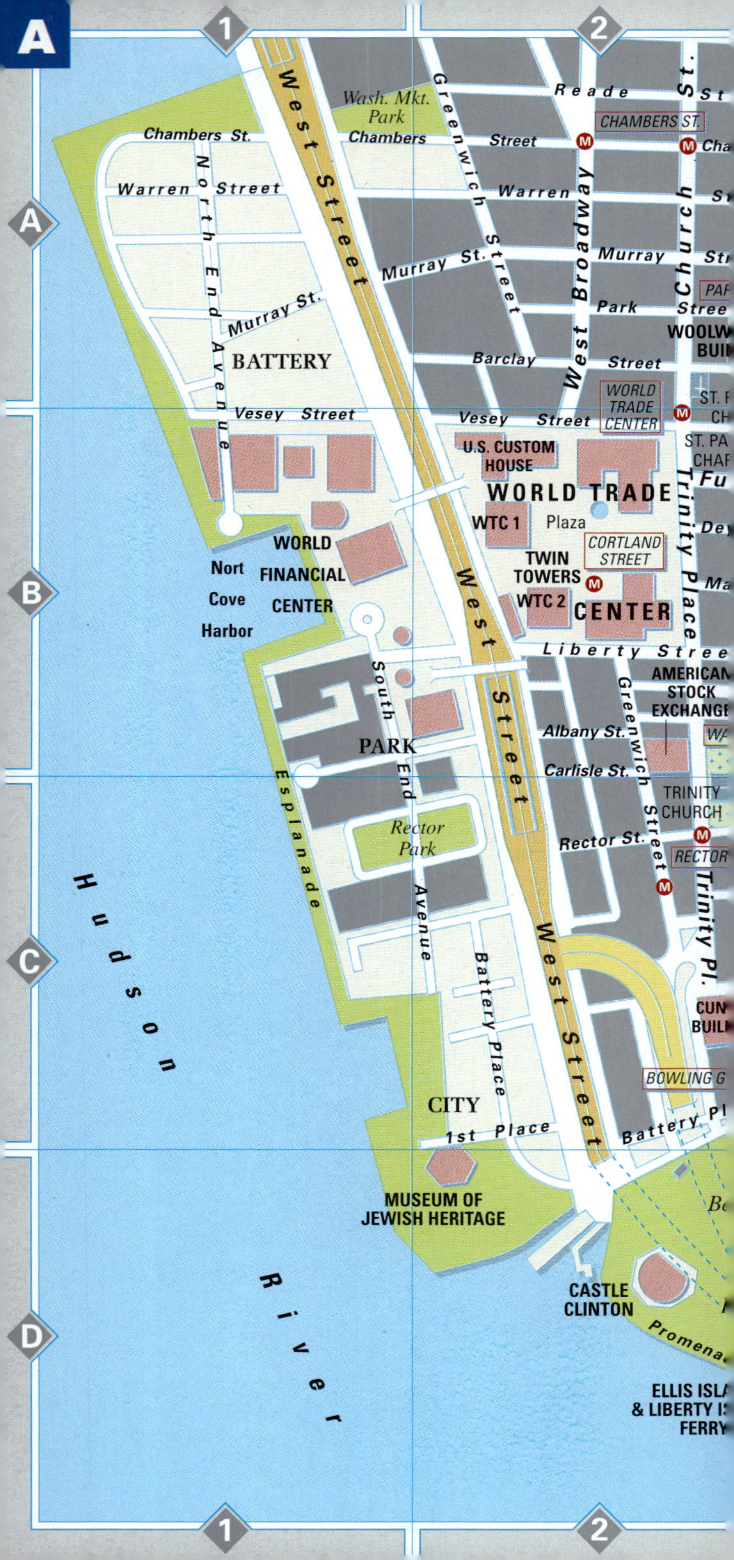
A
1
2
A
B
C
D
Reade
St.
Wash. Mkt. Park
Chambers St.
Chambers
Street
CHAMBERS ST.
Warren Street
Warren
West Street
Greenwich Street
North End Avenue
West Broadway
Church St.
Murray St.
Murray
Park
Street
WOOLW
BUIL
Barclay
Street
BATTERY
WORLD TRADE CENTER
Vesey Street
Vesey
Street
U.S. CUSTOM HOUSE
WORLD TRADE
WTC 1
Plaza
CORTLAND STREET
TWIN TOWERS
WTC 2
CENTER
Trinity Place
WORLD FINANCIAL CENTER
Nort Cove Harbor
Liberty Street
AMERICAN STOCK EXCHANGE
South End Avenue
Albany St.
Carlisle St.
PARK
Greenwich Street
TRINITY CHURCH
Rector Park
Rector St.
RECTOR
Esplanade
Trinity Pl.
Hudson River
Battery Place
West Street
BOWLING G
CITY
1st Place
Battery Pl
MUSEUM OF JEWISH HERITAGE
CASTLE CLINTON
Promena
ELLIS ISLA
& LIBERTY I
FERRY
1
2

3
4
A
B
C
D
U. S. COURTHOUSE
Foley Square
CHAMBERS ST.
SURROGATE'S COURT
Police Plaza
Park Row
POLICE HEADQUARTERS
St. James Place
MUNICIPAL BUILDING
N.Y. CITY COURTHOUSE
CIVIC CENTER
BROOKLYN BRIDGE CITY HALL
CITY HALL
City Hall Park
Wagner Pl.
Brooklyn Bridge
PACE UNIVERSITY
Beekman Street
Gold Street
Dover St.
Pearl Street
Water Street
Front Street
Ann Street
NASSAU ST.
FULTON ST.
Fulton Street
MUSEUM
DOWNTOWN WHITNEY MUSEUM
William St.
John Street
PIER 17 PAVILLON
FEDERAL RESERVE BANK
FULTON FISH MARKET
John St.
South Street
Franklin Delano Roosevelt Drive
Maiden Lane
CHASE MANHATTAN BANK
WALL ST.
SOUTH STREET SEAPORT MUSEUM
Nassau Street
FED. HALL NAT. MEM.
Pine Street
BANK OF NEW YORK
FINANCIAL DISTRICT
BROAD ST.
Wall Street
CITIBANK
William Street
Broad Street
WALL ST. FERRY LANDING
Beaver Street
Hanover Square
INDIA HOUSE
River
FRAUNCES TAVERN
Vietnam Veterans Plaza
Whitehall Street
Broad Street
Water St.
South Street
DOWNTOWN MANHATTAN HELIPORT
WHITEHALL ST.
MUNICIPAL FERRY TERMINAL
East
STATEN ISLAND FERRY
Brooklyn-Battery Tunnel
1:10000
0
100
200 m

B
1
2
A
B
C
D
West 30th Street
East
28TH STREET
28TH STREET
West 28th Street
East 28
Chelsea Park
West 26th Street
APPELLATE COURT
Madison Square Park
West 25th Street
Tenth Avenue
Ninth Avenue
Eighth Avenue
Seventh Avenue
Avenue of the Americas
Fifth Avenue
Broadway
Park Av. South
23RD STREET
West 23rd Street
East
23RD STREET
23RD STREET
CHELSEA HOTEL
GENERAL THEOLOGICAL SEMINARY
FLATIRON BUILDING
West 20th Street
East
CHELSEA
T. ROOSEVELT BIRTHPLACE
West 17th Street
East 17th
PORT AUTHORITY
UNION ISLAND TERMINAL
Union Square Park
14TH ST.
6TH AV.
West 14th Street
East
8TH AVENUE
West 13th Street
14TH ST.
14TH ST.
West 12th Street
West 11th St.
CONSOLIDATED EDISON BUILDING
Gansevoort Street
Eighth Av.
Greenwich Avenue
WASHINGTON ARCH
University Place
East 10
11th Street
ST. JOHN'S CHURCH
GREENWICH VILLAGE
8TH ST.
Hudson
Greenwich
Washington
West
CHRISTOPHER ST.
COLONNADE ROW
Washington Square Park
NEW YORK UNIVERSITY
WEST 4TH ST.
Bleecker
Street
Av.
ST. LUKE'S CHAPEL
Christopher St.
Bedford St.
Bleecker Street
West Street
Hudson Street
Greenwich Street
Sixth
HOUSTON ST.
West Houston Street
South
W. Houston St.
THE NEW MUSEUM OF CONTEMPORARY ART
Prince
ST. ANTHONY OF PADUA
GUGGENHEIM MUSEUM SOHO
Varick
SPRING ST.
Spring
HAUGHWOUT BUILDING
SPRING
Spring St.
Broome Street
SOHO
Hudson
River
Canal Street
Grand
MUSEUM OF HOLOGRAPHY
Mercer
Holland Tunnel
Watts
CANAL ST.
St.
Laight
CANAL ST.
Street of the
Avenue
Street
CIVIC CENTER SYNAGOGUE
ALTERNATIVE MUSEUM
FRANKLIN ST.
Leonard St.
Worth St.
Church St.
Reade
Chambers St.
CHAMBERS ST.
CHAMBERS

3
4
A
B
C
D
East River
Franklin Delano Roosevelt Drive
Second Avenue
First Avenue
Twenty Fourth Street Park
East 20th Street
STUYVESANT TOWN
John J. Murphy Park
Stuyvesant Square
ST. MARY
1ST AVENUE
CONS. EDISON ENERGY MUSEUM
East 14th Street
East 12th Street
UKRAINIAN MUSEUM
EAST VILLAGE
East 10th Street
ST. NICHOLAS
Tompkins Square Park
St. Marks Place
East 7th Street
ALPHABETVILLE
East 6th Street
Avenue A
Avenue B
Avenue C
Avenue D
MERCHANT'S HOUSE
East 3rd Street
Houston Street
East River Park
Hamilton Fish Park
2ND AVENUE
Stanton Street
LOWER EAST SIDE
Chrystie Street
Sara Delano Roosevelt Park
Rivington Street
Clinton St.
ESSEX ST.
DELANCEY ST.
Delancey St.
BOWERY ST.
BIALYSTOKER SYNAGOGUE
Broome St.
LOWER EAST SIDE TENEMENT MUSEUM
BETH HAMEDRASH HAGODOL SYNAGOGUE
LITTLE ITALY
Grand Street
GRAND ST.
Allen St.
Orchard St.
Essex St.
Bowery
Hester St.
W. H. Seward Park
Broadway
Henry Street
Madison Street
Vladeck Park
Water Street
Canal St.
Straus Sq.
Confucius Plaza
EAST BROADWAY
CONGREGATION K'HAL ADATH JESHURUN
CHINATOWN
Pike Street
Cherry Street
Chatham Square
East Broadway
MANHATTAN SAVINGS BANK
Market St.
St. James Pl.
Madison St.
Catherine St.
NEW YORK POST
MUNICIPAL BUILDING
POLICE HEADQUARTERS
South F. D. Roosevelt Drive
MANHATTAN BRIDGE
1:21 000
0
210
420 m

C
1
2
A
B
C
D
Boat Basin
Riverside Park
Henry Hudson Parkway
Riverside Drive
Hudson River
Miller Highway
Twelfth Avenue
West End Avenue
Eleventh Avenue
Tenth Avenue
Amsterdam Av.
Broadway
Columbus Avenue
Ninth Avenue
Ninth Av.
Eighth Avenue
Eighth Av.
Central Park West
Seventh Av.
Seventh Avenue
Dyer Av.
West 79th Street
79TH STREET
AMERICAN MUSEUM OF NATURAL HISTORY
Transverse Road
Central Park
West 76th Street
NEW YORK HISTORICAL SOCIETY
West 75th Street
UPPER WEST SIDE
ANSONIA HOUSE
DAKOTA APARTMENTS
West Drive
The Lake
The Ramble
Cherry Hill
West 72nd Street
72ND STREET
72ND STREET
West 70th Street
Bowling Greens
The Sheep Meadow
NEW YORK SOCIETY FOR ETHICAL CULTURE
Transverse
LINCOLN CENTER
Lincoln Square
Heckscher Playground
FORDHAM UNIVERSITY
West 60th Street
Maine Memorial
Columbus Circle
Central Park
NEW YORK COLISEUM
57TH ST.
West 57th Street
West 57th
59TH STREET COLUMBUS CIRCLE
CARNEGIE HALL
West 55th Street
De Witt Clinton Park
CLINTON
7TH AV.
West 52nd Street
ROCKEFELLER
Passenger Ship Terminal
NEW YORK SCHOOL OF PRINTING
50TH ST.
50TH ST.
49TH ST.
West 48th Street
THEATER DISTRICT
47TH-50TH ROCKEFELLER CENTER
West 46th Street
INTREPID SEA-AIR-SPACE MUSEUM
Duffy Square
MARRIOTT MARQUIS HOTEL
Times Square
West 44th Street
42ND ST.
Hudson River Day Line
West 42nd Street
Port Authority Bus Terminal
TIMES SQUARE 42ND STREET
West 40th Street
West 39th Street
West 37th Street
GARMENT DISTRICT
JACOB K. JAVITS CONVENTION CENTER
34TH ST.
34TH ST.
West 34th Street
West 33th Street
GENERAL POST OFFICE
MADISON SQUARE GARDEN
PENNSYLVANIA STATION
Heliport
West 30th Street

3
4
East 79th Street
UKRAINIAN INSTITUTE OF AMERICA
77TH ST.
UPPER EAST SIDE
East 76th Street
East 75th Street
WHITNEY MUSEUM OF AMERICAN ART
The Glade
Conservatory Pond
Pilgrim Hill
East 72nd Street
FRICK COLLECTION
ASIA HOUSE
68TH STREET HUNTER COLLEGE
East 69th Street
East Green
TEMPLE EMANU-EL
East 66th Street
CHINA HOUSE
ROCKEFELLER UNIVERSITY
ZOO
East 63rd St.
East 63rd St.
E. 63RD ST. FERRY LANDING
KNICKERBOCKER CLUB
LEXINGTON AV.
METROPOLITAN CLUB
Grand Army Plaza
ABIGAIL ADAMS SMITH HOUSE
East 60th St.
5TH AV.
ROOSEVELT IS. TRAMWAY
QUEENSBORO BRIDGE
GENERAL MOTORS BUILD.
59TH ST.
BLOOMINGDALE'S
East 57th Street
TRUMP TOWER
GOLDWATER MEMORIAL HOSPITAL
SONY BUILD.
East 55th Street
MODERN ART
LEXINGTON AV.
ROOSEVELT ISLAND
CITICORP CENTER
SEAGRAM BUILD.
PARK AVENUE PLAZA
51ST ST.
East 52nd Street
CITY HOSPITAL
GENERAL ELECTRIC BUILD.
ST. PATRICK'S CATHEDRAL
East 48th Street
MIDTOWN
46th Street
44th Street
GRAND CENTRAL TERMINAL
CHRYSLER BUILD.
FORD FOUNDATION BUILD.
UNITED NATIONS HEADQUARTERS
East 42nd Street
N.Y. PUBLIC LIBRARY
GRAND CENTRAL
DAILY NEWS BUILDING
Queens-Midtown Tunnel
East 40th Street
East 39th Street
East Side Airlines Terminal
MURRAY HILL
37th Street
St. Gabriel Park
PIERPONT MORGAN LIBRARY
E. 34 TH ST. FERRY LANDING
East 34th Street
33RD ST.
HELIPORT
EMPIRE STATE BUILDING
East 30th Street
Fifth Avenue
Madison Avenue
Park Avenue
Park Av. South
Lexington Avenue
Third Avenue
Second Av.
First Avenue
York Avenue
Sutton Place
Franklin Delano Roosevelt Drive
East River
A
B
C
D
1:20800
0
300 m

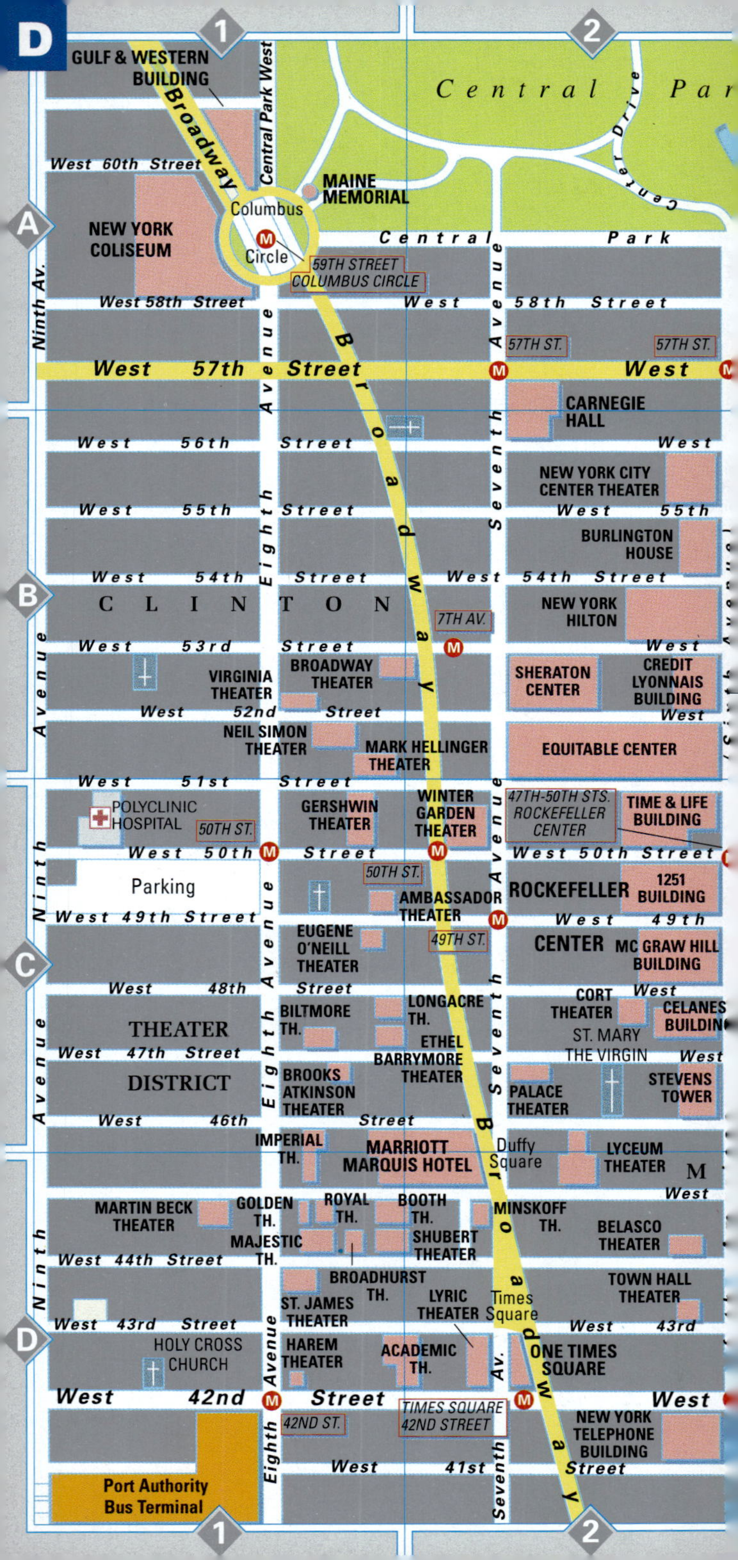
D
1
2
A
B
C
D
GULF & WESTERN BUILDING
Broadway
Central Park West
Central Park
Center Drive
West 60th Street
MAINE MEMORIAL
Columbus Circle
NEW YORK COLISEUM
Central Park
59TH STREET COLUMBUS CIRCLE
West 58th Street
West 58th Street
Ninth Av.
Eighth Avenue
Seventh Avenue
57TH ST.
57TH ST.
West 57th Street
West
CARNEGIE HALL
West 56th Street
West
NEW YORK CITY CENTER THEATER
West 55th Street
West 55th
BURLINGTON HOUSE
West 54th Street
West 54th Street
CLINTON
NEW YORK HILTON
7TH AV.
West 53rd Street
West
Ninth Avenue
VIRGINIA THEATER
BROADWAY THEATER
SHERATON CENTER
CREDIT LYONNAIS BUILDING
West 52nd Street
West
NEIL SIMON THEATER
MARK HELLINGER THEATER
EQUITABLE CENTER
West 51st Street
POLYCLINIC HOSPITAL
GERSHWIN THEATER
WINTER GARDEN THEATER
47TH-50TH STS. ROCKEFELLER CENTER
TIME & LIFE BUILDING
50TH ST.
West 50th Street
West 50th Street
Parking
50TH ST.
ROCKEFELLER CENTER
1251 BUILDING
West 49th Street
AMBASSADOR THEATER
West 49th
EUGENE O'NEILL THEATER
49TH ST.
MC GRAW HILL BUILDING
West 48th Street
CORT THEATER
West
CELANES BUILDIN
THEATER DISTRICT
BILTMORE TH.
LONGACRE TH.
ST. MARY THE VIRGIN
West 47th Street
ETHEL BARRYMORE THEATER
West
BROOKS ATKINSON THEATER
PALACE THEATER
STEVENS TOWER
West 46th Street
IMPERIAL TH.
MARRIOTT MARQUIS HOTEL
Duffy Square
LYCEUM THEATER
M
West
MARTIN BECK THEATER
GOLDEN TH.
ROYAL TH.
BOOTH TH.
MINSKOFF TH.
BELASCO THEATER
MAJESTIC TH.
SHUBERT THEATER
West 44th Street
BROADHURST TH.
TOWN HALL THEATER
ST. JAMES THEATER
LYRIC THEATER
Times Square
West 43rd Street
West 43rd
HOLY CROSS CHURCH
HAREM THEATER
ACADEMIC TH.
ONE TIMES SQUARE
West 42nd Street
West
42ND ST.
TIMES SQUARE 42ND STREET
NEW YORK TELEPHONE BUILDING
West 41st Street
Port Authority Bus Terminal

3
4
KNICKERBOCKER CLUB
East Drive
HOTEL PIERRE
METROPOLITAN CLUB
East 61st Street
LEXINGTON AV.
Pond
East 60th Street
BLOOMINGDALE'S STORE
Grand Army Plaza
5TH AV.
East 59th Street
59TH ST.
A
GENERAL MOTORS BUILDING
East 58th Street
RIZZOLI
East 57th Street
TIFFANY
TRUMP TOWER
East 56th Street
FIFTH AVENUE PRESBYTERIAN CHURCH
SONY BUILD.
East 55th Street
CENTRAL SYNAGOGUE
GOLDWYN INC.
East 54th Street
ST. THOMAS' CHURCH
MUSEUM ... ERN ART
5TH AV.
LEVER HOUSE
ST. PETER'S CHURCH
CITICORP CENTER
B
East 53rd Street
TISHMAN BUILDING
PARK AVENUE PLAZA
SEAGRAM BUILDING
LEXINGTON AV.
East 52nd Street
OLYMPIC TOWER
ST. BARTHOLOMEW'S CHURCH
51ST ST.
INTERNATIONAL BUILDING
East 51st Street
ST. PATRICK'S CATHEDRAL
GENERAL ELECTRIC BUILDING
PAL. D'ITALIA
ATLAS
East 50th Street
Lower Plaza
BRITISH EMP. BUILDING
Promenade
WALDORF-ASTORIA HOTEL
East 49th Street
MAISON FRANÇAISE
EASTERN AIRLINES
WESTVACO BUILDING
C
East 48th Street
270 PARK AVENUE
CHEMICAL BANK BUILDING
East 46th Street
HELMSLEY BUILDING
TOWN
East 45th Street
GRAND CENTRAL POST OFFICE
MET LIFE BUILDING
East 44th Street
East 43rd Street
CITY UNIVERSITY GRADUATE SCHOOL
GRAND CENTRAL TERMINAL
GRAND HYATT HOTEL
CHRYSLER BUILD.
D
GRAND CENTRAL
East 42nd Street
NEW YORK PUBLIC LIBRARY
PHILIP MORRIS HEADQUARTERS
CHANIN BUILDING
MOBIL BUILDING
East 41st Street
1:9250
0 100 200 m
Fifth Avenue
Madison Avenue
Park Avenue
Lexington Avenue
Vanderbilt Avenue
3
4

E
1
2
A
B
C
D
St. Clair Pl.
West 125th Street
125TH STREET
St. Nicholas Park
Convent Av.
St. Nicholas Av.
West 129th St.
West 127th
APOLLO THEATRE
HARLEM
West 125th Street
125TH STREET
Lenox Av.
La Salle St.
Riverside Dr. West
GRANT'S TOMB
Claremont Avenue
Broadway
West 123rd St.
West 123rd Street
RIVERSIDE CHURCH
Morningside Park
Morningside Drive
Morningside Avenue
Manhattan Avenue
St. Nicholas Avenue
Frederick Douglass Boulevard
Adam Clayton Powell Jr. Boulevard
Lenox Avenue
West 120th St.
West 120th St.
LOW MEMORIAL LIBRARY
CASA ITALIANA
BARNARD COLLEGE
COLUMBIA UNIVERSITY
West 118th
West 116th St.
116TH STREET
116TH ST.
West 116th St.
116TH STREET
Phillip Randolph Square
West 115th St.
West 113th St.
West 112th St.
West 112th St.
ST. LUKE'S HOSPITAL
CATHEDRAL CHURCH OF ST. JOHN THE DIVINE
Amsterdam Avenue
Riverside Drive
Riverside Park
Henry Hudson Parkway
Hudson River
CATHEDRAL PARKWAY
Cathedral Parkway
Frederick Douglass Circle
Central Park North
CENTRAL PARK NORTH
West 109th St.
CATHEDRAL PARKWAY
The Cliff
Harlem Meer
LASKER RINK
West 106th Street
Columbus Avenue
Manhattan Avenue
Central Park West
West Drive
The Great Hill
The Loch
103RD STREET
103RD STREET
Central Park
The Pool
North Meadow
East Drive
FIREMAN'S MEMORIAL
West 100th Street
West End Avenue
West 97th Street
Transverse Road No 1
West 96th Street
96TH STREET
96TH STREET
Tennis Courts
West 94th Street
West 93rd Street
West 91st Street
UPPER WEST SIDE
Reservoir
SOLDIERS' AND SAILORS' MONUMENT
West 89th Street
West 88th Street
86TH STREET
West 86th Street
86TH STREET
Transverse Road No 3
Pinetum
THE METROPOLITAN MUSEUM OF ART
West 83rd Street
Summit Rock
The Great Lawn
CLEOPATRA'S NEEDLE
81ST STREET-MUSEUM OF NATURAL HISTORY
West 81st St.
BELVEDERE CASTLE
Turtle Pond
Boat Basin
West 79th Street
79TH STREET
AMERICAN MUSEUM OF NATURAL HISTORY
Transverse Road No 2
Central Park
NEW YORK HISTORICAL SOCIETY
West 76th Street
West 75th Street
West 74th Street
The Lake
The Ramble
Riverside Park

3
4
1:23 500
0
250
500 m
Willis Avenue Bridge
Harlem River Driveway
Harlem River
East 127th Street
125th Street
Louis Guvillier Park
Triborough Bridge
125TH ST.
RANDALLS
Randalls Island Park
ISLAND
J.J. DOWNING STADIUM
A
Paladino Av.
EAST
120th Street
118th St.
116th Street
116TH STREET
115th St.
OUR LADY OF MOUNT CARMEL
Pleasant Avenue
HARLEM
Jefferson Park
112th Street
110TH STREET
East 110th Street
East 109th Street
107th St.
106th Street
PSYCHIATRIC CENTER
B
WARDS
ISLAND
USEO DEL BARRIO
S. OF THE CITY
NEW YORK
103RD STREET
Y. ACADEMY
MEDICINE
Foot Bridge
East 102nd Street
Wards Island Park
Hell Gate
East 99th St.
96th Street
96TH STREET
East 95th St.
Mill Rock Park
LIGHT
LIGHT
East River
C
ERNATIONAL CENTER
PHOTOGRAPHY
East 93rd St.
VISH
SEUM
East 91st St.
PER-HEWITT
EUM
East 89th St.
OMON
UGGENHEIM
SEUM
GRACIE MANSION
86TH STREET
YORKVILLE
86th Street
Carl Schurz Park
LIGHT
NSTITUTE
WISH
ARCH
East 85th Street
COLER MEM. HOSPITAL AND HOME
East 83rd Street
East 81st St.
East 80th St.
D
East 79th Street
NIAN INSTITUTE
ERICA
77TH ST.
UPPER EAST SIDE
John Jay Park
77th St.
ROOSEVELT
ISLAND
East 76th Street
WHITNEY MUSEUM OF AMERICAN ART
East 75th Street
74th Street
Park Avenue
Lexington Avenue
Third Avenue
Second Avenue
First Avenue
York Avenue
East End Avenue
Franklin Delano Roosevelt Drive
(East River Drive)
Triborough Bridge

F
1
2
A
B
C
D
MORRIS HEIGHTS
West 184th St.
Broadway
St. Nicholas Avenue
Cabrini Blvd.
181ST ST.
181ST ST.
Washington Bridge
Cross Bronx
A. Hamilton Bridge
Sedgwick
King J. Boulevard
BUS STADIUM
Audubon Avenue
Amsterdam Avenue
G. Washington Bridge
Fort Washington Park
Henry Hudson Parkway
175TH ST.
Fort Washington Av.
West 175th St.
High Bridge Park
Harlem River Driveway
Major Deegan Expressway
Riverside Drive
W. 170th St.
168TH ST.
MEDICAL CENTER
W. 165th St.
163RD ST.
Sedgwick Ave.
DALAFIELD HOSPITAL
MOTHER CABRINI MEM. HOSPITAL
W. 160th St.
Hudson River
Harlem
157TH ST.
West 156th St.
155TH ST.
W. 155th St.
WASHINGTON HEIGHTS MUSEUM GROUP
TRINITY CHURCH
155TH ST.
West 153rd St.
West 153rd St.
West 150th St.
West 150th St
148TH ST.
Riverside Park
J. Robinson Park
West 147th St.
West 147th
145TH ST.
West 145th St.
145TH ST.
West
Convent Avenue
Hamilton Pl.
West 141st St.
West 141st
CITY UNIVER. OF N.Y.
THE CITY COLLEGE
137TH ST.
St. Nicholas Avenue
St. Nicholas Park
Douglass Boulevard
Frederick Douglass Boulevard
Adam Clayton Powell Jr. Boulevard
West 135th St.
West
135TH ST.
West
West
West 125th Street
125TH STREET
St. Clair Pl.
West 127th St.
APOLLO THEATRE
Riverside Dr. West
Av.
La Salle St.
West 1
GRANT'S TOMB
Morningside Av.
St. Nicholas Av.
West 123
Morning-side Park
Claremont
1:27500
0
275
550 m
RIVERSIDE CHURCH
West 120th Street
West

3
4
A
B
C
D
Spuyten Duyvil
Baker Field
STADIUM
Henry Hudson Parkway
Inwood Hill Park
INWOOD
Broadway
215TH ST.
Isham Park
Tenth Avenue
P. C. RAPID TRANSIT YARD
207TH ST. / INWOOD
W. 207th St.
W. 204th St.
Sherman Av.
207TH ST.
Harlem River
Dyckman St.
NYU COLLEGE OF ENGINEERING
DYCKMAN STREET
Nagle Avenue
THE CLOISTERS
Fort Tryon Park
Hudson River
RADIO TOWER
Harlem River Driveway
GEO WASHINGTON HIGH SCHOOL
High Bridge Park
Major Deegan Expressway
191ST ST.
190TH ST.
Cabrini Blvd.
Fort Washington Avenue
WASHINGTON HEIGHTS
St. Nicholas Avenue
Audubon Avenue
Amsterdam Avenue
181ST ST.
Macombs Road
Jerome Avenue
River Avenue
John Mullaly Park
161ST ST.
YANKEE STADIUM
Fifth Av.
Third Av.
East 138th Street
East 137th St.
138TH ST.
Willis Av.
Brook Av.
St. Anns Av.
BROOK AV.
MOTT HAVEN
Harlem River Driveway
Major Deegan Expressway
Bruckner Boulevard
Third Av. Bridge
Avenue
East 131st St.
Fifth Av.
Madison
Av.
East 127th St.
Willis Avenue Bridge
Triborough Bridge
East 125th St.
125TH ST.
Louis Guvillier Park
Marcus Garvey Memorial Park
Madison Av.
Park Avenue
Lexington Av.
Third Av.
Second Av.
First Av.
120th Street
Paladino Av.
Randalls Island Park

General index

For useful information, travel information, and contact details see pages 6 to 15.

Index

Thanks to Ted Hardin, to the New York Convention & Visitors Bureau (NYCVB), to Christine Silva and to all the establishments presented in this guide for their cooperation.

Picture Credits

1 and cover illustration. J.M. Valat
6 Gall.-Ted Hardin
18 The Paramount
19 1 Soho Grand, 2 The Millennium Hilton, 3 and 4 Marriott Hotels
21 6, 17 Hotel, 7 Chelsea Inn, 8 The Larchmont Hotel, 10 Gramercy Park Hotel
23 11 Hotel Metro, 12 Best Western Manhattan Hotel, 13 Wolcott Hotel
25 18 Morgans, 19 Shelburne Murray Hill
27 22 Hotel Lexington, 23 Roger Smith, 24 Grand Hyatt, 25 Gall.-T. Hardin, 26 Helmsley-B. Summer
29 28 Algonquin, 29 Mansfield, 30 Gall.-R. Berenholtz (bar) and T. Vack (room)
31 34 The Paramount, 36 Michelangelo, 37 Renaissance N.Y.
33 40 Waldorf Astoria, 41 Beekman Tower Hotel, 44 Hotel Intercontinental
35 45 Élysée, 47 N.Y. Palace, 49 Swisshotel
37 50 Shoreham, 51 St. Regis, 52 The Peninsula New York
39 55 Helmsley Windsor-B. Summer, 56 Four Seasons, 58 Parker Meridien
41 60 The Pierre, 61 The Plaza 62 The Westin Central Park South
43 65 The Mark, 66 Carlyle, 67 The Barbizon, 70 Plaza-Athénée
45 71, 74 and 75 Gall.-C. Silva, 73 Empire Radison, 75 Beacon
46 The Terrace
49 1 Gall.-Ted Hardin, 2 The Rainbow Room
51 3 Gall.-L. de Bélizal, 4 Windows-C. Litthe, 5 Gall.-Ted Hardin
53 6 Hudson River Club, 7 Taliesin, 8 Bridge Cafe, 10 Harbour Lights
55 11 Forlini's, 13 Gall.-T. Hardin
57 19 Nobu, 20 Gall.-T. Hardin, 22 Montrachet Steven Freman
59 24 Honmura An, 25 Savoy, 26 Zoë
61 32 Broadway Diner's, 33 2nd Avenue Kosher Deli, 34 Gall.-T. Hardin, 35 Brooklyn USA Diner 36 Carnegie Delicatessen
63 37 Mi Cocina, 39 Home, 41 Cafe Loup
65 44 Union Square Cafe, 45 Zen Palate, 48 Gramercy Park, 49 Verbena M Moran
67 50 Gall.-T. Hardin, 51 P. Page
69 52 B. Smith's, 53 Becco, 54 Gall.-T.Hardin
71 58 M. Moran, 60 Gall.-T. Hardin, 61 Typhoon Brewery
73 63 G. Teuwen, 64 "21" Club, 65 R. Wurman, 67 The Park Room
75 70 Hard Rock Cafe, 71 Jekyll and Hyde, 72 Motown, 73 Planet Hollywood
77 75 Gall.-T. Hardin, 76 Cafe des Artistes, 77 The Regency, 80 Le Régence
79 82 The Lobster Club, 83 Daniel, 85 Gall.-T. Hardin, 86 Park Avenue Cafe, 87 Matthew's
81 88 Rain, 89 Gall.-Ted Hardin, 90 Picholine,
83 94 Wollensky's Grill, 95 Florent, 96 First, 97 Corner Bistro, 99 Empire Diner B. Grant
84 NYCVB
87 2 McSorley's, 3 Fez, 4 I. Lawrence, 5 Nimh-Wass
89 9 Fifty Seven-Fifty Seven Bar, 10 T. Eberle, 13 The Oak Bar, 14 The Promenade
91 19 D. Perdue (ext.) and Gall.-L. de Bélizal (flag), 20 NYCVB (ext.) and E. Patino (Rockettes Girls), 21 SOB's
93 23 Tatou, 26 Catch a Rising Star 28 Caroline's Comedy Club / T. Wheatman (int.)
95 30 Village Vanguard, 31 Blue Note, 33 R.A. Lepley, 34 Gall.-T. Hardin
97 42 M. Lepoer Trench, 41 C. Rosegg, 43 J. Marcus
99 44 S. McNicholas (below) and L. Greenfield (above), 45 R. Foldman, 46 C. Pulin
101 49 Le Bar Bat, 52 Webster Hall, 53 Gall.-L. de Bélizal
103 54 NYCVB (ext.) and W. Klotz (Aïda and int.), 56 C. Lee
104 Battman
107 A, D, I and K Gall.-L. de Bélizal, B Intrepid Sea Air & Space Museum, C Gall.-SD, E Gall.-B. Lenormand, F NYCVB, G Gall.-S. Lenormand, H Gall.-RB, J Gall.-A. Gouessant
108 1 Gallimard, 2 WTC Observatory Deck
111 3 National Museum of the American Indian, 4 Gall.-L. de Bélizal, 5 U.S. Dept of the Interior, 6 Gall. T. Hardin
113 9 and 11 Gall.-B. Lenormand, 10 Gall.-L. de Bélizal
115 15 United Nations, 16 N.Y. Public Library, 17 Pierpont Morgan Library, 18 NYCVB and Battman (top)
117 19 NYCVB, 20 B. Barlow, 21 NYCVB (ext.) and Gall.-T. Hardin (ext.), 22 N.Y. Palace
119 Metropolitan Museum of Art
121 25 Solomon R. Guggenheim Foundation-D. M. Heald, 26 Whitney Museum of American Art, 27 Frick Collection J. Bigelow Taylor, 28 El Museo del Bario, 29 Museum of the City of New York
123 32 American Museum of Natural History (whale) and S. Frances (skeletons), 33 Gall.-L. de Bélizal, 34 N.Y. Historical Society
125 35 Morris Jumel House, 36 Church of St John the Divine and Gall.-L. de Bélizal (details), 37 National Park
127 39 Metropolitan Museum of Art, 40 Dyckman House
128 Gall.-T. Hardin
133 2 Brooklyn Museum of Art, 4 Gall.-L. de Bélizal, 6 Wildlife Conservation Society, 7 NYCVB
135 8 M. Noguchi, 9 D. Sundberg, 10 R. Essel
137 12 Wave Hill, 14 City Island Chamber of Commerce, 15 Wildlife Conservation Society, 16 T. Butt
139 17 Snug Harbour Cultural Center, 19 Historic Richmond Town, 20 R. Erickson
141 21 NYCVB, 23 B. Boss (with kind permission from NFL Photos), 25 NYCVB (Flushing Meadows), Andy Levin (marathon),
142 Niketown
145 A Levi's, B Brooks Brothers, C Warner Bros Studio Store, D Caswell-Massey, E Gall.-S. Lenormand, F Tiffany & Co, G Yankees Clubhouse, H Gall.-E. Guillemot, I Elizabeth Arden, J Nat Sherman, K H&H Bagels, L McCreedy & Schreiber
147 4 Saks Fifth Avenue, 5 Macy's and Gall.-S. Lenormand (details)
149 7 Lost City Art 9 Canal Jean Company 11 Atrium
151 16 S. Risedorph, 18 C. Emilio (int.) and S. Belkowitz (armchair), 19 Portico
153 24 McCreedy & Schreiber, 25 Brooks Brothers, 26 Nat Sherman, 28 Paul Stuart, 31 Worth & Worth
155 33 Metropolitan Museum of Art Shop, 34 Caswell-Massey, 37 World of Golf, 38 Gall.-T. Hardin
157 40 MoMa Design Store, 44 Eileen Fisher, 45 H. Stern
159 47 Belgian Shoes, 48 R. Moore, 49 Bijan, 52 K. Reardon, 53 E. Arden
160 55 Gall.-S. Lenormand, 56 Warner Bros Studio Store, 57 Niketown, 59 Coca Cola Fifth Avenue
163 62 The Original Levi's Store, 65 Crate & Barrel, 66 Revlon Employee Store, 67 Hammacher-Schlemmer
165 69 Ralph Lauren, 71 Gallery of Wearable Art, 72 Calvin Klein
167 78 Maxila & Mandible, 79 Ann Taylor 80, 81 et 83 Gall.-C. Silva
169 86 and 88 Gall.-L. de Bélizal, 87 Gall.-T. Hardin, 90 Gall.-B. Lenormand
170 Gall.-T. Hardin
194 Gall-B. Lenormand